CREATIVE FAMILY THERAPY TECHNIQUES: PLAY, ART, AND EXPRESSIVE ACTIVITIES TO ENGAGE CHILDREN IN FAMILY SESSIONS

Edited by
LIANA LOWENSTEIN

Champion Press
Toronto

Correspondence regarding this book can be sent to:
Champion Press
PO Box 91012, 2901 Bayview Avenue, Toronto, Ontario, Canada M2K 2Y6
Telephone: (416) 575-7836 Fax: (416) 756-7201
Web: www.lianalowenstein.com

Library and Archives Canada Cataloguing in Publication

Lowenstein, Liana, 1965-
    Creative family therapy techniques : play, art, and expressive activities to engage children in family sessions / Liana Lowenstein.

Includes bibliographical references.
ISBN 978-0-9685199-6-7

    1. Family psychotherapy. 2. Systemic therapy (Family therapy).
3. Play therapy. 4. Art therapy for children. I. Title.

RC488.5.L69 2010   616.89'516   C2010-905619-1

Contents

Section One: Engagement and Assessment Techniques

Section Two: Treatment Techniques

Section Three: Termination Techniques

About The Editor

Liana Lowenstein, MSW, RSW, CPT-S, is an author, sought-after speaker, and practitioner who has worked with children and their families since 1988. She completed her Master of Social Work degree at the University of Toronto, and she is a Certified Child and Play Therapist (Supervisor) with the Canadian Association for Child and Play Therapy. She provides clinical supervision to mental health practitioners, runs a play-therapy internship program, and consults to several mental health agencies. She has a reputation as a dynamic workshop leader and has presented trainings across North America and abroad. She is the founder of Champion Press publishing company and has authored numerous publications, including the highly acclaimed books *Paper Dolls & Paper Airplanes: Therapeutic Exercises for Sexually Traumatized Children* (with Crisci & Lay, 1997), *Creative Interventions for Troubled Children & Youth* (1999), *Creative Interventions for Children of Divorce* (2006), and *Creative Interventions for Bereaved Children* (2006). She has also edited the books *Assessment and Treatment Activities for Children, Adolescents, and Families: Practitioners Share Their Most Effective Techniques* (Volumes One and Two).

Contributors

Shlomo Ariel, PhD
Ramat Gan, Israel
Email: wbshrink@gmail.com
Web: http://sites.google.com/site/drshlomoariel

Christopher Belous, MA, LLMFT, CFLE, CCT
East Lansing, Michigan, United States
Email: belousch@msu.edu

Betty Bedard Bidwell, PhD, ATBC, OATR-S., PTR, CPTR-S, CTC-S
Goderich, Ontario, Canada
Email: homestead@betamarsh.com

Amber L. Brewer, PhD-ABD, LMFT
Salt Lake City, Utah, United States
Email: brewer.amber@gmail.com

Paris Goodyear-Brown, MSW, LCSW, RPT-S
Brentwood, Tennessee, United States
Email: paris@parisandme.com
Website: www.parisandme.com

Lois Carey, LCSW, RPT-S
Nyack, New York, United States
Email: ljcarey@optonline.net
Web: www.sandplaytherapy.com

Angela M. Cavett, PhD, LP, RPT-S
West Fargo, North Dakota, United States
Email: acavett@koamentalhealth.com
Web: www.childpsychologicalservices.com

Megan Cowan, MSW, RSW
Toronto, Ontario, Canada
Email: megan.cowan@sympatico.ca

Shannon Culy, BSW, RSW
Estevan, Saskatchewan, Canada
Email: sculy@accesscomm.ca

Gisela Schubach De Domenico, PhD, LMFT, RPT-S
Oakland, California, United States
Email: sandtrayworldplay@gmail.com
Web: www.vision-quest.us

Brian Douglas, MSW, RSW
Kitchener, Ontario, Canada
Email: brian@briandouglastherapy.com
Web: www.briandouglastherapy.com

Sheri Eggleton, BA
Thorold, Ontario, Canada
Email: seggleton@ncys.ca

Rebecca Fischer, PhD
Maumee, Ohio, United States
Email: DrRebeccaFischer@gmail.com

Yuehong Chen Foley, PhD, LPC
Lawrenceville, Georgia, United States
Email: info@responsiblechild.com
Web: www.responsiblechild.com

Catherine Ford Sori, PhD, LMFT
Crown Point, Indiana, United States
Email: katesori@aol.com

Theresa Fraser, MA, CYW (Cert.), CPT
Cambridge, Ontario, Canada
Email: theresafraser@rogers.com
Web: www.theresafraser.com

Karen Freud, BA, A.T.
Toronto, Ontario, Canada
Email: karen@karenfreud.com
Web: www.karenfreud.com

Brijin Gardner, LSCSW, LCSW, RPT-S
Parkville, Missouri, United States
Email: brijingardner@gmail.com

Ken Gardner, M.Sc., R. Psych, CPT-S
Calgary, Alberta, Canada
Email: rmpti@telusplanet.net
Web: www.rmpti.com

Brenda Lee Garratt, T.A.T.I. Intern, A.O.C.A.D., E.C.E.
Goderich, Ontario, Canada
Email: brendalee.garratt@gmail.com

Jacob Gershoni, LCSW, TEP
New York, New York, United States
Email: jacobg12@gmail.com

Lori Gill, BA (SDS), CYW
St. Catharines, Ontario, Canada
Email: Creative.Counselling@bell.net
Web: www.creativecounsellingapproaches.org

Steve Harvey, PhD, RPT-S, BC-DMT
New Plymouth, New Zealand
Email: steve.harvey@tdhb.org.nz

Darryl Haslam, PhD, LCSW, RPT
Springfield, Missouri, United States
Email: DHaslam@missouristate.edu

Katherine M. Hertlein, PhD, LMFT
Las Vegas, Nevada, United States
Email: katherine.hertlein@unlv.edu
Web: www.kathertlein.com

Deborah Armstrong Hickey, PhD, LMFT, RPT-S
Greenville, South Carolina, United States
Email: healingartdoctor@hotmail.com
Web: www.themindgardencentre.com

Linda E. Homeyer, PhD, LPCS, RPT-S
San Marcos, Texas, United States
Email: LHomeyer@txstate.edu

Nikole Jiggetts, MSW, LCSW, RPT
Chesterfield, Virginia, United States
Email: Nikolejiggetts@yahoo.com

Mary Jo Jones, M.S., MFT-Intern
Las Vegas, Nevada, United States
Email: Maryjo08@live.com

Barbara Jones Warrick, M.Ed., CPT-S
London, Ontario, Canada
Email: b.e.jones.warrick@sympatico.ca

Nilufer Kafescioglu, PhD
Istanbul, Turkey
Email: nkafescioglu@dogus.edu.tr
Web: http://psychology.dogus.edu.tr/akademik.htm

Madhu Kasiram, PhD
Durban, South Africa
Email: Kasiramm@ukzn.ac.za

Sueann Kenney-Noziska, MSW, LISW, RPT-S
Las Cruces, New Mexico, United States
Email: info@playtherapycorner.com
Web: www.playtherapycorner.com

Connie-Jean Latam, D.N.M.
Kingsville, Ontario, Canada
Email: connie@cogeco.ca
Website: www.artoflivingresourcecentre.com

Laura Lazarus, MA
Manassas, Virginia, United States
Email: laura.lazarus@nationalcounselinggroup.com

Norma Leben, MSW, LCSW-S, ACSW, RPT-S, CPT-P
Pflugerville, Texas, United States
Email: norma@playtherapygames.com
Website: www.playtherapygames.com

Shirley U. Lindemann, C.A.C.T., S.R.S.P.
Massey, Ontario, Canada
Email: info@artandtherapy.ca
Web: www.artandtherapy.ca

Liana Lowenstein, MSW, RSW, CPT-S
Toronto, Ontario, Canada
Email: liana@globalserve.net
Website: www.lianalowenstein.com

Greg Lubimiv, MSW, CPT-S
Pembroke, Ontario, Canada
Email: glubimiv@hotmail.com
Web: www.lubimiv.ca

Sara Mennen, MS, NCC, LPC, LAMFT, RPT
New Ulm, Minnesota, United States
Email: smennen@siouxtrails.org
Website: www.siouxtrails.org

Cynthia Mota, BA
Las Vegas, Nevada, United States
Email: javiercynthia@embargmail.com

David Narang, PhD
Santa Monica, California, United States
Email: drdavidnarang@gmail.com
Web: www.drdavidnarang.com

Jennifer Olmstead, LMSW, RPT, C-ACYFSW, CAAC
Sault Ste. Marie, Michigan, United States
Email: jhentkowski@saulttribe.net

Susan Perrow, M.Ed.
Lennox Head, Australia
Email: susanperrow@gmail.com
Web: www.healingthroughstories.com

Julie R. Plunkett, LPC, LCPC, RPT-S
Olathe, Kansas, United States
Email: julieplunkett@sbcglobal.net

John W. Seymour, PhD, LMFT, RPT-S
Mankato, Minnesota, United States
Email: john.seymour@mnsu.edu

Angela Siu, PhD, CPT, CTT
Shatin, New Territories, Hong Kong
Email: afysiu@cuhk.edu.hk

Stacey Slobodnick, BSW, RSW
Windsor, Ontario, Canada
Email: Stacey.Slobodnick@glengarda.on.ca

Alison Smith, M.S.
Indianapolis, Indiana, United States
Email: Smith802@umail.iu.edu

Lauren Snailham, MA Clin. Psych
Durban, South Africa
Email: laurensnailham@dbnmail.co.za
Web: www.therapeuticstories.co.za

Barbara Spanjers, MA
Las Vegas, Nevada, United States
Email: barbspanjers@cox.net

Trudy Post Sprunk, LMFT, LPC-S, RPT-S, CPT-S
Tucker, Georgia, United States
Email: trudypostsprunk@charter.net

Rajeswari Natrajan-Tyagi, PhD, LMFT
Irvine, California, United States
Email: rnatrajan@alliant.edu

Heather Venitucci, MSW
Brooklyn, New York, United States
Email: heathervenitucci@gmail.com

Sandra Webb, B.A.Sc.
Cobourg, Ontario, Canada
Email: sandra@sandrawebbcounselling.com
Web: www.sandrawebbcounselling.com

Judy Weiser, R.Psych., A.T.R.
Vancouver, British Columbia, Canada
Email: JWeiser@phototherapy-centre.com
Web: www.phototherapy-centre.com

Lorri Yasenik, MSW, RFM, CPT-S, RPT-S
Calgary, Alberta, Canada
Email: rmpti@telusplanet.net
Web: www.rmpti.com

Pauline Youlin, MS, MFTI
Corona, California, United States
Email: pauliney3@hotmail.com

Foreword

Why work with children in families? After all, they can hardly have an adult conversation with you. They evade making direct answers to questions, they dodge, fall silent and make silly remarks. Often they don't understand what you are getting at, or pretend that they don't. And then there is the matter of their vulnerability. Although they live constantly with their parents, and are being injured and limited by their parents' fights and frustrations, many of us therapists are concerned that kids in conjoint sessions with adults will be victimized by the parents' heightened expressions of distress, anger, or depression. After all, the parents may conclude, there is a therapist present, so why not let loose? We may also be worried that kids will be further disillusioned by their troubled parents and feel less safe than they already do. And then there are the therapist's' concerns about what to do with these difficult little creatures and how to do it.

These are all serious questions and deserve consideration. However, there are compelling reasons for including kids in family sessions. The most powerful reason is that children and teenagers are the emotional heart of the family. If there is tenderness in the family, it is often felt and expressed in relation to the couple's kids. Parents who seem to hate each other can be brought to tears – or at least softened – when they begin to see how much their kids love them, how vulnerable these kids are, and how concerned they are about their parents. So kids are the tender underbelly of the family – vulnerable, and powerful in that vulnerability.

When helped to speak out, even if indirectly, through play, kids are usually honest. This can be especially true of teenagers, one of whom I recall waiting patiently for a long time through many hours of her parents' cheery dissimulation. Then, in the midst of a long, discouraged silence, she said, "The problem with this family is that nobody tells the truth." Then the therapy finally began.

Kids have so much at stake. How their families fare is a matter of life and death for them – their parents may be able to walk away from each other, but whatever protection and solace is possible for kids must usually come from their parents. Aunts and uncles and grandparents and stepparents and even adoptive parents and therapists can help kids, but there is nothing to truly replace a parent in the life of a child. Individual therapy with children is a pale substitute for helping the parents parent, and helping the kids at the same time.

Kids are incredibly loyal to their parents, and to their families. Kids remain committed to their parents through divorce, through being abused by them, through neglect. Even when they are embarrassed by or even ashamed of their parents, they determinably love them.

And they are courageous. Kids will eagerly volunteer to be the scapegoat to protect their parents from the challenges of facing their marital conflicts; they will at their own risk take sides in the interest of marital justice; they will come bravely to the rescue of a vulnerable parent. I remember one woman who described coming home every afternoon as a child and watching television with her depressed father – because she knew he needed her. When I saw her, she was married to a very troubled man whom she took care of. I remember one teenager saying point blank: "I stole the car to make my parents stop fighting."

And they are vulnerable. Daily, they suffer in so many ways at their parents' and sometimes siblings' hands. If we can work with the whole family, assemble and help expose their complex and troubled patterns, we can change the course of kids' lives by helping their parents change their behavior. This may be the most important work we do.

But how do we do it? How can we work more effectively with kids *in* their families, with their parents in the room? The truth is that many therapists were *parentified* kids in their families of origin. We learned to be rational and verbal and to rise above the muck of our families' troubles because they needed us to. Truth is, we may be a little afraid of kids; we tried to get over being kids, and we aren't sure we want to descend to that level again – even if we know how vulnerable and how powerful kids are. We get the logic of working with the whole family; but what can we do about our anxiety?

This book is an encyclopedia (think *Wikipedia*) of helpful ideas about working with kids in family therapy. It is compiled and written by therapists whose liking for kids and whose skill in working with them is obvious and infectious. The authors help us see that working with kids can be fun as well as very helpful to our clients' families. We even begin to suspect that working with families in this way, engaging kids actively in the process, can help us recover from that stiff overidentification with the adult perspective – as if there were really any such thing as an adult. Underneath, we are all kids.

While it is tempting to classify this book as an encyclopedia of techniques for working with families, it is more accurately described as an assemblage of *structured interventions*. The therapist introduces an activity, often labeled as a game or a project, and helps the family "do" the activity. The therapist has a light touch, and humor and creativity are encouraged and allowed to emerge. The activity "Family Genograms Using Miniature Objects," for example, is done with small objects to represent members of three generations of a family, or it can be drawn on a posterboard or created in a sandtray. We all know how provocative creating a genogram can be for adults; involving kids in the project adds an element of unpredictability and honesty. "Creating a Family Timeline" is another intervention that is likely to be lively and cooperative, as well as revealing.

A personal note on the structured interventions. For my dissertation, I did a study of four young couples and the parents of each spouse. I gave all the couples the same structured interview, throwing in questions I thought married couples really needed to talk about; and I tape recorded the discussions. (You can imagine what a huge mountain of data was generated; I wound up focusing on only two couples and their parents.) What I learned is that every couple, even the parent couples, went right to work on the interviews. Most couples spontaneously described their discussions as "therapeutic." "These sessions are helping us," they said. The lesson for me was that, given a useful stimulus and a safe environment, the couples used the occasion to make their own gains. They took the initiative, and they took advantage of the situation provided to them. The same thing obviously happens when families with kids are given useful tools through which to interact – they seize the chance to "work," even though the activity looks like play.

The book is divided into three sections: assessment, treatment, and termination. Yet it seems clear that assessment is also an intervention – families are usually not able to wait for diagnosis; they need to get down to work. And one wonders how, with so much fun going on, the therapist ever gets to termination.

The book begins with an excellent "Theoretical Overview," which is a kind of "manual of engagement" for working with children in their families. It deals with the theory and rationale for this important work, and it includes general strategies in dealing with, for example, disruptive behavior, countertransference issues, client resistance, the unmotivated client; ways of normalizing, reframing, confronting; issues of pacing, identifying strengths and offering psychoeducational information.

As for the encyclopedia of activities, they are wonderfully varied and creative. In the assessment section, there are "Family Strengths and Needs Game," "My Family as Animals," "My Life in the Sandtray," "Our Family Life Scavenger Hunt," "Video Crew," and many others.

The section on treatment encourages family members to reveal themselves to each other, to join together, and to cooperate. It is of course the core of the book. For example, in "Feeling Body Sculpture," a family member (usually a child begins) draws from a container a feeling word. This child then approaches another family member (often a parent) and with the permission of that parent helps the parent assume a posture that reflects that feeling – based on some recollection of the child about the parent. A child helps a parent sculpt a time he – the parent – was disappointed, for example, or proud. The therapist guides discussion and attempts to encourage understanding and empathy across the generations.

Other activities in this section include "Sibling Rivalry," "Royal Family," "Puppet Movie," "Feelings Hide and Seek," "Land of No Rules," and "Let It Rip."

In the termination section, there are indeed some good exercises to help families through the process of ending their therapy sessions.

In reading this book, I sometimes felt sad that my own practice was too adult-focused. If I were to do it all again, I would spend at least a year volunteering in a first- or second-grade classroom, so that I could learn more about young kids and get more comfortable joining with them and working with them. I would read this book and learn these approaches. I would make sure that my office had the requisite materials; I would certainly get a sandtray. I would try not to approach families with a "lesson plan," but would let my own intuition guide me in the activities I suggested. I would add my own wrinkles and variations. I would choose activities that I liked doing. I would approach my work more like play and keep my sense of humor active. I would have more fun, and so would my clients.

Augustus Y. Napier, PhD

Preface

The goal of this book is to provide compelling rationale for the involvement of children in family therapy sessions, and to present engaging assessment and treatment techniques for use in these sessions. When I invited family therapists to contribute their favorite, most successful interventions so that others could use them in their clinical practice, I was delighted with the range of creative ideas submitted. Family therapists from divergent theoretical orientations, work settings, or client specializations will find a wide range of creative and useable clinical interventions in this book.

The material in this text includes a theoretical overview, guidelines for successful practice, special tips for working with challenging situations, and a variety of assessment and treatment techniques.

The interventions have been divided into three sections. The book begins with engagement and assessment activities providing therapists with interventions to join with and evaluate families. The second section presents treatment techniques to facilitate the working through of therapeutic issues. The last section outlines interventions that can be incorporated as part of the family's termination process. A variety of activities are provided within each section to enable therapists to choose interventions that suit their clients' specific needs.

Each technique outlines specific goals. Materials needed to complete the activity are listed. The book includes detailed instructions for all activities and a discussion section that further clarifies application and process.

Practitioners using the interventions in this publication should be well-trained in child-focused family therapy. A warm and caring rapport must be established with the family, and the activities should be implemented using sound clinical principles.

I hope that readers of this book will deepen their understanding of the value of using play and arts activities in family therapy and will find the creative tools helpful in their clinical work.

Liana Lowenstein

Acknowledgments

First and foremost, and without whom this publication could not have been written, I thank the authors who offered so freely their creative techniques to this book. Special thanks to Trudy Post Sprunk who initiated the concept for this book, shared so many wonderful techniques, and provided invaluable support and guidance throughout the development of this publication. I am also grateful to Augustus Napier for his important contribution, and to Terry Trepper, Greg Moffatt, Charles Schaefer, and Chip Chimera for their support of this book.

My heartfelt thanks to Katherine Hertlein and Susan Kelsey, who reviewed the manuscript and provided helpful feedback on the text and activities. Thanks also to Beth McAuley and Patricia Kot for their editorial assistance. Thanks to Kim Bracic and Dave Friesen at Hignell Book Printing for their help in bringing this book to print and to Karrie Ross for designing the cover. Thanks to my family, friends, and colleagues for their continued support and encouragement. I am especially grateful to Steven and Jaime, for their unconditional love and for the joy they bring to my life.

Theoretical Overview

Clinicians using this book should be well trained in issues specific to play and arts therapies, as well as family systems theory. Below is a brief presentation of key theoretical and practical guidelines. A more detailed theoretical presentation is beyond the scope of this book. Readers are therefore encouraged to review standard texts and obtain further training. Suggestions for additional reading can be found in the "References and Suggested Reading" section. A list of organizations that provide relevant training is also included at the back of this book.

THE RATIONALE FOR CONDUCTING THERAPY WITH ALL FAMILY MEMBERS

Many therapists do not include children in family therapy for a variety of reasons. Taibbi (2007) eloquently states, "Some clinicians feel awkward about including children in family therapy. Two cultures, two different worlds, those of the children and those of adults, both need to be explored and understood, yet it's difficult. Parents feel they have to be careful what they say around the children; children, especially if they are young, often feel intimidated by the office, by the questions, by the seriousness of all the talk that they don't understand." Family therapists may exclude children from sessions because they feel uncomfortable working with children or because they feel they lack adequate training in working with children.

And, yet, the family systems perspective contends that the most effective way to work with individuals is in the context of their families. In fact, "from the existing research, it could easily be argued that targeting family issues is the single most important point of intervention for children and adolescents" (Henggeler et al., 1998). In their groundbreaking book, *The Family Crucible* (1978), Napier and Whitaker wrote, "Working directly with the totality of the forces that influence the individual is such a logical idea that it is hard to deny its validity." Ackerman (1970) also stated, "Without engaging the children in a meaningful interchange across the generations, there can be no family therapy." Involving all the children in the family therapy provides the therapist with a more accurate assessment of dynamics, interactional patterns, and rules. Including all the children in family sessions, rather than just the identified patient (I.P.), "shifts the focus away from the I.P., and reinforces the notion that it is a family problem, a product of interaction, rather than the fault of the I.P." (Taibbi, 2007). Moreover, children add their own novel ideas to family problems and solutions.

Moffatt (2004) writes, "In all my years as a counselor, without exception, every one of my clients has spent session time talking with me about issues from childhood. Clients 40 or 50 years of age have shed tears over things that happened when they were children. Often these issues were directly or indirectly the result of something their parents either did or did not do." Family therapy offers clients healing while the children are young instead of waiting forty years.

Parents may need to be educated about a systems approach to therapy. The analogy of a mobile can be used: "When one part is moved all the other parts are set in motion. The same thing happens in families: When one person has a problem it impacts other family members, so everyone needs to be involved in order to accurately determine how each person is affected by the problem" (Sori, 2006). Parents will be more receptive to bringing their children to family therapy if they understand the rationale and benefits.

THE USE OF CREATIVE THERAPIES IN FAMILY THERAPY

The techniques presented in this book incorporate a variety of creative therapeutic approaches, including play, sandtray, art, psychodrama, and PhotoTherapy. Each of these approaches are defined as follows:

Play therapy is the systematic use of a theoretical model to establish an interpersonal process wherein trained play therapists use the therapeutic powers of play to help clients prevent or resolve psychosocial difficulties and achieve optimal growth and development (Association for Play Therapy, 2010).

Sandtray therapy is an expressive and projective mode of psychotherapy involving the unfolding and processing of intra- and interpersonal issues through the use of specific sandtray materials as a nonverbal medium of communication, led by the client(s) and facilitated by a trained therapist (Homeyer & Sweeney, 2010).

Art therapy uses the creative process of art-making to improve and enhance the physical, mental, and emotional well-being of individuals of all ages. It is based on the belief that the creative process involved in artistic self-expression helps people to resolve conflicts and problems, develop interpersonal skills, manage behavior, reduce stress, increase self-esteem and self-awareness, and achieve insight (American Art Therapy Association, 2010).

Psychodrama employs guided dramatic action to examine problems or issues raised by an individual. Using experiential methods, sociometry, role theory, and group dynamics, psychodrama facilitates insight, personal growth, and integration on cognitive, affective, and behavioral levels. It clarifies issues, increases physical and emotional well-being, enhances learning, and develops new skills (British Psychodrama Association, 2010).

Photo Therapy Techniques use people's personal snapshots, family albums, and pictures taken by others (and the feelings, thoughts, and memories these photos evoke) as catalysts to deepen insights and enhance communication during their therapy or counseling sessions in ways not possible when using words alone (Weiser, 1999).

Each of the above modalities has its unique therapeutic properties depending on its application, practitioner, client, setting, and objectives. Play and arts therapies differ from traditional "talk therapy" in that they engage emotions in a direct and physical way, generate creative energy as a healing force, and creatively enable clients to express their problems and conflicts (Malchiodi, 2005). There are several compelling reasons for using art and play when working with children in the context of the family. Expressive therapies "significantly accelerate and deepen the psychotherapeutic process, engaging people more directly and more immediately than do any of the more traditional verbal therapies" (Zwerling, 1979). Additionally, while talk is still the traditional method of exchange in therapy and counseling, practitioners of expressive therapies know that "people also have different expressive styles—one individual may be more visual, another more tactile, and so forth. When therapists are able to include these various expressive capacities in their work with clients, they can more fully enhance each person's ability to communicate effectively and authentically" (Malchiodi, 2005).

Eliana Gil, one of the pioneers of family play therapy, emphasizes that play "can bring people together in a common, pleasurable task, which inherently promotes disinhibition and enjoyment" (1994). Similarly, Bailey and Sori (2000) aptly put it, "Family play therapy moves treatment from the intellectual, cerebral, abstract world familiar to adults, to the world of imagination, spontaneity, metaphor, and creativity that is familiar to children." Family play therapy "lives in the twilight zone between cognition and emotion, where the defenses are not on the alert" (Ariel, 2005).

Harvey's play therapy approach combines play, art, movement, video, and drama. Through these expressive play activities, family interactive patterns, themes, and metaphors are identified. Therapeutic play and art activities encourage family relatedness and help families reconnect on a deeper, more meaningful level. Harvey emphasizes how "families have the creative ability to address their conflicts in a naturalistic manner and that they can and do use play in their ongoing day-to-day life to both problem solve and resolve their basic emotional conflicts. When their emotional distress becomes too high, families lose their resourcefulness, and their everyday playful exchanges become negatively impacted…Play therapy can help families develop resourcefulness to address and problem solve their more specific concerns" (2009). Play and art therapies also help families explore any parallels between the dynamics in session and the interactions at home. This leads to greater insight and, ultimately, to positive changes within the family.

Narrative therapists Freeman, Epston, and Lobovits (1997) use playful approaches to "direct the focus away from the child as a problem and onto the child-problem relationship in a way that is meaningful for adults as well as intriguing, not heavy-handed or boring, for children."

Art therapy is also an effective technique with families because "it bypasses those censors that families may have adeptly construed. A family that did not know how to express feelings directly may find a way to do so when given an opportunity to draw or paint" (Klorer, 2006). When family members engage in an arts or play-based therapeutic activity, they often express thoughts and feelings that they otherwise may not feel comfortable expressing through traditional family talk therapy. Art and play-based activities can unlock a deeper level of communication.

In *A Violent Heart*, Moffat (2002) shares, "A few years ago I was demonstrating this principal for my counseling students. I gave one student Playdough, another Legos, and another crayons and paper. I instructed them to create anything they wanted using the medium that I provided for them and, based on what their creations communicated to me, I would tell each of them something about themselves." As family therapists we too can provide such materials to our clients. Art and play-based family therapy can effectively be used to help clients create and express their internal world and help them to gain insight.

JOINING WITH THE FAMILY

In the initial stages of therapy, the family therapist *joins* with the family. *Joining* means that clients feel a sense of connectedness with the therapist, which usually arises when they feel that the therapist understands, respects, and cares about them. Patterson et al. (2009) stress, "The importance of joining cannot be overstated: It forms the foundation for future work. Failure to successfully join with your clients will hamper all of your efforts, from assessment to treatment. For example, clients will be reluctant to share sensitive information if you have not established a safe and secure relationship with them. Likewise, clients may become highly resistant to or defensive toward suggestions if you have not created a strong therapeutic relationship with them. Ultimately, failure to join with clients will likely lead to premature termination of therapy."

While joining with the family in the beginning phase is critical to therapeutic success, Napier and Whitaker (1978) state, "the therapist must hold fast to his technical skills to avoid becoming entrapped in the family system…He must insist on being the *family's* therapist, drawing his major strength from his status as a professional outsider."

An important element of joining is being sensitive to the family's cultural differences. Clients' racial, ethnic, religious, and cultural backgrounds influence their family structure, roles, decision-making, and values. Respecting cultural differences is an important aspect of rapport building. Therapists need to self-evaluate their own prejudices and areas of inexperience and seek training in multicultural competence. Further, "therapists should be cautioned not to label or generalize behaviors prior to understanding the source of the behavior. In this way, the therapist is more likely to engage more genuinely with clients, thus being more sensitive and aware" (Hoshino, 2003). Bitter (2009) states, "Before we can know the richness and diversity of other families, we must come to know our own heritage. Whether we are part of the dominant culture or of one or more marginalized cultures, both our values and our families have been organized in ways that shape these meanings in our lives."

Research suggests that a positive emotional bond with the therapist is the most important factor in maintaining families in therapy (Hubble et al., 2000). Additional research (Friedlander et al., 2006) suggests that certain therapist behavior is more likely to facilitate a positive emotional bond. This includes listening carefully to each family member, explaining what family therapy is about, and capturing everybody's perspective.

THE ROLE OF THE FAMILY THERAPIST

The therapist plays a pivotal role in effecting changes in the family system. Colapinto (1991) describes the family therapist as playing different roles at different points of therapy, including the roles of producer, stage director, protagonist, and narrator. As a producer, the therapist creates conditions for the formation of the therapeutic system; as a stage director, the therapist introduces situations that challenge the existing structure and push the family toward more functional patterns; as a protagonist, the therapist takes the place of an additional member of the family and unbalances the family organization; as a narrator, the therapist comments on observed interactions and, by questioning each person's attribution of meaning to the behavior of other family members, helps develop new meanings. While taking on these roles, the therapist maintains such qualities as a respectful curiosity, a commitment to help families change, a preference for concrete behavioral modifications over talk about changed feelings, a constant readiness to formulate and modify hypotheses based on information received, and the ability to imbue the sessions with intensity while keeping the clarity of the therapeutic goal.

THE FAMILY LIFE CYCLE

To be most effective in helping children and their families, the therapist must understand the developmental stages of the family and the tasks involved at various stages. For a more thorough summary of the Family Life Cycle Stage Model, the reader is referred to Carter and McGoldrick (1999).

The family's developmental process can be described as a "dynamic one of oscillation between stability and change. Transitions do not include the continuous minor adjustments in the behavior of the family and its members but refer to periods of time when the family becomes used to and adapts to a new set of circumstances" (Rivett & Street, 2009). As an example, when a couple have their first child, there are many changes that the family must adjust to, including the pattern of dependency, the time the couple has together, distribution of household tasks, financial circumstances, and possible introduction of other caregivers into the home.

The typical transitions within a family involve "the setting up of a home together, the birth of a new child, children beginning school and then leaving home, retirement, and the death of a partner" (Rivett & Street, 2009). Families may encounter unique transitional events, such as divorce, a significant promotion, the placement of a child in out-of-home care, chronic illness, the untimely death of a family member, or remarriage. All families must adapt to major transitions, but the pressure to adjust to multiple transitions may be overwhelming. Families may seek therapy when unable to cope with a transitional crisis. When helping families deal with stressful life transitions, therapists must "consider the need for flexibility and adaptability in the face of transitional demands but also consider the family's ability to maintain stability. It is important to concentrate on managing change as well as recognizing the value of maintaining things as they are" (Rivett & Street, 2009).

ESSENTIAL SKILLS IN FAMILY THERAPY

Family therapists employ a variety of core skills in their work with clients. Below is a summary of the common skills of all therapies as they are applied to family therapy. Additional skills will be employed based on the therapist's theoretical orientation and style of working.

Structuring
It is the therapist's role to take the lead with the family and to provide a structure. This includes setting a time, a place, and setting for clients to safely talk about their issues and concerns, initiating discussion about rules in session, intervening if conflict escalates during a session, selecting appropriate interventions for sessions, and regularly reviewing treatment goals.

Empathizing
The therapist must understand and empathize with every member of the family. Rivett and Street (2009) eloquently capture the essence of empathy: "Empathy is essential for engaging individuals in honest and full participation in family therapy. The therapist's empathic response encourages family members to express long felt, but incompletely understood and seldom voiced aspects of their experience. Empathy is therefore a tool for understanding, this being achieved by reflection of feeling and open receptive listening."

Reflecting
The therapist listens and briefly reflects what is said so that each family member feels heard. It is the role of the family therapist to establish an open atmosphere in sessions and to ensure that each family member has an opportunity to express thoughts, feelings, and needs. The therapist conveys to parents that the child must be permitted to express thoughts and feelings openly in session, without fear of reprisal at home.

Hypothesizing and Formulating
During the therapeutic process, the therapist develops a hypothesis or formulation of what is happening within the family. There are different ways of describing the process of hypothesizing. Rivett and Street (2009) characterize a hypothesis as "a theory about how a family pattern contributed to the problem that has brought them to therapy and about what patterns/beliefs/ behaviors might be maintaining the problem now." Hypotheses guide the kinds of questions and issues that the therapist raises in sessions.

Tracking
During the tracking process the therapist listens intently to family stories and carefully records events and their sequence. Through tracking, the family therapist is able to identify the sequence of events operating in a system to keep it the way it is. What happens between point A and point B or C to create D can be helpful when designing interventions.

Using Self-Disclosure
The therapist must ensure that the focus of the therapy is on the client's issues. However, there are times when it is appropriate for the therapist to disclose personal information. The therapist should be aware of his/her own reasons for self-disclosing personal information and attempt to anticipate the impact on the client. Only information that is therapeutically beneficial to the client should be disclosed. The sharing of personal information on the part of the therapist is driven by a combination of personal style, theoretical orientation, and client consideration.

Using Questions

Integrating creative activities into family sessions can lead to rich and meaningful therapy. However, the techniques are not the therapy—they are merely the tools to facilitate the therapeutic process. The therapist uses the activities as a springboard for further discussion and exploration. Questions asked during or after particular activities can uncover clinical information, guide the client to face issues, or facilitate insight. The therapist asks questions that will reveal how the family is interconnected and how it operates as a system. Patterson et al. (2009) outlines four types of questions: lineal, circular, strategic, and reflexive. *Lineal questions* are investigative, deductive, and content loaded, and information gathered from these questions are meant to explain the problem. *Circular questions* are exploratory and uncover patterns in the relationships. *Strategic questions* are challenging in nature and pose new possibilities or positively influence the family system. *Reflexive questions* bring about change in the family without moving the family in any particular direction. Questioning is an important skill in family therapy and, when used appropriately, can foster change and growth in clients.

Normalizing

Clients often feel isolated and alone, or they believe they are crazy or abnormal. An important therapeutic skill is to normalize clients' experiences. To effectively do this, the therapist must have some knowledge of the behaviors, reactions, and experiences that fall within the normal range. Normalizing helps to relieve clients' anxiety about a particular problem and sets a positive tone in therapy.

Reframing

Reframing is when a therapist retells or reconstructs the language used by a family about its problems. An effective reframing provides a new context that gives the problem a new meaning (Rivett & Street, 2009). Creativity is required on the part of the therapist in order to reinterpret symptoms and behaviors presented in therapy.

Confronting

There are times in the treatment process when the therapist needs to confront the client. When confronting clients, the therapist must do so in a careful and sensitive manner, and the timing must be appropriate. Confrontation is necessary in order to bring about change in family systems.

Pacing

Pacing refers to how slowly or quickly material is addressed in sessions. The therapist can influence the pace by "creating opportunities for further exploration of a particular issue, changing the focus to another topic, adding depth or breadth to the discussion, or exploring the emotions related to the issue" (Patterson et al., 2009). *Mirroring* a client's behavior involves moving at the client's pace. *Leading* is when the therapist guides the client in a certain direction. Sessions need to be paced appropriately—if the pace is too slow, clients may feel frustrated that progress is not being made. On the other hand, if the therapist prematurely leads the client in a direction that he/she is not ready for, it can lead to a negative therapeutic response. Specific techniques that hasten the pace of therapy include "asking open-ended questions, leading in a particular direction, identifying the process in the session, and focusing on the here and now" (Patterson et al., 2009).

Identifying and Interrupting Negative Interactional Patterns

Interactional patterns within the family are observed during the assessment process. In later treatment sessions, the therapist employs a number of strategies to interrupt negative interactional patterns. The style and nature of such strategies will depend on the therapist's theoretical model.

Offering Psychoeducational Information

The psychoeducational process is an important element in family therapy. The therapist assesses the family's skill and knowledge in a variety of areas, so that the appropriate role for psychoeducation is clarified. The therapist helps the family gain insight, educates clients about particular issues, and facilitates skill-building. As the family learns and changes, progress is made, and a positive outcome is experienced.

Identifying Family Strengths

Assessment and treatment sessions must focus on identifying and addressing presenting problems within the family. However, it is equally important to focus on family strengths, as this gives the therapist and family "an opportunity to discover, or rediscover, positive qualities about individuals within the family and the family as a whole" (Patterson et al., 2009).

DEALING WITH COMMON CHALLENGES IN CHILD-FOCUSED FAMILY THERAPY

Working With Young Children in Family Sessions

One of the common challenges in family therapy is the discomfort that many therapists have about working with children. Therapists may be anxious about involving children in family sessions because they fear children will be non-communicative or disruptive. Integrating engaging and developmentally appropriate techniques into family sessions can help to involve children and can prevent disruptive behavior.

Therapists may feel they lack the ability to communicate with children in an age-appropriate manner. It is helpful to use simplified language without talking down to children. Using short sentences and concrete terms will be a more effective way to communicate with young children. Pairing age-appropriate verbal explanations with simple visual props is also a good strategy. For example, a poster depicting various emotional states (feeling faces) can be taped to the office wall and referred to during a session that focuses on feelings expression. Puppets, dolls, or figurines can also be used to communicate with young children.

Art and play-based techniques, coupled with the therapist's creativity and playfulness, are key ingredients needed in child-focused family therapy. Hopefully, the techniques presented in this book will provide family therapists with creative tools to engage children and families. Additional techniques can be found in some of the publications listed in the "Suggested Reading" section. Further training in play and art therapy can be found through some of the organizations listed at the end of this book.

Involving Teens in Family Sessions

Adolescents often present in family therapy as hostile and moody. Taffel (1991) suggests avoiding asking teens how they feel about something and refraining from making direct eye contact with them. Empowering teens by giving them an "observer" role can also be a helpful way to involve them in sessions. For example, a teen can be provided with paper and pen and asked to write down what he/she thinks were the three most important things said during the session. Another tip offered by Berg and Steiner (2003) is for therapists to avoid the temptation to teach, lecture, or give advice, and to instead explore the teen's thoughts and beliefs by saying, "You must have a good reason for…" This can initiate conversation and aid in treatment planning.

Engaging the Family in Play and Art Activities

Parents may have difficulty understanding the rationale and effectiveness of using play and art techniques in family therapy sessions. They may view games, drawings, puppets, and the sandbox merely as sources of entertainment for children. Parents may also feel uncomfortable, embarrassed, or silly participating in playful family therapy. It is helpful to meet with parents prior to the first family session to explain the value of using play and arts activities in family therapy and to help them embrace this approach. Wark (2003) outlines the following instructions for the parent session:

1. Inform parents that play and art activities are a part of your family therapy approach. Give examples of the techniques that are usually incorporated into sessions, such as games, drawings, puppets, and sandtray.
2. Ask the parents for their reaction to this method of working. If the parents express doubt or discomfort with this approach, normalize their feelings.
3. Ask the parents for their image and expectations of therapy, i.e., "What are your ideas of how therapy should be conducted with families? What do you think would help your children feel comfortable in therapy? Do you think it will be easy or difficult for your children to talk directly and openly about their thoughts and feelings? Do you think your children will be able to sit still during the entire session? What would help your children participate in the sessions?"
4. Explain some of the key benefits of using play and art techniques in family therapy: (a) children enjoy games, drawing, using puppets and playing in the sand, therefore they will feel comfortable with a play-based approach; (b) since children communicate through play, they will be able to express themselves more easily than traditional "talk therapy"; (c) since play and art activities are active in nature, children's attention is more likely to be captivated and sustained for the duration of the session; and (d) research shows that play helps children develop cognitive, affective, and sensorimotor skills (Singer, 1996).
5. Explain that many parents often feel hesitant to participate in play and art activities in the context of family therapy until they recognize that play is already a part of their behavior.

Provide examples, such as party games, dressing up for a costume party, backyard sports, etc. In addition, many parents already play with their children at home and, therefore, they will have a natural ability to play during therapy.

6. Reassure the parents that they will not be forced to do anything that makes them feel uncomfortable.

7. Provide the parents with printed information summarizing the benefits of playful family therapy.

When introducing play and art interventions into family sessions, "it is helpful to begin with activities that guarantee success; these tasks should be easy and should not require an explicit finished product. In addition, if the family members are asked to work as a group or in pairs, they may feel less conscious of their own contribution" (Revell, 1997).

For family members to feel comfortable participating in play or art activities, they must know that "they are in the presence of a therapist who is comfortable playing. The therapist must be willing to energetically demonstrate, participate and encourage family members in their play" (Revell, 1997). Family members will also feel more at ease engaging in playful interventions if the activities "fit the family style, values, and strengths" (Wachtel, 1994).

Managing Resistance

Anderson and Stewart (1983) define resistance as follows: "All those behaviors in the therapeutic system which interact to prevent the therapeutic system from achieving the family's goals for therapy. The therapeutic system includes all family members, the therapist, and the context in which the therapy takes place, that is, the agency in which it occurs." Resistance within a family session will typically be evident by either critical responses from the family or their non-involvement.

Family therapists need to recognize that all clients feel ambivalent about change. Thus, therapists should not view resistance as a failure but as an expected part of therapy. Nevertheless, there are a number of ways to address resistance. Improving the therapeutic alliance will often engage resistant clients. Another strategy involves further exploring the family's perception of the problem and helping them to set meaningful treatment goals. Family members are more apt to embrace therapy if they are involved in prioritizing the therapy agenda. A further remedy for resistance is to shift from a focus on problems to a focus on strengths. This empowers the family members and can ignite active discussion.

At times clients, particularly children, are resistant because they are bored or feel threatened by traditional "talk" therapy. Incorporating engaging, play-based techniques, such as the ones described in this book, often encourages involvement. On the other hand, parents may be reluctant to engage in play or art activities, and they need to be carefully encouraged. The therapist can meet with parents ahead of time and explain that through play and art activities, children will be able to express many of the emotions that they cannot talk about directly.

Engaging Unmotivated Clients

Some clients come to therapy because they are mandated by the courts to do so. Others are forced to come to therapy by family members. In either case, these clients tend to present in therapy as hostile and unmotivated. The therapist must work harder to join with these clients. Earning the client's trust and respect is an essential element in engaging hostile or unmotivated family members.

Some clients may have poor motivation because they do not feel therapy will be beneficial. Creating a basis for hope will help build motivation. Other clients are resistant to therapy because they believe it is only for crazy people. If this is the case, the therapist must try to reduce the stigma. Patterson et al. (2009) suggest comparing therapy to coaching, in that even the best athletes, such as Olympians or professionals, use coaches. Therapy can also be compared to consulting work, with clients likened to businesses that hire someone with special expertise to help them.

Dealing with Conflict within a Session

It is not uncommon for therapists to struggle with conflicts that erupt in a session. While the personal style of the therapist has an influence here, there are some general strategies that can be employed. If the therapist feels that the conflict might escalate into violence, then ending the session and seeing family members separately might be the appropriate route. The therapist can establish a "no violence" contract with the family. When younger children are involved, the therapist can incorporate an engaging activity to address safety within the home. For example, the family can draw a picture of a "safe home" in which there is no violence and rules for the appropriate expression of anger are followed. Or the family can be asked to create a puppet show to enact the conflictual situation, and then repeat the puppet show to demonstrate a more adaptive resolution to the problem. The therapist might reframe the conflict by saying, *"It is good that you are able to express yourselves and to know that you love each other so much that this will not affect your deep feelings for each other."* Another strategy is to use a positive connotation, for example, "I know that you are choosing to show anger because there is something you really want your family to hear: What might that be?" (Rivett & Street, 2009).

Managing Children's Disruptive Behavior in Sessions

Dealing with acting-out behaviors in family sessions is one of the most difficult issues facing therapists. The child who is non-compliant, disruptive, or aggressive can provoke unpleasant feelings in therapists such as frustration, anger, inadequacy, concern, and fear.

There are many reasons why children act out and there is always a message behind the behavior. Usually, the child's behavior is communicating an unmet need, for instance, a need to be engaged, empowered, nurtured, praised, heard, respected, etc. The therapist should try to decipher the message behind the child's behavior so that the child's needs can be better addressed.

Misbehavior can often be preempted by ensuring that the child is appropriately involved in sessions. The therapist should also be attuned to the child in order to address misbehavior before it escalates. Another strategy is to thank the child for showing his/her difficulties in the session so that the behaviors can be addressed in the present moment. The therapist can ask the parents to show how they handle the child's behavior at home. This provides the therapist an opportunity to assess the parents' child management abilities. The therapist can then give feedback and guidance to the parents.

The therapist can initially assume responsibility for limit-setting in family therapy sessions. This will allow the therapist to model techniques for the caregivers. However, the role of limit-setting should be gradually shifted to the parents as they develop competence in this area. Transferring the major responsibilities for discipline to parents strengthens their position in the family hierarchy.

Discussing rules in the initial session can also prevent misbehavior. Rules regarding safety must be established. A "pass" rule should also be set in the first session so family members do not feel pressured. Rules related to confidentiality should be discussed. For example, asking family members not to share with others what transpires during sessions. Other rules may need to be established, depending on the therapist's style and the circumstances of the family. The family can brainstorm the rules and they can be written on a sheet of paper and taped to the wall. Then when any inappropriate behavior emerges in the session, the therapist can ask the family to look at the sheet of rules, identify which rule is being broken, and discuss what needs to change in that given moment. When working with a family "who continually interrupt and speak on top of each other, a rule can be established that only the one person holding a particular ball, stuffed animal or rock may speak" (Revell, 1997). If the family is chaotic or aggressive, more time should be spent on establishing rules and boundaries.

There are times when a child's acting out behavior is an attempt to seek nurturance. If the therapist suspects that this is the case, then it can be helpful to enable the parents to reach out to their child in a soothing and caring manner.

Shifting Unrealistic Goals
Some clients may have unrealistically high expectations or goals of therapy. For example, parents may express the belief that their child's behavior will be completely problem-free after therapy. In this situation, the therapist must validate the client's goal and then reframe it so that it is more realistic and obtainable. Similarly, individual members within the family may define goals that are incompatible. If this is the case, the therapist needs to creatively reframe the goals so that they are compatible or in some way linked together. For example, parents may want their child to behave better, while the child wants the parents to stop yelling. The therapist could link these goals by suggesting that both the parents and the child have a common desire for mutually respectful behavior.

Dealing with Countertransference
Countertransference issues may lead to problems in family sessions if they are not properly addressed. The therapist may feel more of a natural empathy with the child or with one (or both) of the parents. Or, the therapist may prevent difficult family issues or the family secret from being

openly discussed because of his/her personal discomfort with the issue. Seeking appropriate clinical supervision and exploring one's own family of origin is recommended to address any countertransference issues (Carter & Orfanidis, 1978).

GUIDELINES FOR THE USE OF
CREATIVE ACTIVITIES IN FAMILY THERAPY

Select Activities that Fit the Family's Needs

There are a variety of techniques to choose from in this book. Techniques should be selected that involve all family members and that are appropriate to the developmental capacities of the children in the family. Turn-taking techniques should move fairly quickly, giving each family member a turn in short order (Lubimiv, 2009).

Techniques should be chosen that fit the phase of intervention, beginning with engagement and assessment activities, and then implementing treatment techniques that connect to therapeutic goals. Pacing is also important. The family's level of engagement in therapy and degree of defensiveness should be considered before implementing activities that are more emotionally intense or that require family members to take greater emotional risk.

Therapists are encouraged to be creative and modify the activities to meet the distinct needs of their clients.

Be Well Prepared in Advance of the Session

Prior to using any assessment or treatment exercise, the therapist should first review the activity and gather any necessary materials. If the therapist lacks confidence, then practicing and rehearsing the activity with a colleague before the session may be helpful. However, no matter how well prepared the therapist is for the session, the unforeseen can happen. The therapist needs, therefore, to be flexible and modify the plan according to the family's needs.

Consider Videotaping the Sessions

Videotaping the sessions and showing the family the videotape can be a powerful intervention. Videotape replay can help the family gain insight into their dynamics and understand how they need to change. It can also be helpful in the final stage of therapy to show the family a video of one of their early sessions as a way to highlight the changes the family has made (Trepper, 2002).

It is also helpful for the therapist to review videotaped sessions of clients for their own self-directed learning, as well as for use in clinical supervision. For a thorough list of what to watch for on the videotape, see Bitter (2009). When recording sessions, careful attention must be given to consent, confidentiality, and the security of videotapes.

Be Process Focused

The therapist should focus on the process rather than the techniques so that important family interactions are not missed. Activities must be implemented carefully and sensitively, always keeping in mind the family's treatment objectives.

The therapist should consider how to introduce, process, and bring closure to each activity. When introducing an activity, the therapist should be enthusiastic, expressive, and active in order to engage the family. The purpose of the activity should be outlined and the instructions clearly explained. As the family moves to a more engaged and ready state, deeper issues can be skillfully explored and processed. When the activity has been completed and sufficiently processed, the therapist provides positive feedback to the family on progress made and brings closure to the activity. The therapist should help the family explore how to apply the skills learned in the session to situations at home.

In addition to considering how to introduce, process, and bring closure to an activity in a particular session, the therapist must also be concerned with how the activity will affect the family beyond the session. Although some activities are designed to bring issues and feelings to the surface, care must be taken to ensure that each family member leaves the session in a positive frame of mind and that no one is at risk of being punished or of otherwise suffering consequences for feelings shared or disclosures made during the session.

Section One:
Engagement and Assessment Techniques

Chapter Overview:
Engagement and Assessment Techniques

When families decide to seek professional help, they often feel strong emotions that include being anxious, desperate, embarrassed, inadequate, overwhelmed, or hopeless. Individual family members may have different attitudes about starting treatment. Thus, in the initial session, the therapist must focus on putting the family at ease, praising efforts to seek help at this time, conveying empathy for each individual in the family, assessing each family member's reason and motivation for therapy, illuminating family strengths, and providing a sense of hope about resolving the problems.

The process of rapport-building, joining, or building an alliance between the therapist and the family is essential. The therapist must demonstrate genuineness, patience, respect, support, and empathic understanding. A positive therapeutic relationship is the key to a positive outcome in therapy (Shirk & Karver, 2003). Developing a positive rapport and establishing a safe environment for the family leads to a deeper and more significant level of sharing in family sessions.

In initial sessions, the therapist forms a few hypotheses that provide him/her with areas to explore in future sessions. Assessment activities and key questions should elicit information that will either support or invalidate the hypotheses.

A systemic assessment is critical as it provides the therapist with a thorough understanding of the way the family system works so that appropriate interventions can be selected and implemented. When the assessment and feedback process is done effectively, "it can influence accuracy and engagement in therapy by enhancing the participants' and professionals' appraisals, which in turn impact motivation to change" (Stormshak & Dishion, 2002).

During the assessment phase, the therapist observes issues of competence, cohesion, closeness, and control. In terms of competence, the assessment should focus on the family's ability to organize and manage itself as it accomplishes tasks, as well as the family's ability to problem-solve and resolve conflicts. The family's style of communication is also assessed, including their ability to talk openly and directly in a respectful manner and to express a full range of emotions.

Cohesion is the emotional bonding members have with one another. It is the degree to which family members are affectively connected with one another (Patterson et al., 2009).

Closeness refers to the parents' abilities to provide developmentally appropriate nurturance and care for their children. This includes the family's capacity to enjoy interactions with one another, and the parents' abilities to provide their children with appropriate affection and praise. It also relates to the parents abilities to focus on the emotional needs of their children.

When assessing control, the therapist should explore how decisions are made within the family, the way in which discipline is handled, whether consequences for misbehavior are appropriate and consistent, and whether the children take on age-appropriate responsibilities in the home (Patterson et al., 2009).

Assessment activities provide a window for therapists to observe process and content within family interactions. Process information relates to how the family interacts, the verbal and nonverbal expressions, and stylistic idiosyncrasies. Content information focuses on what is being said, including the symbolic meaning conveyed through the metaphor. It also includes the actual product created by the family (Gil & Sobol, 2000; Sori, 2006).

In addition to observing the process and content that evolves during an activity, the therapist should also observe nonverbal cues, such as facial expressions, tones of voice, energy level, amount of enjoyment, and degree of engagement (Sori, 2006).

A comprehensive assessment will facilitate a more accurate picture of the family. However, it is not enough to simply assess the family. The value of the assessment is in how it is used to develop a treatment plan that guides the therapy (Odell & Campbell, 1998). Assessment is also an ongoing process. It does not end after the first few sessions. The family therapist collects information and observes systemic functioning throughout the entire intervention process.

A variety of play and arts techniques are presented in this section to engage and assess families. Children are usually comfortable participating in play and arts activities. However, the parents may not be as comfortable. It is up to the family therapist to present these interventions in a way that helps parents accept them as legitimate and helpful approaches.

Basketball
Source: Liana Lowenstein

Goals
- Increase open communication among family members
- Identify positive aspects of family life and pinpoint areas for change

Materials
- Basketball net and hoop (or garbage can and crumpled paper)
- Question cards (included)
- Blue and yellow cardstock or index cards
- Adhesive labels
- Masking tape
- Prizes (optional)

Advance Preparation
To make the basketball question cards, photocopy the happy face questions provided onto yellow cardstock and cut them into cards. Or copy the questions onto yellow index cards. Color a happy face on the other side. Photocopy the sad face questions provided onto blue cardstock and cut them into cards. Or copy the questions onto blue index cards. Color a sad face on the other side.

Set up the basketball net and hoop. Place masking tape along the floor to create a "throw" line.

Copy each job from the list below onto a separate self-adhesive label:

Police Officer:	Ensures family members are following rules for good behavior such as listening when others are talking.
Consequencer:	If a family member exhibits inappropriate behavior during the session, the Consequencer leads the family in a discussion about a fair consequence.
Cheerleader:	Cheers the family member on when he/she is shooting a basket.
Reader:	Reads the questions aloud to the players.
Summarizer:	Summarizes significant information learned during the game about each family member.

Description

Explain to the family that they are going to play a special version of basketball, which will help them to discuss happy and sad experiences. The rules are explained as follows:

"Family members take turns shooting a basket. If a player successfully throws the ball through the basketball hoop, he/she picks a card from the 'happy face' pile. These questions relate to happy experiences. If a player misses the basket, he/she picks a card from the 'sad face' pile. These questions relate to unhappy experiences. The game continues until all the questions have been answered, or until each family member has had a pre-chosen number of turns. If all of the question cards are answered before the game is over, the pile of cards can be shuffled and re-used."

As an optional component of the game, give a small prize for each question answered.

Prior to the start of the game, assign one job to each family member (see above list of jobs). Have family members stick their labels onto their shirts and explain their designated jobs to them.

Active discussion among the family is encouraged during the game. Stop the game periodically to expand on feelings or issues disclosed by the family members.

After the game, facilitate discussion by asking the following process questions:

1. What new information did you learn about your family?
2. What was the most interesting or surprising response?
3. Name something you liked about a family member's response.

Discussion

Closed communication within a family is often a major factor preventing healthy family functioning. This game increases open communication among family members, particularly when children need help to express their feelings to their parents or siblings. Modifying the traditional game of basketball can engage the family and involve them in playful interaction. The questions can be modified to suit the needs of the family. It is also useful to "ask family members, including children, to make up a few of their own cards to be included in the game, involving questions they think other families or children might find useful or fun. This exercise of creating cards is projective in nature, and often gives the clinician added insight into children and their families" (Gil, 1994).

The therapist can use this game to assess the family's relationships and style of interaction, their playfulness or rigidity, and the roles members assume. The assessment information is used to intervene therapeutically to address issues raised by the family.

Each client is assigned a "job" such as Police Officer or Cheerleader. This facilitates participation of all family members and maintains their interest in the game. The jobs can be randomly assigned or the therapist can be more purposeful in assigning them. For example, the oppositional child can be asked to be the Police Officer in order to encourage appropriate behavior. Assigning the role of Cheerleader to a parent can help that parent provide the children with positive reinforcement.

The process questions at the end of the game facilitate discussion among family members and encourage insight.

The use of prizes is an optional part of the activity, but the prospect of "winning" something during the course of the game may lower defenses and incorporates an additional component of engagement and playfulness into the technique.

References

Gil, E. (1994). *Play in family therapy*. New York: Guilford.

Lowenstein, L. (1999). *Creative interventions for troubled children and youth*. Toronto, ON: Champion Press.

About The Author

Liana Lowenstein, MSW, RSW, CPT-S, is a social worker and Certified Play Therapy Supervisor in Toronto. She maintains a private practice, provides clinical supervision and consultation to mental health professionals, and lectures internationally on child and play therapy. She has authored numerous publications, including the books *Paper Dolls and Paper Airplanes: Therapeutic Exercises for Sexually Traumatized Children, Creative Interventions for Troubled Children and Youth, Creative Interventions for Bereaved Children*, and *Creative Interventions for Children of Divorce*.

Basketball
Happy Face Question Cards

What is your favorite meal?	What do you like to do for fun?	When was the happiest moment of your life?
What's something that money can't buy that brings you happiness?	Tell about a time someone in your family did something nice for you.	Tell about a time you and your family did something fun together.
Name one kind or loving thing you do for someone in your family.	Name someone outside your family whom you care about.	What's one of the best things that has happened in your family?
Tell about a time your family was able to solve a problem.	Tell about a family holiday or celebration that you enjoy.	What are you looking forward to doing together as a family?

© Liana Lowenstein

Basketball
Sad Face Question Cards

What is your least favorite meal?	What is something you really don't like doing at home?	Tell about a sad moment in your life.
What's one of your biggest worries?	Tell about a time someone in your family made you angry.	What would you say to someone who smiled even when they felt upset?
What is something you do that bugs others in your family?	Tell about a time you did something that made someone in your family angry.	What's something sad or difficult your family has experienced?
Tell about a problem your family is experiencing.	When was the last time you cried? What happened that made you so upset?	What is something you would like to change about your family?

© Liana Lowenstein

8

Beach Ball Game
Source: Trudy Post Sprunk

Goals
- Establish a safe and open therapeutic environment
- Identify the family interactional patterns that are contributing to the problematic behavior
- Increase open communication among family members.

Materials
- A small beach ball that has 4-6 colors
- Questions (included)

Advance Preparation
Arrange the therapy space so that tossing a small beach ball causes no damage.

Description
Ask the family members to sit in a circle (on chairs or on the floor). Request that, while seated, a family member gently tosses the ball to another family member. The family member who catches the ball notices the color his/her right thumb is on at the time of the catch. The color is reported to the therapist who reads aloud one of the open-ended questions found in the corresponding color category. The therapist is always free to choose which open-ended question to read or to create one for the client.

After an individual responds, other family members can share their thoughts and/or feelings, or add additional information. Then the ball is gently tossed to the next person and the pattern is repeated.

As an aid to helping the family process this experience, ask the following questions:

1. Name something you liked about a family member's response.
2. If you could change a person's response, how would you change it?
3. Tell something new you learned about another family member.
4. Who do you feel you know better since playing the game? Who would you still like to know more about?

Discussion
The experience of tossing a beach ball during therapy creates a playful environment that decreases defensiveness. The therapist reads the open-ended questions and the family members' responses serve as an assessment tool that can aid in uncovering areas of distress. In addition, through each individual's response, greater insight is acquired.

The order and pacing of questions in this game is important. The therapist should begin with neutral questions, such as "My family likes to…" Feelings questions can come next, such as "I like the way…" As the family begins to feel more at ease, questions that involve greater risk-taking can be posed, such as "I feel bad when my family…" Since this is an engagement activity, the therapist should be in tune with the family's readiness to respond to questions that may feel threatening. End the game on a positive note with a question such as "At home I really like…"

About The Author

Trudy Post Sprunk, LMFT-S, LPC-S, RPT-S, CPT-S, is a Licensed Marriage and Family Therapist and Supervisor who has been practicing psychotherapy since 1971. She has presented at international, national, and local conferences and has been interviewed on radio and television. She is certified as an EMDR Specialist and is a Registered Play Therapist Supervisor. She is past-president of the Association for Play Therapy and president and co-founder of the Georgia Association for Play Therapy.

Beach Ball Game
Questions

Red
- My family likes to...
- My family is proud of me when...
- I feel bad if my family...
- I let someone in my family make me feel...
- I wish my family...

Orange
- My happiest memory with my family is...
- I need...
- I feel hurt when...
- I would not like to have...
- I'm expected to...

Yellow
- Something funny that happened in my family was when...
- Someone in my family gets angry when...
- I feel disappointed when...
- I hate it when...
- When a person is sad, he/she should...

Blue
- I love to give...
- Once someone helped me...
- When something is hard for me I...
- I don't like to...
- I would hate to lose...

White
- I like the way...
- Something I appreciate about my family is...
- I'm sad when...
- I get angry when...
- My mother and I like to...

Green
- I just love to...
- I'm the kind of person who...
- My father thinks I...
- If someone loves you, they...
- At home I really like...

© Trudy Post Sprunk

Boat-Storm-Lighthouse Assessment
Source: Trudy Post Sprunk

Goals
- Gather information about the family, especially issues pertaining to danger and rescue
- Create an opportunity to express feelings such as fear, helplessness, hopelessness, bravery, etc.
- Identify ways to access support

Materials
- Large sheet of white paper or poster board
- Markers
- Paper and pencil for each family member

Advance Preparation
Provide a large flat surface for the drawing activity. Place the large sheet of paper or poster board so all family members can easily reach it. Arrange seating to insure privacy while writing.

Description
Explain to family members that they are to fill a poster board with one drawing of a boat, a storm, and a lighthouse. They are to complete the task silently. Upon completion, ask each to write a story about what he/she thinks happened before, during, and after the storm. A young child can quietly dictate a story to the therapist. After each person shares his/her story, the therapist guides the family in a discussion involving fears, rescue, danger, and how to access family support when needed. The therapist models acceptance of the diverse beliefs and experiences within the family.

The therapist may help the family experience the process by exploring the following:

1. What do you think it would have been like to be in the boat with your family during the storm?
2. Who would have been most helpful to you during the storm?
3. Can you name three feelings you might have had during the worst part of the storm?
4. If you believed that a rescue would occur, how did you think it would happen?
5. In what ways could you have asked for help?

Discussion

Boat-storm-lighthouse assessment is an engaging activity. The drawing provides a glimpse into each family member's inner world, including traits, attitudes, behaviors, and personality strengths and weaknesses. More specifically, the drawing enables the therapist, as well as the family members, to learn such things as who tends to be optimistic and upbeat or who might be more pessimistic or morbid. It also uncovers the ability to mobilize inner resources and access external support when faced with danger and conflict. A family art activity "is a tool that provides the therapist and the participants with a vehicle for exploration. During the evaluation phase the art task offers the family a focus for an interactional experience. This technique, which delineates communication patterns, is viewed primarily through the process and secondarily through the content… From the moment the family is involved in creating a product, a record of each action is documented onto the construct. Thus, cause and effect are observable, enabling the clinician to assess both the strengths and weaknesses of the total family and the members therein" (Landgarten, 1987).

Family differences can be openly discussed, as well as some of the reasons these differences exist in the family. The therapist models support for the individual differences and encourages the family to support a member who is not thinking or feeling positively. A discussion of how to access family support is the final stage of this activity.

Reference

Landgarten, H.B. (1987). *Family art therapy: A clinical guide and casebook*. New York: Routledge.

About The Author

Trudy Post Sprunk, LMFT-S, LPC-S, RPT-S, CPT-S, is a Licensed Marriage and Family Therapist and Supervisor who has been practicing psychotherapy since 1971. She has presented at international, national, and local conferences and has been interviewed on radio and television. She is certified as an EMDR Specialist and is a Registered Play Therapist Supervisor. She is past-president of the Association for Play Therapy and president and co-founder of the Georgia Association for Play Therapy.

Bull's Eye Assessment
Source: Julie R. Plunkett

Goals
- Define the presenting problems that led the family to therapy
- Expand the presenting problem outward and away from the individual
- Begin defining goals for treatment

Materials
- Scissors
- Pens or pencils
- Dartboard (included)
- Dart Template (included)
- Tape

Advance Preparation
Copy (and enlarge, if desired) the dartboard onto white paper. Tape it to the wall. Make multiple copies of the dart templates. Cut out the darts.

Description
Instruct the clients to brainstorm problems within the family that have led them to therapy. Describe the three circles as follows:

Current Problems in Our Family: These are the problems that led you to come to therapy. For example, the children are having difficulty accepting their new stepfather.

Past Problems in Our Family: These are the problems in your past that have led up to the current problems. For example, Johnny is angry about his parents divorce and this makes it hard for him to become close with his new stepfather.

Problems Outside Our Family: These are the influences outside the family that add to the current problems. For example, the mother's family is against the new marriage and the children are aware of this.

Once a person has written his/her problem on a dart, instruct him/her to shoot the dart at the target (this is simply done by having a family member walk it up to the bull's eye). The person will then attach the dart with tape to the section of the bull's eye that it relates to (Current Problems in Our Family, Past Problems in Our Family, or Problems Outside Our Family). They can do as many or as few as needed.

Facilitate a discussion that focuses on the above process. Ask questions such as:

1. What problems were *targeted* (defined)?
2. Which problems did you agree on? Disagree on?
3. How can this activity help you and your family?
4. Which problems would you like to *shoot for* (focus on) in therapy?
5. How will you feel once some of the problems are addressed?

Discussion

This intervention assesses salient problems within the family and identifies goals for future therapy sessions. It allows each member to have a voice and encourages family discussion. The activity helps the family *target* the presenting problem as well as look at the larger framework. By including the family in formulating treatment goals, the family can take ownership of the problems and enhance their motivation to find solutions.

The use of the target adds a playful element and allows all family members, even young children, to be meaningfully involved in the session. As Hardaway (1994) states, "Small children have important messages to share, and play is the medium through which small children, and in fact, some older individuals, are best able to work and express themselves."

The therapist can normalize feelings that are raised during the session. Empathic statements suggesting how difficult things must be for the family can help the family feel supported.

Reference

Hardaway, T.G. (1994). Family play therapy as an effective tool in child psychiatry. In C.E. Schaefer & L.J. Carey (Eds.), *Family play therapy*. New York: Jason Aronson.

About The Author

Julie Plunkett, LPC, LCPC, RPT-S, is a Licensed Counselor and a Registered Play Therapist Supervisor in Kansas. She provides counseling to children and their families. Her clinical practice focuses on issues such as foster care, adoption, chronic illness, and divorce. She is an instructor and supervisor for the Play Therapy Certificate Program at the MidAmerica Nazarene University.

Bull's Eye Assessment
Dartboard

Bull's Eye Assessment
Dart Template

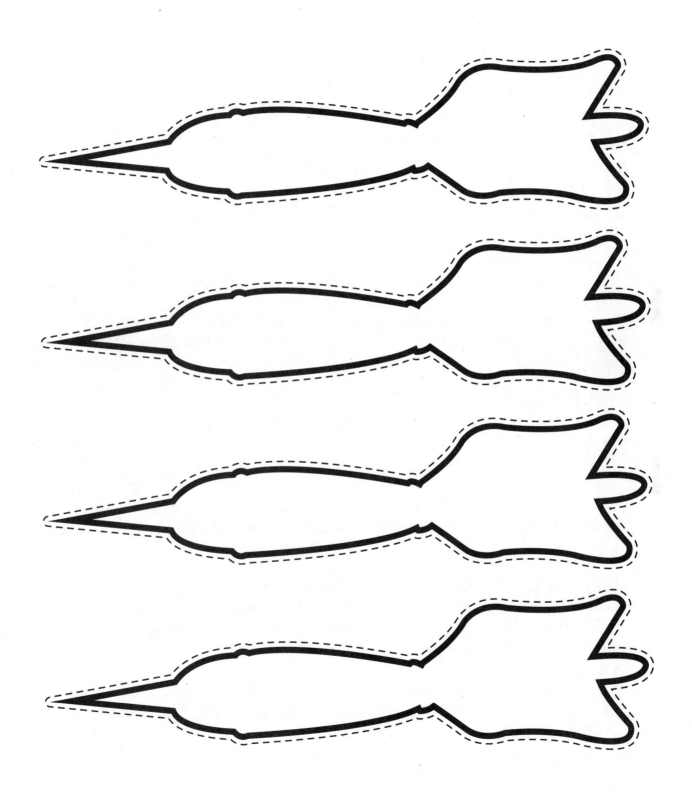

Create-A-Family Collage
Source: Trudy Post Sprunk

Goals
- Establish a safe and open therapeutic environment
- Identify the family interactional patterns that are contributing to the problematic behavior
- Increase open communication among family members

Materials
- White poster board
- Large variety of pictures cut from magazines
- Scissors for children
- Scissors for adults
- 1-3 glue sticks
- Paper and pencil for use by one of the parents

Advance Preparation
Arrange a flat space for the poster board so that each person has easy access. Arrange the magazine pictures face up near the flat surface so all family members can easily see them.

Description
Ask family members to silently cut out pictures and/or words that describe how they feel about their family life. Next, ask them to randomly glue their picture and/ or word choices on the poster board.

Ask members to explain the reasons for their choices. Encourage them to explain their perceptions about their family life, supporting their enjoyment of the positives and exploring solutions when problem areas are presented.

Request that family members each select one of the pictures from the collage to be used to create a story about their family. After the pictures are chosen, explain that the goal is to incorporate all the pictures into one story. The completed story needs to have a title, beginning, middle, and end.

Have family members decide on the order for the storytelling: who will begin the story, who will go next, and so on. Once each family member has had a turn (or multiple turns) contributing to the story, ask the family to decide together on a title for the collage and the story.

Using the pencil and paper, one of the parents writes and then reads the completed story. The family processes their feelings and thoughts about their experience and their story. The following process questions can guide the discussion:

1. In what way(s) does your story remind you of your family life?
2. What was it like to work together toward the goal of creating a story?
3. Can you name a picture you wish you could have added to the story?

Discussion

This technique offers opportunities for families, in the safety of the therapeutic environment, to express positive and negative perceptions of their family life. Incorporating the art process into family sessions "allows participants to simultaneously express their thoughts and feelings through individual and group art activities. Individual and family beliefs can be communicated within a single art expression" (Riley & Malchiodi, 2003). Thus, the therapist as well as the family is able to assess family issues and needs. Once concerns are shared, the family can work to correct misperceptions or problem-solve any anxieties.

In addition, mutual storytelling provides masked opportunities to tell one's story, which can include ideas, needs, emotions, beliefs, hopes, and so on. As the completed story is read aloud, each person can hear his/her part of the story, take in the input of others, and compare and contrast the family's responses.

Reference

Riley, S., and Malchiodi, C.A. (2003). Family art therapy. In C. Malchiodi (Ed.), *Handbook of art therapy*. New York: Guilford.

About The Author

Trudy Post Sprunk, LMFT-S, LPC-S, RPT-S, CPT-S, is a Licensed Marriage and Family Therapist and Supervisor who has been practicing psychotherapy since 1971. She has presented at international, national, and local conferences and has been interviewed on radio and television. She is certified as an EMDR Specialist and is a Registered Play Therapist Supervisor. She is past-president of the Association for Play Therapy and president and co-founder of the Georgia Association for Play Therapy.

Family Genograms Using Miniature Objects
Source: Lois Carey

Goals
- Identify intergenerational roles, patterns, and issues
- Increase open communication among family members

Materials
- 2 large sheets of white paper or poster board
- Pencil with eraser
- Markers
- Large selection of miniature non-breakable objects such as small items in and around the office, nature items, character figurines, small toys, plastic animals, costume jewelry, etc.
- Sandtray half-filled with sand (for sandtray version)
- Camera

Advance Preparation
Arrange a flat space for the poster board so that each person has easy access to it. Arrange the markers and miniature objects near the flat surface so all family members can easily access them.

Set up an example of a genogram that covers three generations.

Description
Explain the use of genograms to the family, using the example. Outline that the purpose of the activity is to help the family members see themselves and each other in relationship to the others and to help them understand what some of the underlying problems may be within the family. Describe the steps of the activity as follows:

"First, I would like each one of you to show me what your family is like compared to the one I illustrated for you. I have laid out a large piece of paper and I would like you to draw your family – use squares for males and circles for females. (It might be helpful to first draw the genogram with a pencil in case an error is made, and then trace over the pencil with the marker.) You can add the age of the person on the symbol if it is known. Please include all of the children, the parents, and the grandparents, along with any other significant relatives (aunts/uncles/cousins). The whole family can contribute to the making of the genogram. After the genogram is drawn, I would like you to select an object from those that are laid out that reminds you of each person on the genogram and place it on the genogram where that person is shown. It is important that the maker select an object for him/herself as well. Each of you is to choose an object for each person on the genogram and place it on the genogram. Comments about another member's choice are not permitted at this time. You will have an opportunity to discuss the various choices later during the discussion part of this activity."

When the genogram is complete, ask process questions such as:

1. Why does so and so remind you of that object/figure/animal/etc.?
2. What new information did you learn about your family?
3. What made you the most curious?
4. How did you feel when you described your choices?
5. Where do you see the strengths in your family?
6. What do you think needs to be changed in your family?

Following the question period, the family can use the chosen objects and make a scene with them. If the therapist is trained in sandplay work, then the scene can be portrayed in the sand tray. If not, a scene can be created on top of another large-sized clean piece of paper.

Once the scene is completed, continue by asking the maker about his/her thoughts/feelings regarding what he/she has produced; that is, what is it about the person that suggests a tiger or a bear (or other object)? Then each family member is invited to add his/her interpretation. An especially important figure is the one chosen for the maker–for example, does he/she see him/herself as vulnerable, strong, helpless, and so on? Finally, the therapist can add his/her thoughts, especially by noting where the alliances in the family are and/or where there may be conflict.

Take a picture of the genogram for the family and for the clinical file.

Note: Depending on the size of the family (more than three or four), it may be easier for each family member to create his/her own genogram on a separate piece of paper.

Discussion

Family therapists frequently do not include young children in family therapy sessions and are thus excluding a most important part of the family. In addition, many family therapists are uncomfortable with "play," an essential component to working with children in a family. A genogram is a familiar technique for family therapists and can help ease the transition from an adult treatment approach (verbal) to one that includes an attitude of "play" for all family members, young and old alike. It has been found that play is the language of children and when families can see the value of communicating with their children in this way, often symbolically, significant improvements are possible. When one makes a genogram "come alive" through the use of objects, it is more possible to see, depending on the placement and type of objects used, who is in the role of the scapegoat, the patient, the leader, the controller, or the follower, and if there is a "family secret" or if there are family alliances, and so on.

A wealth of information about the family can be revealed through the use of the genogram when combined with three-dimensional objects. It is also important to notice who has been left out and ask the maker why that person(s) is (are) not included. This is especially helpful if the case is one of a death in the family, or the parents are divorced, or it is a stepfamily.

This technique is suitable for diverse types of cases – for example, families that are intact; single-parent, homosexual/lesbian, and divorced families; families that have experienced a death, sexual abuse, or depression. This technique can be used during the assessment stage as well as during the treatment process by addressing the problems that have been revealed by the genogram.

References

Carey, L. (1991). Family sandplay therapy. *Arts in Psychotherapy* 18: 231–239.

Carey, L. (1999). *Sandplay therapy with children and families*. New York: Jason Aronson.

Gil, E. (2006). *Helping abused and traumatized children.* New York: Guilford.

Imber-Black, E., Roberts, J., & Whiting, R. (Eds.). (1988). *Rituals in family therapy.* New York: W.W. Norton.

McGoldrick, M., Gerson, R., and Petry, S. (2008). *Genograms: Assessment and intervention (3rd ed.).* New York: W.W. Norton.

About The Author

Lois Carey, LCSW, RPT-S, is a Licensed Clinical Social Worker, a Registered Play Therapist Supervisor and Provider. She is in private practice and conducts ongoing training and clinical supervision through the Center for Sandplay Studies. She has lectured internationally and throughout the United States. She is an Approved Provider for the Association for Play Therapy and grants Continuing Education Units for that association. She has authored and edited four books, two of which have been translated into Korean and Chinese, and authored numerous chapters and articles in books and journals.

Family Strength Genogram
Source: Angela M. Cavett

Goals
- Identify strengths of individual family members and the family as a whole
- Broaden the view of family members to include positive attributes
- Increase the rate of positive verbal comments and pleasurable exchanges between family members

Materials
- Large piece of paper or poster board
- Pencil with eraser
- Marker
- Large selection of miniature non-breakable objects such as small items in and around the office, nature items, character figurines, small toys, plastic animals, etc.; or a variety of pictures cut from magazines
- Scissors
- Tape
- Camera

Advance Preparation
Arrange a flat space for the poster board so that each person has easy access to it. Arrange the markers and miniature objects (or magazines) near the flat surface so all family members can easily access them.

Set up an example of a genogram that covers three generations.

Description
Explain the concept of genograms to the family, using the example. Then have the family draw their own genogram, using squares for males and circles for females. (It might be helpful to first draw the genogram with a pencil in case an error is made, and then trace over the pencil with the marker.) Ask them to begin with the parents and then add the children, grandparents, aunts, uncles, and other significant relatives. Names and ages (if known) should be included for each person added to the genogram.

After the genogram is drawn, the family is introduced to an array of miniature objects or magazine pictures. The family is asked to pick a miniature object (or magazine picture) for each person on the genogram that represents that persons positive attributes or "something that everyone likes about them or something he/she is good at." The family must decide together on one object for each person on the genogram. (If they do not agree, the therapist can encourage negotiation.) The miniature object or picture is placed on the paper where that person is represented with either a circle or a square. The parent or therapist may help younger children with the placement of the figure/picture.

23

Take a picture of the Family Strength Genogram for the family and for the clinical file.

The following process questions may be used with adaptations for the developmental stage of the child:

1. Describe the miniature objects/pictures chosen to represent the strengths of each person on the genogram.
2. Do all your family members have some positive characteristics?
3. Who are you most like? Who are you least like?
4. Who is most supportive of you? What characteristics does that person have?
5. If someone in your family has hurt or upset you, can you still appreciate their strengths?
6. Do you tend to focus more on the strengths or weaknesses of others in your family?
7. What would change in your family if you focused more on the strengths of individual family members?

Discussion

The genogram is a powerful therapeutic tool to assess relationships among family members and familial patterns. For a thorough review of the genogram, see McGoldrick and Gerson (2008). Gil (2006) developed the Play Genogram as an extension of the genogram in which the child uses miniature objects to depict his/ her view of family members. The Play Genogram allows children to process thoughts and feelings about their family and the relationships between themselves and family members.

In therapy, clients at times restrict discussion about some of their emotional experiences. These restrictions may be a result of the individual feeling that some information should not be shared. At times, cultural differences may restrict one's sharing of information in therapy. When sharing their personal or familial narrative, clients may be reluctant to talk about salient issues in the family. The original Play Genogram allows for a lessening of these restrictions and facilitates a more open discussion of family issues and relationships. This lessening of the restrictions may stem from the nature of the activity that allows the representation of significant others and relationships to be discussed symbolically through miniature objects or magazine cut-outs. In the Family Strength Genogram, the same process of symbolic representations of people or relationships could allow for a lessening of the restriction and help clients talk more openly, particularly about family strengths.

The Family Strength Genogram challenges the family to focus on the positive qualities within their family. This can create a positive shift for the family and help to create a more positive atmosphere.

Great care and clinical judgment must be used before, during, and after the Family Strength Genogram intervention if there is a history of child maltreatment. The child should be asked to think of positive characteristics only when the therapist has fully heard the child's experiences with different family members, especially if the child has been abused or neglected. If the therapist feels that the intervention is minimizing the child's abusive experience, the intervention should not be used.

References

McGoldrick, M., Gerson, R., and Petry, S. (2008). *Genograms: Assessment and intervention (3rd ed.).* New York: W.W. Norton.

Gil, E. (2006). *Helping abused and traumatized children*. New York: Guilford.

About The Author

Angela M. Cavett, PhD, LP, RPT-S, is a Psychologist in private practice providing evaluation and therapy to children, adolescents, and families. She is an adjunct faculty member at the University of North Dakota in the Department of Counseling Psychology. She is a Registered Play Therapist Supervisor and provides training and supervision related to child psychopathology and treatment, including play therapy. She is the author of *Structured Play-Based Interventions for Engaging Children and Adolescents in Therapy* (2010).

Family Strengths and Needs Game
Source: Stacey Slobodnick

Goals
- Identify strengths and needs within the family
- Increase open communication among family members

Materials
- Gameboard (included)
- Game cards (included)
- Blue and red card stock or construction paper
- Blue, red, and yellow markers
- Scissors
- Treats (small individually wrapped candies)
- One die

Advance Preparation
Photocopy the question cards onto blue card stock and cut them into cards, or write the questions onto blue construction paper. Photocopy the "Person in My Family Who…" cards onto red card stock and cut them into cards, or write the questions onto red construction paper. Copy (and enlarge, if desired) the gameboard onto white paper. Color in the squares blue and the circles red. Stars can be colored yellow. Use a treat as the single play piece to start the game.

Description
Begin by explaining that families often focus only on problems, and rarely discuss their strengths. Introduce the Family Strengths and Needs Game by indicating that the game will help the family focus on strengths within the family as well as on areas for change. Explain that the game involves answering questions related to strengths within the family. When a family member is unable to answer a question, then that is an area of need.

The person whose birthday is coming up next starts the game by rolling the die and moving the treat clockwise around the board the number of spaces indicated on the die. Since there is no start space, the first player can start anywhere he/she likes.

When a player lands on a blue square, that player takes the top card on the blue pile and answers the question by filling in the blanks or completing the statement.

When a player lands on a red circle, that player takes the top card on the red pile and answers the question by filling in the name of the family member.
When a player lands on a yellow star, that player follows the directions on the star or, if it states TREAT, that player distributes a candy to each player.

This game has no finish line and is not intended to be competitive so players can end the game after a designated time period or after each player has had a pre-chosen number of turns.

The following questions can be helpful when processing the activity:

1. What is a family strength that was identified in this game?
2. What is a need or area of change that was identified through this game?
3. How is playing this game together different from playing other games as a family?

The therapist can summarize the various strengths and needs identified by the family members and recount as necessary throughout the course of treatment.

Discussion

It is important that a family be able to identify its strengths so they can be used as part of the treatment methodology. It is equally important to regularly talk about strengths in the family so that negative perceptions do not interfere with relationships.

Parents are often overwhelmed with their child or emotionally disengaged, and they need support and guidance. It is important to help parents recognize their strengths, such as their love and concern for their child, and their commitment to help their child.

Children and parents alike will enjoy getting positive feedback from one another. Generally, families do not perceive this as a threatening activity as it encourages positive feedback by acknowledging the nice things family members do for each other. The star spaces allow family members to have fun and laugh together.

The game can be used to facilitate further discussion among the family members. An important concept of game play "is points of departure, in which players leave the game to discuss psychological issues expressed during game play. For the therapist, a key aspect of game play therapy is managing and guiding discussion back and forth between the safety of the game and the realistic discussion of issues through points of departure" (Schaefer & Reid, 2001).

As with other therapeutic games, rules should be established at the outset, such as a "pass" rule if a family member does not feel comfortable answering a particular question.

Reference
Schaefer, C.E, & Reid, S. (Eds). (2001). *Game play: Therapeutic use of childhood games* (2nd ed.). New York: John Wiley & Sons.

About The Author

Stacey Slobodnick, BSW, RSW, is a clinical social worker at Glengarda Child and Family Services, a children's mental health agency in Ontario, Canada. She provides clinical services and case management in the Day Treatment Program to children and their families. She is pursuing certification as a Play Therapy Associate through the Canadian Association for Child and Play Therapy.

Family Strengths and Needs Game
Blue Question Cards

I like it when my mom/dad...	Something my brother/sister is good at is...
I wish I could _____ like my brother/sister	My mom/dad knows how to...
_____, you made me smile when...	My family and I are looking forward to...
Something good I learned from my mom/dad is...	I feel happy when someone in my family ...

Family Strengths and Needs Game
Blue Question Cards

When my _____ listens to me I feel...	In the future, my family...
When my _____ supports me I feel...	I'm like my mom/dad when I...
We never fight when we...	My _____ is a good person because he/she...
We have fun together when we...	When my _____ pays attention to me I feel....

© Stacey Slobodnick

Family Strengths and Needs Game
Red Question Cards

The person in my family who Hugs me is...	The person in my family who Helps me is...
The person in my family who Plays with me is...	The person in my family who Knows me the best is...
The person in my family who Loves me is...	The person in my family who Is most like me is...
The person in my family who Listens to me is...	The person in my family who Believes in me is...
The person in my family who Cares about me is...	The person in my family who Cheers me up is...
The person in my family who Spends time with me is...	The person in my family who Makes me feel good about myself is...

© Stacey Slobodnick

Family Strengths and Needs Game
Game Board

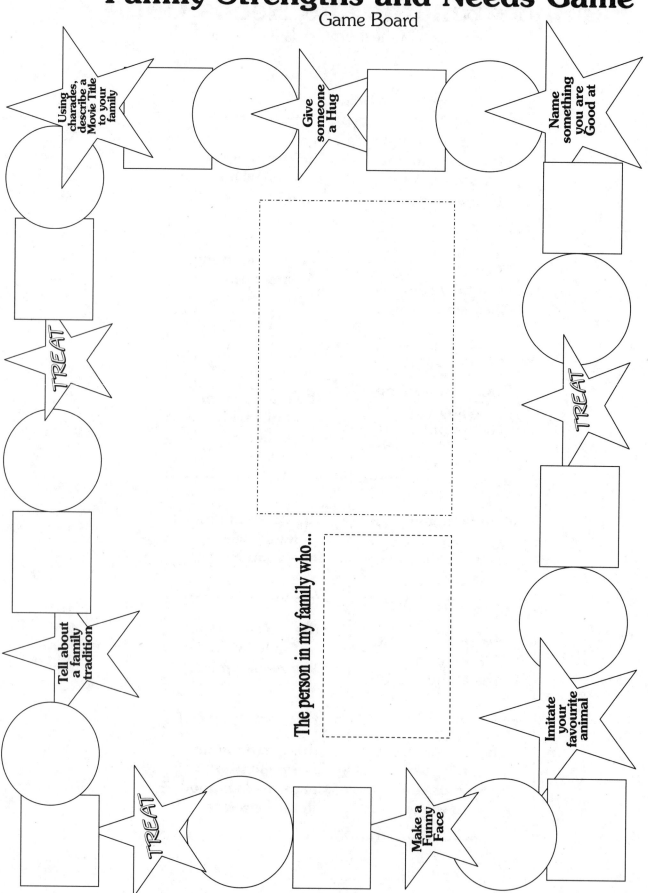

Using charades, describe a Movie Title to your family

Give someone a Hug

Name something you are Good at

TREAT

TREAT

Tell about a family tradition

The person in my family who...

Imitate your favourite animal

TREAT

Make a Funny Face

© Stacey Slobodnick

Family Timeline
Source: Liana Lowenstein

Goals
- Identify significant life events experienced by the family
- Assess family relationships and dynamics
- Normalize that everyone has both positive and negative life experiences

Materials
- Transparent tape
- Paper
- Ruler
- Self-adhesive labels (2" x 4")

Advance Preparation
Tape together several pieces of paper to make one long sheet. Use the ruler to draw a line across the middle of the paper from one end to the other.

Description
Introduce the activity by stating that all families experience both positive and negative life events. Then explain to the family that they are going to make a time line that depicts the positive and negative events they have experienced together. Ask the family members to think of three to five positive life events they have experienced together, and three to five negative life events they have experienced together, and to write each of these events down on separate adhesive labels. A parent or older sibling can write for younger clients, or the younger clients can draw the life event and have their parent write a brief description of the event underneath their picture.

If the family has difficulty thinking of significant events, the therapist can prompt with statements such as, "Write about a happy event you have experienced together." "Write about a sad event you have experienced together." "Write about a holiday or family celebration you remember." "Write about a time your family accomplished something." "Write about a time you were pleasantly surprised by something someone in your family did for you." "Write about a bad argument that happened in your family." "Write about a family trip or outing." Write about a loss or write about a hurt." "Write about the funniest moment." Write the date the event occurred at the top of each label.

Once the family has completed writing or drawing the memories and events on the labels, each label is attached to the sheet of paper in chronological order. Positive events are placed above the line, negative events below the line.

The therapist then guides the family in a more detailed discussion of each memory and their feelings associated with each memory. The following probes can be helpful when processing the activity:

33

1. What is your favorite memory and why?
2. Tell us about a bad memory and describe the feelings this memory evokes as you think about it.
3. What or who has helped you get through the tough times?
4. What is a good memory you hope to add to the timeline in the future?

Discussion

This activity is a valuable assessment tool because it gathers information about significant events the family has experienced. Some families will enjoy completing this exercise, and will openly share their life experiences in the session. Other families may struggle with the activity, because they may feel too anxious or ashamed to talk about their experiences. The therapist can deal with client resistance by making supportive comments that validate and normalize the client's feelings. If the therapist knows of significant negative events the family has experienced that they have not included in the time line, the therapist should wait until the activity is completed, and then state, "Some memories may be too difficult for you to share right now. You can always add to your time line when you are feeling more comfortable."

In processing traumatic or difficult events the family has experienced, it is important to validate the family's resilience. For example, the therapist can state, "Even though your family has been through tough times, you're still here. . .you survived something really difficult!" The therapist can then ask, "How have the tough times made you stronger? How can you use this strength to get through any tough times you experience now or in the future?"

In addition to its diagnostic value, this activity can be used as a therapeutic intervention to facilitate discussion of various issues, such as change and loss, family relationships, and personal achievements.

About The Author

Liana Lowenstein, MSW, RSW, CPT-S, is a Social Worker and Certified Play Therapy Supervisor in Toronto. She maintains a private practice, provides clinical supervision and consultation to mental health professionals, and lectures internationally on child and play therapy. She has authored numerous publications, including the books *Paper Dolls and Paper Airplanes: Therapeutic Exercises for Sexually Traumatized Children, Creative Interventions for Troubled Children and Youth, Creative Interventions for Bereaved Children,* and *Creative Interventions for Children of Divorce.*

© Liana Lowenstein

Family Trivia Game
Source: Trudy Post Sprunk

Goals
- Increase open communication among family members
- Increase feelings of family connectedness

Materials
- Multiple strips of white paper or multiple white note cards for each person
- Pencils
- Container, shoebox, or empty wastebasket

Advance Preparation
Arrange the seating so that each person has privacy to write his/her questions.

Description
Have family members quietly and privately write trivia questions about family members and/or family events on each strip of paper. (The therapist may need to help young children by writing for them.) Examples of trivia questions include:

1. Whose favorite food is pizza?
2. Who gives the best back rub?
3. Who is older, Mom or Dad?
4. Who in the family snores?
5. Who laughs the loudest?

Ask that they sign each paper, fold it, and place it in the shoebox or other container.

When the paper strips have all been put into the container, the therapist reads one of the trivia questions. The family members try to answer the question. The person who wrote the question waits patiently while others try to answer.

Once all of the questions have been answered ask:

1. What was the funniest trivia question?
2. Were any of the questions uncomfortable or embarrassing? If yes, which ones?
3. Which trivia questions about you did you like the most?

Provide time for the family to process positive and negative feelings created by this activity.

35

Discussion

The purpose of this activity is to encourage a sense of family unity. This feeling can occur because only family members can provide the answers to the trivia questions correctly.

In addition, family trivia provides opportunities for laughter and learning more about each other. Through this experience family members can have a more positive relational experience.

Families come for therapy often as the result of a child who is the symptom-bearer for the family. There may be marital issues, enmeshment, triangulation, hierarchy of power conflicts, miscommunication, disengagement, and so on. This activity can be incorporated into initial family therapy sessions to allow participants to feel "more alive" and playful as they interact with one another. The playfulness decreases defensiveness and enhances relationships. As the family relationships improve, the therapist can then use other more explorative techniques to assess family functioning.

About The Author

Trudy Post Sprunk, LMFT-S, LPC-S, RPT-S, CPT-S, is a Licensed Marriage and Family Therapist and Supervisor who has been practicing psychotherapy since 1971. She has presented at international, national, and local conferences and has been interviewed on radio and television. She is certified as an EMDR Specialist and is a Registered Play Therapist Supervisor. She is past-president of the Association for Play Therapy and president and co-founder of the Georgia Association for Play Therapy.

First Session Family Card Game
Source: Liana Lowenstein

Goals
- Join with the family
- Assess family relationships and dynamics
- Identify positive aspects of family life and pinpoint areas for change

Materials
- Question cards (included)
- Card stock or index cards
- Scissors
- Standard 52-card deck
- Cookies

Advance Preparation
Photocopy the question cards provided onto cardstock and cut them into cards, or copy the questions onto index cards.

Description
Introduce the activity by stating, "We are going to play a game that will help me get to know your family." The rules are explained as follows:

"Take turns picking the top card from the deck of cards. If you get a card with an **even number**, pick a card from the question card pile and **answer the question**. If you get a card with an **odd number**, pick a card from the question card pile and **ask someone in your family to answer the question**. If you do not feel you can answer the question, you can ask your family for help. If you pick an ace, ask someone in your family for a hug. If you pick a jack, do 10 jumping jacks. If you pick a Queen or King, you get a cookie. At the end of the game, everyone who played gets a cookie."

Active discussion among the family is encouraged during the game. The therapist may wish to stop the game periodically to expand on feelings or issues disclosed by the family members.

After the game, facilitate discussion by asking the following process questions:

1. What new information did you learn about your family?
2. What new information did you learn about family therapy?
3. What was the most interesting or surprising response?
4. Which was the most difficult question?
5. How do you feel now, compared to how you felt at the beginning of the session?

Discussion

Therapeutic techniques that involve children or the entire family can be challenging, particularly if the therapist relies on the usual modus operandi of therapy–talk. This activity provides a means by which talk is integrated into an engaging game. Game playing "is a form of play and is, thereby, a form of amusement and source of enjoyment to the participants" (Schaefer & Reid, 2001). Clients can express themselves through this playful game format. The information gleaned from the game can be used to open communication among family members.

The question cards in this game have been specifically designed to facilitate therapeutic rapport and to help the family identify treatment goals. The game is used as a "stimulus for expression of otherwise unattainable information" (Schaefer & Reid, 2001). During the game, there is ample opportunity to observe family dynamics, which further assists in treatment planning. Pro-social behaviors are also assessed through the game, such as turn-taking, eye contact, adhering to rules, and listening.

Added elements of the game include jumping jacks to channel anxious feelings into a positive outlet, hugs to encourage nurturing interactions in the family, and cookies to entice members to participate.

The therapist provides supportive feedback and validates feelings that emerge during the course of the activity.

References

Lowenstein, L. (2006). *Creative interventions for bereaved children*. Toronto, ON: Champion Press.

Schaefer, C.E., & Reid, S.E. (2001). *Game play: Therapeutic use of childhood games*. New York: John Wiley & Sons.

About The Author

Liana Lowenstein, MSW, RSW, CPT-S, is a Social Worker and Certified Play Therapy Supervisor in Toronto. She maintains a private practice, provides clinical supervision and consultation to mental health professionals, and lectures internationally on child and play therapy. She has authored numerous publications, including the books *Paper Dolls and Paper Airplanes: Therapeutic Exercises for Sexually Traumatized Children, Creative Interventions for Troubled Children and Youth, Creative Interventions for Bereaved Children*, and *Creative Interventions for Children of Divorce*.

First Session Family Card Game
Questions

Fill in the blank: **Our family is here today because...**	**Fill in the blank:** **A good therapist is someone who...**	**Ask the therapist a question that will help you feel more comfortable working with her/him.**
Define family therapy. (You can ask the therapist to help.)	**What sorts of problems usually bring a family to therapy?** (You can ask the therapist to help.)	**What would need to happen in the session today to make you feel like it was worthwhile coming?**
Say one word that best describes how you feel about being here today.	**Who decided you should seek help at this time?**	**What is a question or worry you have about family therapy?**
Explain what you've done before to try to solve the main problem that brought you here today.	**Tell about a time when things at home were better.**	**Switch seats with the person who you think is the most affected by the problem.**

© Liana Lowenstein

39

First Session Family Card Game
Questions

Who, outside of your family, has helped you in the past?	**What would your parent or sibling say needs to change in your family?**	**What do you think needs to change in your family?**
Describe what it would be like in your family with problems all gone.	**True or False: When families see a therapist they often feel nervous, embarrassed, and overwhelmed.**	**Of the goals that have been identified today, which is the most important to you?**
True or False: Everyone in our family plays a part in making it better.	**Switch seats with the person you think is most willing to change in your family.**	**What is the most important thing for the therapist to know about your family?**
True or False: Only crazy people go to therapy.	**Switch seats with the person who is the easiest to talk to about problems and worries.**	**How will you feel if you or your family gets the help you need?**

© Liana Lowenstein

The Flowers and the Weeds
Source: Greg Lubimiv

Goals
- Establish a safe and open therapeutic environment
- Identify issues that are contributing to the problematic behavior
- Identify strengths within the family
- Set goals to be addressed in treatment

Materials
- Story: "The Flowers and the Weeds" (included)
- Assorted colors of construction paper or tissue paper
- Green or grey cardboard or card stock
- Pipe cleaners or Popsicle sticks
- Flower templates (included)
- White poster board
- Black marker
- Several pairs of scissors
- Transparent tape

Advance Preparation
Make a flower using the colored construction or tissue paper. Use a pipe cleaner or a Popsicle stick for the stem. This will be used as a sample to show the family during the session.

Make several copies of the flower templates.

Description
The activity begins by reading "The Flowers and the Weeds" story to the family.

Explain to the family that our lives can be very much like Belle's. We sometimes have weeds (problems) that grow and get in the way of our flowers (our healthy growth). However, weeds, or problems, can be very powerful and very difficult to get rid of, especially when we try to pull them all out (deal with them) at the same time.

Have the family members create flowers from the colored construction or tissue paper. Use pipe cleaners or Popsicle sticks for the stems. The family can use the flower templates to make it easier to create the flower shapes.

Each family member should make at least three flowers.

Have the family members cut out some weeds using the green or grey cardboard.

41

Each family member should create at least four weeds.

Ask family members to write on a flower something that is a strength for the family or something that is going well. The family may need prompts to assist them in identifying strengths, for example, motivated to get help, able to have fun together. Each family member should identify at least one strength; but try to elicit two or three from each family member.

On the poster board, draw several lines for the earth using a black marker. Have the family members tape the flowers on top of the earth.

Next, have the family members identify the problems in the family and write each problem on one of the weeds. Try to cover all the main problems the family or member of the family is having. Have the family members tape the weeds over the flowers so they are covered.

Ask the family if they think the flowers will grow strong and beautiful. The answer should be no. Ask why and relate this to the story.

Ask the family if they can deal with all of the problems at the same time, and why it might be difficult to do so. The correct response is that they need to deal with one weed/problem at a time.

Through discussion have the family identify which weed/problem they will work on first. It is often best to guide the family to a problem that is likely to succeed to provide them with a sense of hope and positive energy. Develop a plan to deal with that weed/problem.

It is helpful to identify the first three weeds/problems that will be addressed in later sessions so that after the first is "pulled out" everyone knows which will be dealt with next.

In later sessions, the metaphor of weeds and flowers can be referred to, with an emphasis on the family's positive growth and change.

Discussion

Storytelling has been used for centuries as a tool to entertain and teach as well as to create a connection between generations. Over the last half century it has been used in therapy to help children, youth, and adults heal. As Okri (1996) states, "It is easy to forget how mysterious and mighty stories are. They do their work in silence, invisibly. They work with all the internal materials of the mind and self. They become part of you while changing you."

Therapeutic stories can be used in a variety of ways. In this activity, the story "The Flowers and the Weeds" is used as a way to help the family clearly identify problems and to set realistic treatment goals.

"The Flowers and the Weeds" is particularly helpful when problems seem overwhelming, or when there does not seem to be any hope for things to get better.

Incorporating an art activity adds an additional element of engagement and brings the metaphors from the story to life. Family art therapy "enhances communication among family members and uncovers, through the process as well as the content of the art task, family patterns of interaction and behavior" (Riley & Malchiodi, 2003). "The Flowers and the Weeds" is a useful intervention to assess families and to help them to communicate more openly and effectively.

References
Okri, B. (1996). *Birds of heaven*. London: Phoenix.

Riley, S., & Malchiodi, C.A. (2003). *Family art therapy*. New York: Guilford.

About The Author
Greg Lubimiv, MSW, CPT-S, is the Executive Director of the Phoenix Centre for Children and Families, a children's mental health centre in southeastern Ontario, Canada. As well, he is involved with Invest In Kids, assisting in the development of an innovative parenting program that starts in pregnancy and continues to the child's first birthday. He has worked in the field of children's mental health since 1981 and has been involved as a clinician, trainer, and administrator. He has specialized training in the field of play therapy and family therapy and has authored a number of books and articles on this and other topics, including *Wings for Our Children: The Essentials of Becoming a Play Therapist* and *My Sister Is An Angeline,* a book helping children cope with sibling death. He has a Masters of Social Work and is a Certified Play Therapist Supervisor with the Canadian Association for Child and Play Therapy. He has been presented with the Monica Hebert Award for contributions to the field of Play Therapy.

The Flowers and the Weeds
Story

Once upon a time, there was a small flower named Belle who lived in the corner of a large garden. As Belle grew up she did not notice that around her were some weed seeds that had blown from another garden. The weeds had already begun to sprout, but, still, they were not in the way, so Belle did not think about them.

One morning Belle woke up – it was still dark and she was cold and very thirsty. She thought it must be too early in the morning so she went back to sleep. She woke up a few hours later, but it was still dark and cold and dry. What had happened to the sun, she wondered. Suddenly she noticed a flicker of light above her. It was the sun…but something was in the way. She then noticed that all around her the little weeds had grown into huge weeds and now they were taking away her sunlight, her water, and her space to grow.

Belle asked the weeds to leave but they said they would not. Belle reached down and grabbed a bunch of them. She pulled and pulled but they were too strong. If only she had pulled them out when they were tiny and had no roots.

As the weeds grew bigger and stronger, Belle became weaker and less colorful. Belle felt there was no hope. Then one dark morning she heard a voice from below her. "Hi there," the voice said.

Belle looked down and saw a ground hog. Belle told the ground hog to go away, but it just sat there and looked at her. "Why don't you get rid of these weeds and enjoy the beautiful sun…it is a great day out," said the groundhog.

Belle cried and cried and then told the groundhog her story. The groundhog nodded his head in understanding. He said there was a way to solve the problem and asked the flower if she wanted to have some help. Belle nodded yes.

The groundhog said if they worked together he could help her pull out the weeds. They grabbed a bunch of weeds and started to pull together. They pulled and pulled and pulled, but the weeds did not budge. Belle was ready to give up. Suddenly, the groundhog started to laugh out loud and said, "I am so silly. I forgot the lesson my grandfather taught me about weeds. He told me if I ever faced strong weeds to pull them out one at a time, never in a bunch."

Belle nodded. That made sense. Belle chose one of the weeds and they pulled together. They pulled and pulled and slowly, but surely, the weed came out of the ground. She then picked another weed and together they pulled. Soon all the weeds were gone. Belle looked up at the beautiful sun and the warmth of the sunlight felt so good. She took a big drink of water from the earth. She started to grow again and soon she bloomed into a strong, beautifully colored flower.

Every morning from then on, Belle would wake up and take a big stretch. She would then look around her and pull out any small weeds that may have grown overnight, because when they were small they were easy to pull.

Groundhog would come by from time to time for a visit and both of them would lie out in the sun and talk.

© Greg Lubimiv

The Flowers and the Weeds
Flower Template

I'm an Animal
Source: Connie-Jean Latam

Goals
- Assess family relationships and dynamics
- Identify positive aspects of family life and pinpoint areas for change
- Increase open communication among family members

Materials
- Large variety of plastic animals, including domestic, farm, jungle, sea, insects, and dinosaurs or, alternatively, have family members draw or create their own animal using assorted craft supplies or Playdough
- Statements (included)
- Scissors
- Container, shoebox, or basket

Advance Preparation
Copy the statements, cut out each one and fold and place in the container. Display the animals so that each member can see them and select one.

Description
Explain to the family that they are going to play a special version of being an animal and imitate/animate the attitude and behavior of that animal in a playful manner. The activity is explained as follows: "Choose from the collection of plastic animals one that seems to feel good to you. Take turns selecting a card with a question or statement written on it. Read it aloud, then answer the question or complete the sentence as if you are that animal."

Next, process this experience by asking the following questions:

1. Which question did you like the most?
2. Name something you liked about a family member's response.
3. In what ways do you think (name of family member) is similar to or different than the animal he/she chose?
4. What do you think it would be like to be the animal that you chose?
5. What was easy for you to say as the animal you chose?
6. What was most difficult for you?
7. Do you wish that (name of family member) was always like the animal that he/she chose?
8. Do you think that (name of family member) could be another animal? If so, which one and why?

Discussion

Each member of the family will have his/her unique way of communicating within a family unit. In some cases some or one of the members may be guarded and non-expressive. This activity engages the family in a playful manner in order to facilitate communication and determine attitudes and interactions.

This activity can be integrated into the assessment process. Gil (2003) emphasizes the value of using play in family assessment: "Family play therapists pay attention to the family's language, isolating and then pursuing play metaphors or metaphor language. They also observe how families approach a play activity and the outcome of their efforts. The result is that families may provide a deeper level of communication that can assist clinicians in their formulation of, and response to, the presenting problem."

References

Gil, E. (2003). Family play therapy: "The bear with short nails." In C. Schaefer, (Ed.), *Foundations of play therapy*. New York: John Wiley & Sons.

Latam, C.J. (2010). *Everything is food! Art and play therapy exercises of wisdom and peace*. Kingsville, ON: Self Published by Connie-Jean Latam and Art of Living Resource Centre Inc.

About The Author

Connie-Jean Latam, D.N.M., is a Doctor of Natural Medicine, accredited by the American Naturopathic Association, and a Certified Trauma and Loss Counselor, Certified Addictions Counselor, Certified Hypnotherapist, Certified Grief and Bereavement Counselor, Certified Healing Touch, Therapeutic Touch Practitioner and Teacher, a Reiki Master, and a Theraplay® and Art Therapy Practitioner. She is the author and illustrator of *Everything Is Food!* She has been in private practice since 1990 serving adults, adolescents, and children. She owns the Art of Living Resource Centre Inc., located in Kingsville, Ontario.

I'm an Animal
Statements

I am just like this animal because I…

I wanted to be the (animal name) because…

My first choice of animal was not here and this made me feel…

I like to…

I am good at…

I enjoy the season (winter, spring, summer, or fall) because I like to…

When I get angry I…

When I am sad I…

I am frightened when…

I protect myself from danger by…

I stay away from…because…

For the child: When Dad's or Mom's animal is angry I…

I liked it when (another animal in the game) did or does…

I (make the sound of the animal) when…

I (move like the animal) when I am…

I want /need…

I want to be this animal in real life because…

© Connie-Jean Latam

My Family Edible Animal Farm

Source: Paris Goodyear-Brown

Goals
- Establish a safe and open therapeutic environment
- Assess family relationships and dynamics
- Increase open communication among family members

Materials
- Paper plates
- Napkins
- Plastic knife
- Graham crackers
- Peanut butter or Nutella
- Animal crackers
- Camera (optional)

Advance Preparation
Arrange seating so that each family member can work privately on a flat surface. Arrange the materials so that each family member has easy access to them.

Description
Provide family members with several graham crackers and instruct them to lay them side by side on their paper plates. Give each member peanut butter (or Nutella) and explain that this will act as mortar to attach the graham crackers to each other. Have the family members spread peanut butter (or Nutella) across the top of the graham cracker "plate" to provide a sticky base for the animal crackers. When this step is finished, present the members with several different kinds of animal crackers. Examples include domestic animals, jungle animals, and icing-covered animals. Prompt the clients to choose an animal cracker to represent each family member. They are to include themselves as an animal on the farm. Once the members have chosen an animal for each family member, ask them to pretend that the animals live on a farm together. Instruct the clients to arrange the animals "on the farm" doing something together. Then have each member make up a story about his/her animals on the farm. Present the following rules: The story must have a beginning, a middle, and an end. All the characters on the farm must be mentioned at some point in the story.

Once the family members have created their animal farm and story, they are asked to share their creations. While discussing the animal farms, ask questions such as:

1. How does it feel to be a particular animal on the farm?
2. Take each animal, one by one, and describe it using as many adjectives as you can.
3. If your farm could be changed in some way, how would you change it?

50

Take a photograph of the animal farms for the family (as well as for the clinical record). Then the family members can eat their animal farms!

Discussion

My Family Edible Animal Farm is an engaging way to help clients explore their perceptions of family dynamics while nurturing them through the use of food.

Younger children may need a prompt with each family member, such as "Pick an animal to be your mom." They may also need more prompts during the story, such as "And then what happened?" or "What does the elephant do in your story?"

Important assessment information can be gleaned through this activity. For example, the therapist can uncover the following:

1. How close together or far apart are family members?
1. Are they facing each other or are their backs turned?
1. Are there alliances or outcasts?

Food-based interventions may not be appropriate for clients with eating disorders or food allergies, or for clients suffering from obesity.

Reference

Goodyear-Brown, P. (2002). *Digging for buried treasure: 52 prop-based play therapy interventions for treating the problems of childhood.* Available at www.parisandme.com.

About The Author

Paris Goodyear-Brown, MSW, LCSW, RPT-S, is a Social Worker and Registered Play Therapist Supervisor residing in Nashville, Tennessee. She is an Adjunct Instructor of Psychiatric Mental Health at Vanderbilt University, guest lecturer for several universities in middle Tennessee, maintains a private practice, and has an international reputation as a dynamic speaker and innovative clinician. She is best known for developing clinically sound, played-based interventions that are used to treat a variety of childhood problems and has received the APT award for Play Therapy Promotion and Education. She is the author of *Digging for Buried Treasure: 52 Prop-Based Play Therapy Interventions for Treating the Problems of Childhood; Digging for Buried Treasure 2: 52 More Prop-Based Play Therapy Interventions for Treating the Problems of Childhood; Gabby the Gecko; Play Therapy with Traumatized Children: A Prescriptive Approach;* and co-author of an original DVD of prescriptive play therapy interventions entitled *10 Peas in a Pod.* She is also editor of *The Handbook of Child Sexual Abuse.*

My Life in the Sandtray
Source: Sandra Webb

Goals
- Assess the child's understanding of their life path
- Encourage the child to identify and express feelings about significant life events and about the places he/she has lived
- Increase the caregivers understanding of the child's significant life experiences

Materials
- Sandtray
- Sand
- Variety of miniature objects or figurines representing different categories such as people (varied ages, races, abilities and occupations), animals (pets, farm, and wild), vehicles, plants and things from nature (rocks, shells), furniture/household objects, buildings, fantasy figures; or, use different shapes and different sizes of marbles and stones
- Paper
- Pen
- Camera

Advance Preparation
It is helpful if the therapist has some understanding of the child's early life history, but this is not vital as the focus of this activity is the child's perspective of his/her life.

Description
Note: This activity involves one child and his or her caregivers.

This activity is best done without too much description or discussion as the aim is to have the child spontaneously create a sandworld about his/her life. The therapist may have conducted other sessions with the child in which they have discussed the child's life but, for this session, begin the sandworld without further talk of the child's history.

Ask the child to create a sandworld about his/her life. Have the child include significant life events (positive and negative), places the child has lived, people who have been in their lives (positive and negative), and so on. Ask the child to divide the sandtray in a way that makes sense for him/her. For example, the child may wish to divide the sandtray according to age (i.e., a six-year-old may divide the sandtray into six segments) or a foster child may divide the sandtray into three to illustrate the two foster homes and the birth family in which he/she has lived. The child can draw a line in the sand to make different sections (vertical or horizontal) and the child can decide the size of the different sections. Clarify with the child how he/she has divided the sandtray. The child may choose to make printed signs for each section or verbally delineate the different sections.

Next, ask the child to choose figures and objects that remind him/her of the events, memories, places lived, and so on. As the child is building, listen to what he/she says but do not engage in any detailed discussion about the facts of his/her life (unless the child asks and, if he/she does ask, then keep the discussion brief at this point). The child may ask the parents/caregivers to participate. Part of the assessment will be to notice who leads, who follows, how much the child freely contributes, and how the family interacts during the process.

Once the child is finished, ask the child to tell a story about the sandworld and write the story that the child dictates. If the child does not want to do this, that is fine. The child might not want to do this part of the activity, or he/she might become distracted by other things as he/she is creating. The child may put few things in one section and more in another. Make note of these things and trust that the child is processing the experience in his/her own way. The child will continue to process the experience between sessions. Accept what the child does and know that he/she is integrating his/her life experiences at a pace that feels safe. Encourage the child and the parent/caregiver to think about the new things they have learned during the activity.

Take pictures of the sandworld for the child/family if the child wants pictures as well as for the clinical record.

Discussion

This activity helps a child to "see" his/her life in a visual, kinesthetic manner. It gives the child a linear view of his/her life that is not segregated into good/bad/before/after sections. The child is able to share these memories with the caregiver who is present and possibly gather new facts and experiences about his/her life. Through this experience, the child will begin to integrate the difficult memories with the happy memories and be more amenable to looking at the future.

It is important to help children integrate and understand more fully what has happened to them in their lives. Children have a much better chance of living more coherent, satisfying lives when they can co-create a coherent narrative of their lives with their caregivers. Sandplay is one way to help children find a way to share their "stories" with their caregivers.

This method is helpful with children in biological, foster, or adoptive families. It can be a helpful intervention to use with more than one set of caregivers. The child and caregivers often get a better understanding of what each one remembers, how life has been in each part of the child's life, and how the child has understood what has happened along the way.

The sandplay method allows the child to bring some of the unconscious memories into the conscious realm so he/she can begin to understand and process them in a new way. Sandplay is a natural activity for children. Adults often need more time to comfortably explore this medium, but children usually move into sandplay with little effort.

In future sessions, the child can create a world about one of the parts of his/her life. It is helpful to record (on a form or through photographs) some of the figures that the child uses in his/her sandworld and to notice which ones he/she uses again and which ones change.

About The Author

Sandra Webb, B.A.Sc. (Child Studies) is a Certified Child Psychotherapist and Play Therapist Associate and Certified Theraplay® Therapist.She facilitated and completed six years of Sandtray-Worldplay® training with Gisela Schubach De Domenico and advanced training in Dyadic Developmental Psychotherapy (DDP) with Dr. Daniel Hughes. She is an Adoption Practitioner approved by the Ministry of Community and Social Services and she works with domestic and international adoption. She has presented workshops on Adoption, Play Therapy and Sandtray-Worldplay® in North America and abroad. She has written articles for several magazines and she produced a DVD and CD called *Building the Bonds of Attachment* with Dr. Daniel Hughes. She has been in private practice since 1995 working with children, families and adults specializing in attachment based therapy using Play Therapy, DDP, Theraplay® and Sandtray-Worldplay®. She received the Monica Herbert Award for her outstanding contribution to the field of play therapy and the Cobourg and District Chamber of Commerce President's Award.

Our Family Life Scavenger Hunt
Source: Angela M. Cavett

Goals
- Join with the family
- Develop an understanding of the family's life and home environment
- Assess family relationships and dynamics
- Assess the family's coping skills and available resources

Materials
- Scavenger Hunt list (included)

Advance Preparation
Make a copy of the Scavenger Hunt list.

Description
Note: This activity is completed over two sessions.

Introduce the Scavenger Hunt activity by explaining that it is a fun way to get to know the family. Ask the family if they enjoy scavenger hunts. If some of the family members have never been on a scavenger hunt, explain the concept to them. Give the Scavenger Hunt list to the family. Ask them to review the list and to discuss what they might choose to bring for specific items. Then ask them to consider who will be responsible for collecting each item on the list, that is, will they collect the items together, divide the list, how will decisions be made regarding which items to bring, and so on.

Encourage the family to do the Scavenger Hunt at home and bring the items back for the next session. A specific way to bring the items may be discussed with the family and/or the parent. For families who use public transportation, the Scavenger Hunt can be adapted to include smaller items that are easier to transport or the family could bring photos or drawings of the items.

The family returns to the following session with the items they collected for the Scavenger Hunt. Ask them to present and discuss each item. If items were not collected, the reasons and underlying feelings are discussed. Ask questions to guide the discussion, such as:

1. Who made most of the decisions during the Scavenger Hunt?
2. Who had the most fun collecting the items?
3. Did anyone become upset during the Scavenger Hunt and, if so, how was this handled?
4. Give an example to show how your family worked together during the Scavenger Hunt.

5. What was your favorite item to collect?
6. What was the hardest item to collect?
7. What do you think was the purpose of this activity?

Discussion

The joining and assessment process may be enhanced by playfully engaging the family in a Scavenger Hunt. The Scavenger Hunt allows the clients to present important aspects of their family life. The playfulness of the intervention decreases resistance and allows the family to lead the engagement process. Therapeutically, the Scavenger Hunt enables the therapist to answer the following questions:

1. Does the family follow through on therapeutic homework?
2. Does the parent assist or direct the child? Is the interaction supportive? Does it facilitate sharing?
3. How are decisions made within the family?
4. What role has each family member adopted within the family?
5. What is the communication style in the family?
6. Does the family have the capacity to have fun together?
7. Does the child have access to reminders of his or her life story?
8. What do the family members do to relax and self soothe?
9. What interests do the family members have?
10. Does the family participate in positive time together?

Rich assessment information is obtained through this activity. It brings family issues and dynamics to the surface so that they can be explored, discussed, and treated. During the activity, the therapist shows interest in the items brought by the family and asks open-ended questions to further explore underlying thoughts and feelings.

About The Author

Angela M. Cavett, PhD, LP, RPT-S, is a psychologist in private practice providing evaluation and therapy to children, adolescents, and families. She is an adjunct faculty member at the University of North Dakota in the Department of Counseling Psychology. She is a Registered Play Therapist Supervisor and provides training and supervision related to child psychopathology and treatment, including play therapy. She is the author of *Structured Play-Based Interventions for Engaging Children and Adolescents in Therapy* (2010).

© Angela M. Cavett

Our Family Life Scavenger Hunt

List

1. Family photograph

2. Baby picture of each child with the parent(s)

3. Baby picture of each child with another adult

4. Picture of someone important to your family

5. Picture from a family vacation or outing

6. A recipe used for a favorite family meal

7. Something that helps you relax

8. Something funny

9. Souvenir from a family trip

10. Something homemade

11. The biggest and the smallest shoes in your family

12. Something that represents your family's heritage or culture

13. A family heirloom

14. Something that represents what your family does for fun

15. Something important to your family that money cannot buy

16. Something that represents a problem or worry in your family

17. Something that represents the love in your family

18. Something that can help your family

Our Family Has a Whole World to Play With

Source: Gisela Schubach De Domenico

Goals

- Involve the family members in a communal, non-therapist directed activity
- Stimulate each family member's unique creativity, receptivity, and innate wisdom
- Stimulate each family member's capacity and interest to help the family grow into wellness
- Remove the focus on the identified patient

Materials

- Sandtray, minimum size of 20" x 24" x3" to 5" deep, filled halfway with 60-mesh play sand
- Comprehensive collection of miniature toys, natural objects, and symbols that depict the complexities and diversity of human life experiences. These images may be stored on shelves or in individual baskets. (See De Domenico, 2004)
- Pitcher of water
- Large candle
- Matches
- Digital camera

Advance Preparation

Place the sandtray with the sand on the surface of a low table in the center of the room, close to the miniatures.

Have two to six chairs of the appropriate height nearby.

Description

Introduce the use of Sandtray-Worldplay as a means of allowing the family to have a communal (that is, a joint) play experience. On one hand, joint family sandtray play invites everyone to show up and bring their freely chosen, uniquely individual contribution into the world in the sand. Everyone's play characters are welcomed. On the other hand, joint family sandtray play invites everyone to dynamically receive the unique contributions of the other members of the family. Instead of ignoring or boxing off play characters contributed by the others, everyone is encouraged to get to know them and to actually interact and play with them. This supports the unfolding story of the family's play world. The family is given the opportunity to relate in a natural, dynamic, interactive way in present time.

Often there is no time and place for families to play: some families get stuck in blaming one another or simply demanding a "change." Families are relational, living entities that grow and develop when they actively engage in spontaneous relational activities. During this therapeutic hour, it is important to recognize, nurture, and care for the family.

Directives to the Family at the Beginning of the Building Cycle: "I invite all of you to build a family world in this tray of sand: the sand may be moved, you can see the blue surface on the bottom. You may use water to mold the sand in any way you like. Here are small toys, natural objects, and images of all sorts that each one of you may use to make the family world the way you want it to be for today. When making your family world in the sandtray, each one of you chooses what/ whom to bring into the world. Choose whatever 'calls you,' whether you like it or not. There is no need to know what anything means: focus on playing together. Each mountain, lake, car, animal, tree, monster, magician, and so on that you bring and place into the family world is a gift to the family world. The family world always belongs to everyone. Everyone shares equally. Everyone can play with all of the characters in the world: so you can arrange and rearrange everything as many times as you like. And yes, you can take characters out of the world any time you want to. In fact, do place the characters where you think they belong. You may talk to one another while playing or you may play in silence. Find the way you want to play today. As all of you play together, your world will change from moment to moment until everyone has the sense that the family world is the way it needs to be for today."

Directives at the Completion of the Building Cycle: "Now that the family world has come to be, silently look at the world together and remember the way this world came to be.

Let us take turns: each one of you may share the way you experience the story of what happened and what is happening in today's family world. We will first listen to everyone. Then you can share and discuss your experiences, your ideas and your feelings about the world with one another."

Directives at the End of Playtime and Sharing Time: "Before we leave this family world, I invite each one of you to explore what today's family world and your own inner wisdom tell you about what your family needs at this time. What does this play tell us about our goals for family play therapy?"

Closing the Session: As the therapist photographs the world, he/she may acknowledge the different aspects of the world that brought the family world/story to life. Repeating the teachings that each member of the family noted, the therapist then lights a candle next to the world. Everyone is encouraged to look once more at the family world and its teachings. The family is instructed to congratulate one another and to honor the validity of each person's experience. The lit candle invites everyone to honor the sacred/awesome aspects of the family's world.

Discussion

The free and spontaneous Sandtray-Worldplay Family Session sets the tone for the course of Dynamic Expressive Family Play Therapy. The family is acknowledged as an intelligent, creative, sensitive, action-oriented being. Therapeutic play in the sandtray stimulates the family's innate capacities to meet their collective needs for survival, nurturing, harmony, health, joy, and so on. Capacities to problem-solve and receptivity to professional counseling may significantly increase as the family explores many different possibilities of change and transformation in their communal play.

It is recommended that a non-directed Sandtray-Worldplay approach be used initially with families so that the family is bonded to their own creative problem-solving potential. This type of play session may be used at any time during the course of treatment and during the termination phases. As the family becomes more adept at playing together, each member of the family may take turns in playing with the whole family world while the others are watching. No characters are removed, no characters are added: the family plays with the existing family world! This is a wonderful way of discovering the infinite possibilities inherent in any given circumstance.

During the family session, it is helpful for the therapist to be as non-directive as possible and to support everyone's creative expression. There is no need to expect a "certain type" of world. Focus, hold, and encourage the process of playing with the possibilities. Let the family engage in their own "self-assessment." Let them get to know one another. Let them get a sense of what they are seeking and what they have to work with.

Discourage and do not reflect any blaming or judgmental statements or personal references – for example, "You always make such a mess." Instead, redirect the speaker to the world and what the characters in the world are doing, saying, feeling, and so on. Remind each member that if they want the characters doing something else, they are free to let that happen.

The therapist may ask other questions of the family at the end of the session:

1. Today, your family came and played together. This is a great accomplishment. I wonder what it was like for each one of you to be together and to play together as a family?
2. Did you notice how each one of you brought special contributions to your family world today? Please reflect on what each of you contributed. You can help one another remember.

3. When you played together today, each one of you had an opportunity to receive the contributions from other members. Some gifts come as welcome surprises, some are difficult to receive, and some we find irritating and upsetting. Can you reflect and share how you received the play from the others?

Observe the world, the family at play and the evolving interaction, and notice and support manifestations of their
- spontaneous, experimental play – the spirit of playfulness and differentiation
- ability to receive and play with others' play
- curiosity, interrelatedness, joining
- expressions of respect, affection, trust
- ability to receive another's story
- suffering and caring

When being with the family world, notice
- those beings who have the capacity to go on a "heroic quest" so that the characters in the world can meet their needs more effectively
- the presence of wisdom keepers, helpers, and learning opportunities
- the appearance of obstacles, destructive forces, and agents of change

Notice your own countertransference strivings by
- the way you are moved by the session
- the degree to which you can support each family member's play
- your need to change the world, the play, or the family's story

Special Considerations and Modifications
When the family finds it too difficult to create one world together either because someone is "too weak" to show up or because others are "too blaming," authoritarian or angry, then consider offering each member of the family their own personal sandtray. There, each one can create a world that no one else may touch or play with. Using this play process, everyone shares their own individual world with the members of the family. Family members learn to develop curiosity and empathic responsiveness to each other's experiences. Individual worlds created within family sessions give clues as to how the family can best support the individual strivings and needs of each family member. (See De Domenico [2005] for more instructions.)

Note: It is helpful when the play therapist has received Sandtray-Worldplay training experience and has participated in individual, family, and group Sandtray-Worldplay processes.

References
De Domenico, G.S. (2004/1982). *Sandtray-Worldplay Therapy: Levels 1-6 training hand-outs.* Oakland, CA: Vision Quest Into Symbolic Reality.

De Domenico, G.S. (2005). *Sandtray-Worldplay: A comprehensive guide to the use of the sandtray in psychotherapeutic and transformational settings.* Oakland, CA: Vision Quest Images.

De Domenico, G.S. (2008). *Sandtray-Worldplay: An experiential home study course for individuals and groups: Volume 1.* Oakland, CA: Vision Quest Images.

About The Author

Gisela Schubach De Domenico, Phd, LMFT, RPT-S, is a Licensed Marriage and Family Therapist, Family Counselor, and a Registered Play Therapist Supervisor. She developed and teaches phenomenological, process-oriented Dynamic Expressive Play Therapy, Sandtray-Worldplay and Nature-Worldplay Therapy in a 32-day Foundations Methods Course through Vision Quest Into Symbolic Reality. In private practice in Oakland, California, she offers transformational and clinical trainings, consultations, and supervision throughout the United States and Canada. She is an approved provider for the Association of Play Therapy, the National Board of Certified Counselors, and the California Board of Behavioral Sciences. Co-founder and editor for the Sandtray Network and the *Sandtray Network Journal*, she has authored numerous articles, six training manuals, and two Sandtray-Worldplay Therapy Texts.

Rappin' Family Puppet Interview
Source: Catherine Ford Sori

Goals
- Engage reluctant adolescents, children and families in the therapy process
- Observe and assess family dynamics (e.g., their level of enjoyment, communication, structure, and ability to organize around a task)
- Identify how the rap puppet story may reflect issues in the family

Materials
- Paper
- Pen or pencil for each family member who has good writing skills
- Wide variety (at least 20 to 30) of puppets to represent animals, people, and mythical figures that are aggressive, nurturing, and timid (see Gil & Sobol [2000] for a more detailed list). (Note: if puppets are not available, inexpensive stuffed animals may be substituted, which can be found at resale shops.)
- Play microphones (optional)
- Video (or audio) recorder (optional)

Advance Preparation
The puppets can be spread out on a table or carpet before the family arrives. The other materials should be close by so they are easily accessed when needed.

Description
The Family Puppet Interview (FPI) was first developed by Irwin and Malloy (1974), and it involves having family members select puppets and then create stories using the puppets to act out the stories. After the story is performed Irwin and Malloy ask clients cognitive questions, such as what the title of the story might be, or what each person thinks the moral of the story is. Gil (1994) has expanded the basic FPI by "staying in the metaphor" when she processes the activity. She talks directly to the puppets and encourages the puppets to reply, or to talk something over together, or perhaps to consider trying to do something different together, all before coming out of the metaphor. Only later will she move from the metaphor to reality by asking questions about the title, moral of the story, or if the family sees any similarity between the puppets' story and their lives.

In giving instructions to clients Gil emphasizes that they are to use the puppets they have selected to *act out*—not simply narrate their stories (1994). "Rappin' the Family Puppet Interview" is a cultural and musical adaptation of Gil's use of the Family Puppet Interview, in that the family members will write their story (with a beginning, a middle and an end) as a rap, and then use their chosen puppets to perform the rap (instead of acting it out).

63

To introduce the activity explain to the family that you have a special activity for them to do as a family that involves puppets and rap. First ask each person to select a puppet. The therapist should stand back and observe the process of how each member chooses the puppets, making note of puppets that are selected but then discarded. After everyone has chosen their puppets the instructions are as follows:

"Now as a family you are to make up a story that has a beginning, a middle, and an end, but it cannot be a story you already know, like *Cinderella* or *Toy Story*. You are going to write your story as a Rap, practice it, and then have your puppets perform the rap for me."

It does not matter if the puppets all rap together, or if each puppet performs a part of the story and then all the puppets join in for a "chorus." It is up to the family to negotiate how they will do this. Give the family about 30 minutes to complete the task. (Note: Since this activity may take more than the session hour some families may finish their rap in the following session.)

The therapist should then disengage while the family works on the rap, either by leaving the room and observing behind a one-way mirror (if available), or by sitting quietly and unobtrusively in a corner while pretending to be engaged in another task, while really taking note of how the family organizes around the task, their level of engagement and enjoyment, how decisions are made, their patterns of communication, noting any structural issues (such as coalitions, enmeshment, disengagement, etc.), who dominates and who is left out, as well as if a leader emerges, and how the rap is written and by whom (see Gil & Sobol, 2000). These process observations are important in assessing the family.

Before the family begins the performance the therapist can ask each puppet to introduce him/herself. When the family performs the rap, the therapist should note any differences between how the activity was rehearsed and how it was performed (Gil & Sobol, 2000). The activity should first be processed by "staying in the metaphor" (Sori, 2006). For example, the clinician may ask the mother's lamb puppet what it is like to have a bumblebee for a son, or how a monkey and an octopus play together when one lives in the trees and the other lives in the ocean. Questions should be formulated that are specific to the family and the story, including how the puppets overcame adversity, worked together, and what strengths each puppet possessed. (See Gil, 1994; Gil & Sobol, 2000 for more suggestions on questions to process the FPI.)

The discussion can then focus on the following questions:

1. What was it like to write the rap and to perform it using puppets?
2. What surprised you in doing this activity?

3. What was the best and the most difficult part about the activity?
4. What similarities did you notice between the activity and your own lives?

Video (or audio) tapes of the rap can be used in subsequent sessions to expand the metaphor or to address themes and issues that have emerged. Many families (especially children) enjoy seeing themselves perform, and it may take repeated viewings for the therapist to grasp all the meaning (Gil & Sobol, 2000) in the Rappin' Family Puppet Interview.

Discussion

Rap has been used in general to engage and treat adolescents and families (Sori, in press; 2008). Rap is relevant to many cultures and age groups, and is an extremely useful way to involve reluctant adolescents and children in therapy. It is also a medium that many parents relate to, and can be used to elicit the "expertise" of younger family members in writing and performing raps.

This activity is an effective way to assess a family's ability to work together, their boundaries and structure, their communication style, and even their levels of attachment. Because this is a playful activity but is culturally relevant for many of today's parents, teens, and children, it is an excellent way to engage and empower them to be active participants in the therapy process. Using puppets and rap are ways to sidestep client's natural defensiveness or reluctance to disclose information to a therapist.

For a follow-up activity the therapist may choose to write his/her own rap, using the same puppets chosen by the family or new puppets to address issues that emerged in the previous session, or to write a better ending to the family's rap/story.

While the Rappin' Family Puppet Interview is an excellent activity to use in the early stages of therapy to engage and assess families, it can also be used at termination (or [w]rap up!), where the family could be asked to use the same (or new) puppets and to write a rap that reflects on their experience in therapy. The therapist can use this story to punctuate change, perhaps by creating his/her own puppet rap about the family and their hard work, their strengths, progress, and future goals (Sori, in press).

References

Gil, E. (1994). *Play in family therapy*. New York: Guilford.

Gil, E., & Sobol, B. (2000). Engaging families in therapeutic play. In C.E. Bailey (Ed.), *Children in therapy: Using the family as a resource*. New York: W. W. Norton.

Irwin, E. C., & Malloy, E.S. (1975). Family puppet interviews. *Family Process, 14,* 170-191.

Sori, C.F. (in press).Using hip-hop in family therapy to build "rap"port. In H. G. Rosenthal (Ed.), *Favorite counseling and therapy homework assignments* (2nd ed.). New York: Routledge.

Sori, C.F. (2008). "Kids-rap:" Using hip-hop to promote and punctuate change. In C.F. Sori & L.L. Hecker (Eds.),*The therapist's notebook:Vol. 3.More homework, handouts, and activities for use in psychotherapy.* New York: Routledge.

Sori, C.F. (2006). Family play therapy: An interview with Eliana Gil. In C.F. Sori (Ed.), *Engaging children in family therapy: Creative approaches to integrating theory and research in clinical practice.* New York: Routledge.

About The Author

Catherine Ford Sori, PhD, LMFT, is Associate Professor and Leader of the Marriage and Family Counseling track at Governors State University, and is also Associate Faculty at the Chicago Center for Family Health (an affiliate of University of Chicago).She completed her doctorate degree at Purdue University West Lafayette in Child Development and Family Studies with a Specialization in Marriage and Family Therapy. She specializes in family systems and health care, and was Director of Children and Family Services at a cancer support center. Other special areas of interest include integrating play in family therapy, training counselors to work with children and families, child bereavement, integrating music and dance in couples and family therapy, divorce and stepfamily issues, ethics, and spirituality. She is the author/editor of 6 books, including *The Therapists' Notebook for Children and Adolescents, The Therapist's Notebook II* and *The Therapist's Notebook III* (co-edited with Dr. Lorna Hecker) and *Engaging Children in Family Therapy: Creative Approaches to Integrating Theory and Research in Clinical Practice*, as well as Volumes I and II of *The Therapist's Notebook for Integrating Spirituality* (co-edited with Dr. Karen Helmeke). She has authored numerous additional book chapters and journal articles and has presented nationally, regionally, and locally on topics such as those above. She is a licensed Marriage and Family Therapist and an approved supervisor with the American Association for Marriage and Family Therapy, a member of the Association of Play Therapy and the American Counseling Association, and serves on several journal editorial boards.

Recipe for Success
Source: Katherine M. Hertlein

Goals
- Increase self-awareness related to individual and family needs
- Identify strengths and weaknesses within the family
- Develop future goals for treatment sessions

Materials
- One sheet of scrapbooking paper (any style)
- Writing instruments such as pen or marker
- Scrapbooking decorations (these decorations might be related to cooking, food, recipes, or characteristics about the family member's completing the activity)
- Supplies to create a chef's hat or an apron for each family member (optional)

Advance Preparation
Arrange a flat space for this activity and place the materials so that each family member has easy access to them.

Description
Ask the family to collaborate on developing a recipe for success, that is, a recipe that includes the necessary ingredients for a happy, successful family. Have them include ingredients, quantities, and cooking instructions. The ingredients should not be directly related to food but rather to emotions, thoughts, sensations, and behaviors. For example, one family included portions of some ingredients such as, "love," "fun times," "trust," "respect," and "hugs."

To add to the appeal of this activity, each family member can create a chef's hat or an apron. This will help the family members have a tangible reminder of the activity and therapeutic goals.

Once the family outlines the recipe, ask process questions such as:

1. Describe the process of how the recipe was composed. Who contributed what elements?
2. What thoughts emerged as you constructed the recipe?
3. What feelings emerged as you constructed the recipe?
4. Did any of the ingredients surprise you? If so, in what ways?
5. Describe the process of generating the cooking instructions. What is the most important step? What is the least important or most changeable?
6. How was the final determination made regarding the ingredients included and the process to make the recipe?
7. What can each person in the family do/change to ensure the recipe turns out well?

What can the therapist do in his/her role as "Assistant Chef" to help bring this recipe to fruition?

Once the task is processed, ask the family to describe how they want to see their recipe. What ingredients does the family want to increase or decrease? What ingredients does the family want to add or remove completely? What would be the steps that they would like to change? Discuss what would be included in the new recipe and steps involved to complete the dish. Work with the family to construct their new recipe using the scrapbook paper and the decorations.

After completing the recipe, follow up with the remaining process questions:

1. Who else will know this recipe? With whom would you share it and under what circumstances?
2. What side dishes might go well with this recipe?
3. How would you know when you need to add another ingredient or alter the cooking instructions?
4. What needs to happen in order for you to make a change in the ingredients? In other words, how might you add more _____ in your family life?
5. What tools might you need to be able to complete the recipe?

Discussion

This activity assists both family and therapist in understanding how they see themselves, as well as the issues to be addressed in treatment. The scrapbook page serves as a visual reminder of the goals to be achieved in therapy. It addresses goals in treatment by presenting a way to develop a plan to achieve the goals identified in the success recipe.

This activity also addresses process issues within the family in the discussion of how the recipe was constructed. Additionally, it gives the family an opportunity to collaborate with one another on a joint activity related to reaching their goals and creates the beginnings of a positive history.

One challenge that may arise is the inability of a family to come to agreement about one recipe. Address this challenge by asking each of the family members to generate his/her own recipe as homework and bring it to session. During the session, focus on the commonalities around the recipes and develop a shared vision of what the recipe might include. The therapist might also advance the idea that the goal at the completion of treatment would be to complete one unified family recipe. The closer the family gets to being able to complete the unified recipe, the closer they are to the termination of treatment.

About The Author

Katherine M. Hertlein, PhD, LMFT, is an Associate Professor in the Department of Marriage and Family Therapy at the University of Nevada-Las Vegas. She received her Master's Degree in Marriage and Family Therapy from Purdue University Calumet and her doctorate degree in Marriage and Family Therapy from Virginia Tech. She is a member of the American Association for Marriage and Family Therapy, the Association for Play Therapy, and the America Association for Sexuality Educators, Counselors and Therapists. She formerly served as president of the Nevada Association for Play Therapy. She has published fifty articles and book chapters and five books, including *The Therapist's Notebook for Family Healthcare* and *The Couple and Family Therapist's Notebook*.

Thought Bubbles
Source: Trudy Post Sprunk

Goals
- Assess family relationships and dynamics
- Indentify how each family member perceives family dynamics such as communication styles and feelings
- Increase open communication among family members
- Increase family cohesion
- Increase coping strategies

Materials
- Pencils
- Thought Bubbles Worksheet (included)

Advance Preparation
There are five versions for this activity. Decide in advance which version to use in the session.

Make multiple copies of the Thought Bubbles Worksheet for each family member. If the family consists of more than four, give each person two pages of the worksheet.

Arrange seating so that each family member can write privately on a flat surface.

Description for Version 1: Funny Behavior
Request that members of the family silently write their names on their worksheets. Next, ask that they write the names of family members below the stick figures.

Have each member of the family write something in each thought bubble that he/she and other family members have said and/or done that was funny.

After each person has written in each thought bubble, ask each person to share what he/she wrote about a family member. For example, the family might agree to first share the funny things Dad has said or done. After sharing what family members have written about themselves and others, ask them to review their thoughts and feelings about their fun times together.

Another option is for the therapist to collect the completed pages, read the responses, and ask the family to guess who wrote each response.

Description for Version 2: Repeated Comments
In the thought bubble above each figure's head, ask family members to write

comments or questions that each person in their family, including themselves, repeats frequently.

Upon completion, have each person share what he/she wrote. As this information is shared, guide them in discussions regarding the effect of and effectiveness or ineffectiveness of each person's repeated comments.

Description for Version 3: Feelings
In the thought bubble above each figure's head, ask family members to write the feeling that they and other family members seem to experience most often.

After family members indicate they have completed the task, encourage them to share what they wrote, to give examples of when they usually observe that feeling in a family member, and how it affects them.

Description for Version 4: Worries
In the thought bubble above each figure's head, ask family members to write what they think each family member worries about and what they do to decrease the worry.

Family members then share their responses. After everyone has had a turn to share their responses, ask them to list additional techniques for decreasing worry behavior.

Description for Version 5: "Unsaids"
In the thought bubble above each person's head, ask family members to write the things they believe other people want to say, but cannot for some reason.

Family members then share their responses. After everyone has had a turn to share their responses, discuss what might make it easier for family members to communicate more openly.

Discussion
The use of the Thought Bubble, Version 1, provides an opportunity for family members to share and laugh together. This increases feelings of family connectedness, which decreases feelings of isolation that may exist in one or more family members.

In Version 2 of the Thought Bubble, family members share their perceptions of what others say repeatedly and the effect of these repeated comments. This provides a reality check as others may validate or invalidate one's self-perception. During the discussion, the therapist encourages family members to explore the reasons for these repeated comments, as well as techniques to avoid unnecessary repetition.

During the family's experience of completing the task in the Thought Bubble, Version 3, everyone provides information about themselves and their perception of each family member's primary feeling state. This opens up communication about feelings and perception of feelings. It engages each member, aids in assessing, and increases understanding. Version 5 also enhances communication within the family.

Children are often acutely aware of their parents' emotional states and are deeply affected by their parents' stressors and worries. The Thought Bubble, Version 4, provides the venue in which family members share their worries and what they do and/or think to decrease their worries. This tool deepens family awareness and enriches the therapeutic dialogue about coping strategies.

About The Author

Trudy Post Sprunk, LMFT-S, LPC-S, RPT-S, CPT-S, is a Licensed Marriage and Family Therapist and Supervisor who has been practicing psychotherapy since 1971. She has presented at international, national, and local conferences and has been interviewed on radio and television. She is certified as an EMDR Specialist and is a Registered Play Therapist Supervisor. She is past-president of the Association for Play Therapy and president and co-founder of the Georgia Association for Play Therapy.

Thought Bubbles

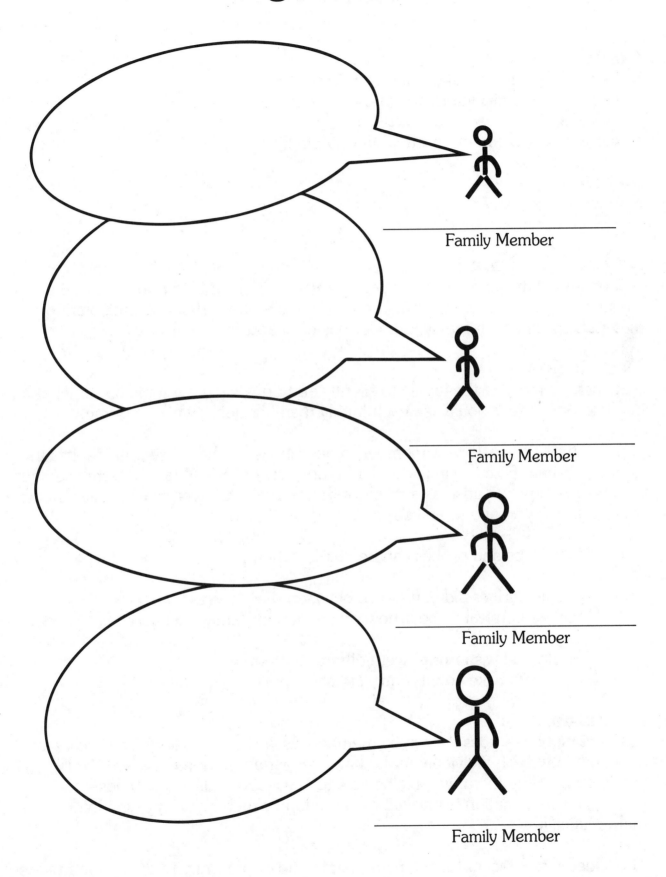

Family Member

Family Member

Family Member

Family Member

Video Crew
Source: Trudy Post Sprunk

Goals
- Establish a safe and open therapeutic environment
- Identify the family interactional patterns that are contributing to the problematic behavior
- Increase open communication among family members

Materials
- Sheets of paper
- Colored pencils, markers or crayons

Advance Preparation
Arrange a flat drawing space for each family member. It is important that the sheets of paper are not in direct eyesight of each other. Arrange the coloring materials so that each family member has easy access to them.

Description
Ask each member of the family to silently and privately draw a picture of what an invisible video crew would see each family member doing while at home.

Upon completion, ask each member to describe what they drew that depicts their family at home. Discuss similar and different perceptions of family members and process feelings that arise as a result of this activity. Ask what each family member is feeling, thinking about, and so on.

The following tips and probes can be helpful when processing the activity:

1. What similarities did you notice between the pictures?
2. What did you learn about how others in your family feel about life in your family?
3. How do you wish things were different at home?
4. What do you like about family life at home?

Discussion
This technique provides the family members as well as the therapist a means of assessing how each individual in the family experiences home life and family relationships. The therapist may be able to learn about alliances, triads, roles, and so on. This information is invaluable to the family therapist as he/she intervenes therapeutically.

The Video Crew technique offers the family the opportunity to discuss and process their feelings about family life, both how they perceive it as well as how they would like it to be different.

As a result of asking family members to engage in right hemisphere activity, such as art, left-hemisphere activity (analytical, cognitive, rational) is often provoked. When clients engage in art activities, they often provide spontaneous insights about the work they have completed (Gil, 2003). Moreover, drawings offer family members the opportunity to project their inner self onto an external surface. The trained therapist can use this visual record to understand individual beliefs and feelings. Understanding each family member's inner world can help the therapist see how each person can affect the family's functioning. This insight can help the therapist write treatment plans, set goals, and provide effective therapy.

Reference
Gil, E. (2003). Family play therapy: "The bear with short nails." In C.E. Schaefer (Ed.), *Foundations of play therapy*. New York: John Wiley & Sons.

About The Author
Trudy Post Sprunk, LMFT-S, LPC-S, RPT-S, CPT-S, is a Licensed Marriage and Family Therapist and Supervisor who has been practicing psychotherapy since 1971. She has presented at international, national, and local conferences and has been interviewed on radio and television. She is certified as an EMDR Specialist and is a Registered Play Therapist Supervisor. She is past-president of the Association for Play Therapy and president and co-founder of the Georgia Association for Play Therapy.

What Is My Role in the Family?
Source: Heather Venitucci and Jacob Gershoni

Goals
- Reveal roles and relationship dynamics within the family
- Increase open communication within the family
- Build trust and create safety among family members
- Encourage role exploration and discussions about role experimentation

Materials
- Paper
- Black marker
- Pens, pencils, and markers
- Questions (included)

Advance Preparation
Write the following titles on white or colored paper, one per page.

- The Scapegoat	- The Positive Thinker
- The Dominator	- The Negative Nelly
- The Nurturer	- The Hater
- The King of The House	- The Lover
- The Pleaser	- The Secret Keeper
- The Goofball	- The Excuse-maker
- The Entertainer	- The Quiet One
- The Money Maker	- The Talker
- The Housekeeper	- The Mystery
- The Worry-er	- The Wizard
- The Planner	- The Mediator
- The Organizer	- The Ignorer
- The Fighter	- The Ignored
- The Complainer	- The Boss
- The Diva	- The Fairy Princess
- The Baby Bear	- The Observer

Spread the sheets of paper out on the floor with the titles facing up.

Review the questions below and modify them as needed to fit the particular family's situation.

Description
Explain the activity as follows: "Today, we are going to play a game that will help you to identify roles that you play in the family. As you can see there are a lot of papers on the floor with different titles on them."

Ask the family members to take turns reading the titles and to discuss what the titles mean to them. Then say, "Now, I would like each of you to choose two or three titles that you feel describes the roles that you play in your family. For example, let's pretend that in *Sally's* family, both her older brother and younger sister come to her when they have a problem, but they ask her not to tell anyone else or they will get mad at her. Her first choice might be The Secret Keeper. At the same time, she might also be the one in the family that is always performing and telling funny stories, so her second choice might be The Entertainer or The Goofball. She might also feel like she gets blamed for everything when things go wrong, so her third choice might be The Scapegoat."

Once family members have chosen two to three titles, ask them to take a seat and place the titles in front of them. Say, "Now, I am going to read a question and I want you to hold up the sign that represents the best answer for you." If none of the roles supplied fit, offer paper for family members to write or draw their own titles or characters. This may offer a wonderful opportunity for the family to join together in creating an entire set of titles/roles in relation to a favorite book, movie, or song.

Read each question and allow family members to acknowledge one another and their responses. This can be done in silence, with one-word statements to express their feelings, or with more sharing and fuller discussion of each answer.

The following probes can be helpful when processing the activity:

1. What did you learn about the roles played by each person in your family?
2. How do you wish things were different at home?
3. What do you like about the roles played by each person in your family?
4. Which role would you like to try for a day?
5. What is one thing you could do to change the role you play in the family?
6. Who could you ask to help you with your role?
7. Who do you want to thank for the role they play?

If time is left at the end, supply markers and ask members to choose the title that they feel most connected to and write words, thoughts, feelings, and images around the title on the page. Ask members to share what role they enjoy, dislike, and would like to try, to change, or to give away.

Discussion
This activity was adapted from similar exercises developed by Dayton (2003) and Lipman (2003).

Jacob L. Moreno (1977), creator of sociometry and psychodrama, believed that each one of us is born into a system in which we learn behaviors based on roles assigned within our family of origin. He called this our "social atom" and believed that we take our social atoms with us wherever we go, recreating role relationships learned within the family unit. Action methods were Moreno's response to this belief, offering a playful and spontaneous way for people to explore their assigned roles, to express feelings about those roles, and to encourage choice and change in relation to unwanted or dysfunctional roles (Lipman, 2003).

The activity presented facilitates the first step toward role exploration, offering a structured way for family members to identify their family roles and to contemplate and verbalize feelings associated with them. Together, family members are encouraged to support one another through active listening, while sharing information about each role's challenges, acknowledging different role's strengths, and considering the possibility of changing a role. This often enhances family connection and communication and deepens family trust.

"By exploring roles, we can explore aspects of the self [in relation to other].... Well adjusted people tend to play a variety of roles.... When we experience a balance of roles in our lives, and can move in and out of them with ease and fluidity, we guard against feeling burned out, depressed, or stuck.... We can look at our lives...and write our own prescriptions simply by naming the roles that we play and seeing if the roles feel in balance" (Dayton, 2003). Role satisfaction and role balance within the family unit offers the possibility for healthier, more satisfying relationships both in and outside of the family unit.

References

Dayton, T. (2003). *Treatment of addiction and trauma in women*. In J. Gershoni (Ed.), *Psychodrama in the 21st century: Clinical and educational applications.* New York: Springer Publishing.

Lipman, L. (2003). *The triadic system: Sociometry, psychodrama, and group psychotherapy*. In J. Gershoni (Ed.), *Psychodrama in the 21st century: Clinical and educational applications*. New York: Springer Publishing.

Moreno, J.L. (1977). *Psychodrama. Vol.1*. Beacon, NY: Beacon House.

About The Authors

Jacob Gershoni, LCSW, CGP, TEP, is a Psychotherapist certified by the American Group Psychodrama Association. He works with individuals, couples, and groups both in private practice and at the Psychodrama Training Institute in New York City, where he is a co-director. He is also on the staff of the Columbia Presbyterian Medical Center. A Trainer, Educator and Practitioner (TEP) certified by the American Association of Group Psychotherapy and Psychodrama, he offers training classes for group therapists and others interested in Action Methods in psychotherapy. He graduated from the Hebrew University in Jerusalem (1971) and the University of Michigan (1975). His postgraduate training has been in Family Therapy and Psychodrama. Since 1980, he has maintained an active affiliation with two counseling services for the Gay, Lesbian, Bi-sexual, and Transgender community in New York City: Identity House and the Institute for Human Identity. His employment history includes work at the Fred Finch Youth Center in Oakland, California, and at the Queens Child Guidance Center in New York City.

Heather Venitucci, MSW, received her Master of Social Work degree in 2010 from Hunter College School of Social Work, where she graduated with honors. While at Hunter, she trained with Jacob Gershoni and Nan Nally-Seif at the Psychodrama Training Institute where she facilitated groups and worked with individuals and couples dealing with depression, anxiety, trauma, and addiction. Before graduate school, she used creative writing and role-play with inner-city school-age children to address issues of abuse, violence, depression, addiction, and family conflicts. From 2000 to 2005, Heather and her husband built a theater in New York City, where they housed their theater company, The Actor's Playground. In that time she worked with Broadway veterans such as Tony Award–Winner Norbert Leo Butz, and actors such as Sandy Duncan, Didi Conn (*Grease*), Katherine Narducci (*Soprano's*), and Julie Bowen (*Parenthood, Boston Legal, and Ed*). An early version of Heather's one-woman show, *Dad and Me* (the final version is titled *Father/Daughter*), was a finalist in *The Strawberry One-Act Festival* in 2006 where she was nominated as Best Actress and chosen to be part of the festival's publication of *The Best Plays From The Strawberry One-Act Festival: Volume 4*.

What Is My Role in the Family?
Questions

1. Which role are you good at?

2. Which role do you struggle with?

3. Which role feels good to you?

4. Which role gets you the most attention?

5. Which role hurts?

6. Which role do you think is the easiest?

7. Which role do you think is the hardest?

8. Which role would you like to give away?

9. Which role do you want to improve on?

10. Which role makes you feel [angry, sad, anxious, lonely, tired, mean, happy]?

Section Two:
Treatment Techniques

Chapter Overview:
Treatment Techniques

The treatment phase of intervention is a time to help the family work on therapeutic goals. A treatment plan should be developed for each family and be tailored to the unique needs of the clients. It is best not to mass produce treatment plans, even if clients have similar problems (Dattilio & Jongsma, 2010). The treatment plan ought to identify the family's treatment needs, desired goals, and the strategies for achieving these goals. Well-informed treatment goals are defined as being (a) important to the family, (b) realistic and achievable for the child and family, and (c) behaviorally measurable and specific. Although a variety of issues may surface during the assessment, the therapist must prioritize the goals on which to focus during the treatment process.

Once a treatment plan has been developed and goals formulated, the family works on the actualization of their goals. At times, goals need to be added or reformulated.

During the treatment phase, the family invests in therapeutic work, makes changes within the system, and consolidates these changes. The therapist helps the family to develop skills and reinforce changes until they are a part of the family's patterns. The treatment phase is also a time when deeper issues may surface, as clients have developed trust in the therapeutic relationship.

Therapists focus on both the content as well as the process during sessions. The content refers to what family members say, and the process is how these ideas are communicated. By focusing on the process of their discussions, therapists can help families improve the way they relate and thus enhance their own capacity to deal with the content of their problems.

Ultimately, family therapy helps to strengthen family dynamics, enhance communication, process feelings, provide psychoeducation, improve parenting, and restructure boundaries. A wide variety of activities are included in this section to help families address their treatment issues.

Attachment Sandtray
Source: Barbara Jones Warrick

Goals
- Increase the frequency of positive interactions between the parent and the child
- Increase open communication between the parent and the child
- Broaden the caregiver's understanding of the child

Materials
- Sandtray half-filled with sand
- Small objects or figurines representing different categories such as people (varied ages, races, abilities and occupations), animals (pets, farm, and wild), vehicles, plants and things from nature (rocks, shells), furniture/household objects, buildings, fantasy figures, etc.

Advance Preparation
Set the sandtray on a table where parent and child can sit side by side. Have the small objects easily accessible to the child.

Description
Note: This activity is for one parent and one child.

Inform the parent and child that the child will be building a *world* in the sand, an activity designed to help them feel closer. Tell the parent that his/her role will be to watch and listen and to be curious about the *world* the child builds. Let the parent know that you will be supporting him/her in developing curiosity about the child's *world* by modeling this before asking the parent to ask questions.

Position yourself and the parent across the tray from the child. Instruct the child to build a *world* in the sand using the available objects. The *world* may be about anything the child wants. Let the child know that you and the parent will be watching and ask the child to indicate when he/she is finished.

When the child is finished ask him/her to talk about the *world*. Using the child's terms and labels, ask the child to say more about any part of the *world* you are curious about (thus modeling the process for the parent). For example, if the child uses the word "wolf" in referring to a dog, ask the child to tell you more about the "wolf." As the child describes the feelings, thoughts, and experiences of the "wolf" invite the child to "notice how that feels" or ask "Who in this world knows about that (feeling, thought, experience)?" In talking about the *world,* keep the focus on the *world* and make physical gestures toward the *world* (using your hand/finger to point to or draw a circle in the air around the object[s] you are referencing). Do not assume to label any object or action in the *world* that the child has not specifically identified him/herself.

Turning to the parent, ask him/her what in the child's *world* he/she would like to know more about. Reframe the parent's questions to ensure that the questions carry no assumptions about, and are respectful of, the *world* and the child. Repeat this process until you sense the child has had the opportunity to fully share his/her experience of the world with the parent or until you come to the end of your session. (Ensure there is ample time to complete the steps below.)

Gesturing to the *world,* ask the following question: "If this *world* were a story, or if we were to learn something from this *world,* what would the title of that story be? What would we learn from this *world*?" For example, a child might title the *world* "The Happy Day" or describe the learning as "How to Make Friends."

Based on the child's response, ask the child and the parent to notice times between now and the next session when the title of the world or the learning shows up. For example: "Notice when you are having a *happy day*." Or, "Notice when you (know *how to*) *make friends*."

At the end, thank the child for his/her hard work and praise the parent for his/her curiosity.

Discussion

The research on attachment (Webster-Stratton, 1992) identifies the importance of child-led play in enhancing child self-esteem and strengthening the parent–child bond. The main purpose of this technique is to strengthen the parent-child bond through a structured sandtray activity. By using the sandtray for this work, a nurturing and contained environment is provided. In modeling curiosity and reframing the parent's questions, the integrity of the child's *world* ensures that the child experiences being seen, heard, understood, and valued.

Where a second sandtray is available, the activity may be repeated by the parent with the child becoming the observer. This application is contra-indicated both early in therapy and with children who due to age or attention deficits are unable to focus while the parent builds. In working with two *worlds*, it may be necessary to schedule a longer session or be prepared to do this over two sessions.

An additional variation has each builder identify a figure from his/her *world* that would like to visit the other builder's *world*. Start by inviting the child to see if a figure from his/her *world* wants to visit the parent's *world*. Check for permission from the parent, and then have the child move the object that has been selected into the other *world*. Then ask both (starting with the child) to "notice how the *world* has changed." Then repeat the process, inviting the parent to choose a figure to visit the child's *world*. If either builder is unwilling to receive a visitor into his/her *world*, explore what will be allowed (the figure is placed next to or on the edge of the tray without being in the *world)*. Then ask both child and parent to notice what that is like. Even if one builder refuses to admit a figure into his/her *world*, ask both builders to notice what that is like and how that feels.

Reference

Webster-Stratton, C. (1992). *The incredible years: A trouble-shooting guide for parents of children aged 2–8 years.* Lancaster, UK: Umbrella Press.

About The Author

Barbara Jones Warrick, M.Ed., CPT-S, is a Child and Family Therapist and Certified Play Therapist Supervisor who has been working in both agency and private practice settings since 1988. She has trained with Dr. Margareta Sjolund in the Erica Method of Sandtray Assessment and has completed the six-year training program in the Sandtray-Worldplay™ Method with its creator Dr. Gisela De Domenico. She has presented workshops on sandtray therapy in both Canada and the United States.

Avoiding Landmines
Source: David Narang

Goals
- Increase the child's appropriate use of impulse control and other coping techniques
- Teach the child to control impulses by using parental directions as support
- Teach the parent how to give clear, supportive, specific instructions to the child
- Improve interaction between parent and child so that clarity and non-punitive qualities of the parent's directions result in the child becoming open to and seeking more parental feedback

Materials
- Bandana or pillowcase for use as blindfold
- Cardboard for cutting out squares as landmines
- Scissors
- Marker

Advance Preparation
Cut out approximately 10 cardboard squares to be used as landmines. If using the word "landmine" is either insensitive or too intense for your particular client, please create a different metaphor. That intensity, however, often helps children engage in the activity. On the cardboard squares, use a marker to write down problems that reflect low trust in authority, emotional regulation errors, cognitive errors, or poor coping skills. For example:

1. Stopped taking slow deep breaths when feeling angry or stressed.
2. Pushed/hit a peer instead of using respectful words.
3. Yelled at someone when felt angry.
4. Assumed the teacher doesn't like me.
5. Refused to tell my mom/dad what was bothering me.
6. Forgot that I can handle being bored sometimes.
7. Forgot that some people at school want me to succeed.
8. Lost hope after making one mistake, and so made many more.
9. Felt unlovable when I made a mistake.
10. Forgot to fix it, after I made a mistake.

Arrange the therapy space so that the cardboard squares can be spread out on the floor.

Description
Note: This activity is for one parent and one child.

Explain to the child/teen and parent that sometimes life has a lot of landmines we have to avoid, because if we don't, parts of our lives can blow up. Part of a parent's job is to help a child/teen predict and avoid landmines, and part of a child/teen's job is to accept that guidance from a parent.

Review the landmines written on the cardboard squares, noting each landmine problem the child will attempt to avoid stepping on during the activity.

Set up the labeled "landmines" on the ground in an open and flat area. With child and parent expressing willingness for the activity (children and early teens are usually eager to try this), ask the parent if he/she is willing to take responsibility for child safety during the activity. If so, have the parent tie a bandana around the child's head as a blindfold.

The parent now needs to use instructions (e.g., forward, left, right, stop) to help the child get from one side of the minefield to the other side, without stepping on a landmine.

During the activity, coach the parent if his/her instructions are unclear, anxiety laden or harsh, or otherwise difficult to follow. Coach the child if he/she is not responding well. Count how many mines the child steps on.

Repeat the activity, this time, without parental guidance, and count how many mines the child/teen steps on this time. Some youth are very surprised about the increase in the number of mines they step on without guidance, creating an opening within them to consider accepting parental guidance.

Increase process awareness and generalization of skills to other contexts with the following questions:

1. For the parent: What did you learn about how to be most effective in giving your child instructions?
2. For the child/teen: What do you think of the difference in how many mines you stepped on when your mom/dad was and wasn't helping?
3. For the child/teen: How would you know in real life if things were getting bad enough at school or at home that you should ask for help?
4. For parent and child: What makes it easier for (child's name) to ask for help when he/she is stuck?

Discussion

Children who are oppositional and/or hyperactive receive a lot of negative feedback about their behavior. That repetitive criticism often results in more anger toward and distrust of authority figures and ever lessening of attachment security. If this pattern continues, many children can deteriorate toward severe disturbances in their conduct.

The therapist can use this activity as a method to help the parent learn how to give guidance in a specific and supportive style. The child/teen gets immediate feedback on how much listening to his/her parent can improve his/her performance.

Following the activity, the therapist can help the child and the parent to discuss how the child would know it is time to ask for help (e.g., conflict with teachers escalating into daily frequency), and how the parent would respond when the child asks, contributing to a foundation of trust. The child learns that he/she could seek help before his/her behavior escalates.

About The Author

David Narang, PhD, is a psychologist in Santa Monica, California. He has served as the director of a large community mental health clinic in Los Angeles. Currently, he supervises a school-based mental health program operated through Saint John's Child and Family Development Center. He also maintains a private practice. He has supervised psychotherapists, co-authored a book chapter in *Latino Children and Families in the United States: Current Research and Future Directions* (Contreras, Narang, Ikhlas, & Teichman, 2002), and published several journal articles.

Beat the Record Routine Race
Source: Liana Lowenstein

Goals
- Establish consistent rules and routines
- Reduce tension and conflict between parent and child

Materials
- Instruction sheets (included)
- Props (see suggested props below)
- Stopwatch or watch
- Paper
- Pen
- Prizes (optional)

Advance Preparation
In the session prior to this activity, discuss the list of props required for the activity (see below) and decide which props the family will bring to the following session, and which props the therapist will bring. Modify props as needed.

Print the three instruction sheets and cut out each one, or copy the instructions onto paper or index cards. Set up the following three stations with the instruction sheets and the appropriate props:

Station #1: The Morning Routine:

Task	Prop
Wake up	Pillow placed on the floor
Wash	Toothbrush, washcloth, comb
Get dressed	Oversize shirt
Eat a healthy breakfast	Paper plate, plastic fork
Leave for school on time	Backpack

Station #2: The Afterschool Routine:

Task	Prop
Eat a healthy snack	Paper plate and fork
Complete homework with focused attention	Paper and pencil
Free time	Small toy
Eat dinner together as a family	Plate and fork for each family member

Station #3: The Bedtime Routine:

Task	Prop
Wash	Toothbrush, washcloth
Change into pajamas	Pajama top
Story time	Storybook
Bedtime	Pillow, blanket

Description

This activity is designed for children who have difficulty following daily routines. It is best to conduct the activity with one child and one parent. The other family members can observe and then have a turn. (Alternatively, the other family members can act as cheerleaders and cheer the child on during the race.) Explain to the family that they are going to participate in a fun activity to help them with routines at home. Outline the activity as follows:

The child and parent will begin at station one, The Morning Routine. The parent will read the instructions to the child and coach the child to complete each task. The child will complete each task as quickly as possible. Once all the tasks at station one are complete, the child and parent will quickly move to station 2, The After School Routine, and the parent will coach the child to complete each task at this station. Once complete, the child and parent will proceed to station 3, The Bedtime Routine, and the parent will again coach the child to complete each task as quickly as possible.

Explain that this activity is a race and the child will be timed to see how quickly he/she can complete all the tasks at the three stations. The therapist will set the timer once the child begins to complete the first task at station one and will stop the timer as soon as the child has completed the last task at station three. The therapist will write down the time it took for the child to complete this race.

Once the child has completed all the tasks at the three stations, the child will start again, and see if he/she can beat his/her record. As an optional component to this activity, the child can be awarded a small prize if he/she beats his/her record.

Most children will complete the race faster the second time. The therapist can point out that the child was able to beat the record because, once the tasks are familiar, they are easier to complete.

The parent is encouraged to praise the child throughout the race. The therapist can model labeled praise such as: Great job getting ready for bed; I like how you focused on your homework.

After the game, facilitate discussion by asking the following process questions:

1. Which task was the most fun to complete?
2. What are some examples of healthy breakfast and snack foods?
3. (For the child) Is it usually easy or difficult for you to complete your homework with focused attention? If it is difficult, what strategies would make it easier?
4. (For the child) What are your favorite things to do in your free time?
5. (For the parent) Do you have a rule at home that homework must be completed before your child has free time? If not, is this a rule that you think

is important to enforce?

6. Does your family eat dinner together? If yes, what do you enjoy about this time? If no, is this something you would like to incorporate into your daily routine?

7. Is story time a part of your bedtime routine? If yes, what are your favorite books? If no, is this something you would like to incorporate into your daily routine?

8. Was it easier to complete the tasks faster the second time and, if yes, how come?

9. How do you think this activity can help you at home?

Discussion

Conflict between parents and children often escalates around daily routines. This intervention helps parents establish and enforce consistent routines, using a playful and engaging activity. Kaduson, Cangelosi, and Schaefer (1997) emphasize that children learn and remember better when instruction is made fun and enjoyable. Additionally, children derive a unique sense of competency through play.

The discussion questions facilitate exploration of current routines and encourage the integration of appropriate family rituals such as eating together as a family, story time, and so on.

It can be helpful to meet with the parents in a separate session prior to activity implementation to assess current routines and to discuss desired changes in routines. The parents can also be prepped to take on an appropriate coaching role during the activity, and to learn labeled praise. The therapist and family are encouraged to be creative and to modify the props to further enhance the level of engagement.

Reference

Kaduson, H.G., Cangelosi, D., & Schaefer, C.E. (Eds.). (1997). *The playing cure: Individualized play therapy for specific childhood problems.* New York: Jason Aronson.

About The Author

Liana Lowenstein, MSW, RSW, CPT-S, is a Social Worker and Certified Play Therapy Supervisor in Toronto. She maintains a private practice, provides clinical supervision and consultation to mental health professionals, and lectures internationally on child and play therapy. She has authored numerous publications, including the books *Paper Dolls and Paper Airplanes: Therapeutic Exercises for Sexually Traumatized Children, Creative Interventions for Troubled Children and Youth, Creative Interventions for Bereaved Children,* and *Creative Interventions for Children of Divorce.*

Beat The Record Routine Race
Instruction Sheets

Instruction Sheet for Morning Routine:

(The race will begin with the child wearing a pajama top and laying down with head on the pillow, pretending to be asleep.)

1. Wake up and get out of bed
2. Wash face (rub cloth on face for 10 seconds), brush teeth (10 seconds), comb hair (10 seconds)
3. Change out of pajamas into clothes (remove pajama top and put on oversized shirt, or if it seems inappropriate for the child to undress in the session, then modify i.e., tie the shirt around child's waist)
4. Eat a healthy breakfast (pretend for 20 seconds, using the plate and fork)
5. Go to school or daycare (put on backpack, walk out the door)

Instruction Sheet for Afterschool Routine:

1. Arrive home, have a healthy snack (come back into the room, go to station 2, and pretend for 10 seconds to eat a healthy snack using the paper plate and fork)
2. Complete homework (modify to child's age, such as write the alphabet, or write first and last name)
3. Free time (modify to child's interest, such as complete a puzzle, or throw a ball back and forth from parent to child three times)
4. Eat dinner together as a family (pretend for 30 seconds using the plates and forks)

Instruction Sheet for Bedtime Routine:

1. Wash, (rub cloth on face for 10 seconds), brush teeth (10 seconds)
2. Change into pajamas (remove shirt and put on pajama top, or if it seems inappropriate for the child to undress in the session, then modify i.e., tie the pajamas around child's waist)
3. Parent read a story to the child (parent reads first page of book aloud), parent tucks child into bed (child lays on pillow and parent covers child with blanket), kisses goodnight.

© Liana Lowenstein

92

Behavior Remote
Source: Rebecca Fischer

Goals
- Decrease the child's behavioral problems
- Teach parents how to implement effective child management strategies
- Increase the frequency of positive interaction between parents and child

Materials
- TV/DVD remote control (or create one using art supplies)
- Paper or cardboard
- Scissors
- Glue or tape
- Markers or crayons

Description
Explain to the family that they are going to learn about a special tool that will help them to deal with problem behaviors. Show the family the remote control and discuss its use for televisions, DVD, and music players. Explain that the remote brought to the session is a special "behavior remote" that controls behavior and thoughts just like the regular remote controls the television. Go through the various buttons and explain what each button may represent in terms of behavior. This can be modified based on the child's presentation, but may include:

- Pause button: Can be used for a child (or parent, never a sibling) to "pause" a child's out of control or anxious behavior to give the child time to decide on his/her next course of action or which coping skill to use (e.g., deep breathing) that he/she is having trouble using in real-life situations.
- Fast Forward button: The child/parent can "fast forward" to see what the potential consequences of his/her behavior will be while in "pause" mode.
- Stop button: If the child/parent decides during "pause" mode that his/her behavior may result in negative consequences, he/she can choose to stop that behavior and switch to a new behavior.
- Play button: The child/parent can choose to continue the original behavior after "pause" mode or begin a different behavior.
- Rewind button: The child/parent can "rewind" or think about what he/she could have done differently to have reached a better outcome than what is currently being experienced.
- Volume buttons: Can help the child/parent choose how loud to be in a given situation (e.g., turn down yelling voice and talk in a lower voice).
- Mute button: A child may decide that he/she needs to "mute" his/her behavior (e.g., whining).
- Channel-changing buttons: The child/parent can look through different stations (behaviors) to select the best choice.

Next, the family works together to make their own behavior remote out of craft supplies, putting on whatever buttons are relevant to their particular problem behavior. (Fewer buttons are recommended for families with very young children.)

The child and parent can then role-play various scenarios and practice using the behavior remote. For example:

1. Child asks for a cookie, parent says no as it is too close to dinnertime. Child throws a tantrum. Parent yells and sends child to his/her room.
2. The children are arguing over what television show to watch and the argument escalates into a physical fight.
3. The parent is helping the child complete his/her homework. The child becomes frustrated as he/she does not understand the homework assignment. The child throws the homework across the room. The parent becomes upset and yells at the child.

The family can be encouraged to come up with their own scenarios to role-play. A discussion can then take place, using the following questions to guide the process:

1. In what ways can the remote help each of you with your behavior?
2. Which button on the remote can you press when you are feeling frustrated or angry and you feel like you are about to lose your temper?
3. (To the child) What might be some situations in which your parents may need to help you remember to use your behavior remote? What will your response be when they remind you?
4. What positive changes might occur in your family if each member uses the remote?

It is important to establish a rule with the family that it is never appropriate for a sibling to attempt to control a co-sibling's behavior by using the remote.

At the end of the session, the family takes the remote home to use as a reminder. In the following session, follow up with the family to explore the effectiveness of this technique.

Discussion

Most clients are familiar with remote controls and understand the various functions such as pause, rewind, and mute. In this activity, the remote control provides a concrete, visual tool to help family members control negative behaviors and implement appropriate coping skills. The use of an internal remote to control negative or impulsive behavior helps clients feel empowered and take control of their own behavior. Additionally, the "fast forward" and "rewind" components encourage clients to think about the cause-effect link of their behavior before acting impulsively.

Many parents find that although children learn coping skills in treatment, they do not use them in real-life situations. Taking the remote control home enables the family to put into practice the coping skills that they have learned in treatment.

About The Author
Rebecca Fischer, PhD, received her doctorate degree from the University of Toledo. She has worked with children, adolescents, and families in both inpatient and outpatient settings. She currently works in private practice as a Psychology Postdoctoral Trainee and is working toward psychology licensure in the state of Ohio.

Birthday Celebration
Source: John W. Seymour

Goals
- Highlight the value of the individual child in the life of the family
- Increase parents' ability to nurture their child
- Help family members renew or begin similar family traditions in their home life

Materials
- Craft supplies to make birthday cards such as construction paper and markers
- Whiteboard or large piece of paper with suitable marker
- Simple refreshments (optional)
- Party hats, blow horns, etc. (optional)
- Small birthday cake with candles (suitable for the cultural background and accommodating any health concerns), matches to light the candles, knife to cut the cake, plates, napkins, and forks (optional)

Advance Preparation
Set up any party games that will be incorporated into the birthday celebration.

Description
This activity is divided into several segments: Planning a birthday observance in session, implementing the observance in session, and briefly identifying what the family might do to incorporate this experience at home.

Planning
Play therapy theories vary in the degree to which sessions are more therapist-or client-directed and in guiding how and when to involve family members. This activity may be adapted to reflect many of these variations. In some cases, the activity may be introduced in a spontaneous way during the course of a family play therapy session. For others, it may be incorporated into a more structured approach, being planned first with the parent(s) and then incorporated into a later play session.

However the activity begins, the therapist introduces the purpose of the activity to the family by stating the importance of family traditions in both nurturing individual family members and developing a greater sense of togetherness between family members. The introduction should include a review of the common ingredients of strong family traditions: supportive family and friends, recognition of personal and family strengths, and the sharing of play, refreshments, and gifts. Family members may be encouraged to give examples.

With family members in a small circle, ask them about their family birthdays: How were the parents' birthdays observed when they were children? How has this family observed birthdays? Who was invited? What activities were planned? What refreshments were served? What gifts were exchanged? If the family has a very limited history of observing birthdays, then ask them to imagine how they would like to observe a birthday.

With the whiteboard or large piece of paper, list the four parts of a birthday observance: Inviting, Playful Activities, Refreshments, and Gifts. Ask the parents what they can do today in the session to enact a simple birthday observance for their child. Guide the discussion as follows:

Inviting: Who else would be invited? In a well-equipped play therapy room, puppets, dolls, or stuffed animals might be used as "stand-ins" for family members and guests not at the session. Therapeutic issues may include who is included/ excluded and reasons for those choices (these can range from a simple absence to issues such as awkwardness around post-divorce multiple households, chemical use, or safety matters such as family violence).

Playful Activities: Help family members use available play materials and their imaginations to plan several simple party games. Simple foam-ball games can be created, or old familiar games such as "Duck, Duck, Goose" can be used. Therapeutic issues may include encouraging adults' abilities/willingness to plan and engage in nurturing play and the child's abilities/willingness to engage in play.

Refreshments: This can be "pretend" refreshments or simple refreshments provided by the therapist. Therapeutic issues may include affirmation of the child's or family's favorite traditional foods, tying into cultural strengths, and affirming the child's special value to the family in a rousing chorus of "Happy Birthday to You," or some other family selection.

Gifts: Each family member uses the available craft materials to make the child a Happy Birthday card and think about what to say to the child when the child is presented with the card. For the child observing the birthday, have him/her make a card that represents what it will mean to him/her to be his/her new age. One variation that can be very affirming is to have all family members create cards with an acrostic of the child's name, spelling out the child's name and using each letter as the first letter of a word or phrase that illustrates the child's different qualities. Therapeutic issues may include family members' abilities to put affirmations into words with the child, and the child's ability to receive the affirmations.

Implementation

As family members finalize their plans for each of the four parts, the therapist or a family member can fill in the outline on the whiteboard or planning paper. The therapist then encourages the family to implement the plan in session, providing only the encouragement needed to facilitate the observance, and noting therapeutic issues for addressing at the end of the session or in a future session.

Transferring from the Session to Home Life

When the observance is completed, the therapist has the family return to a discussion circle. Family members are encouraged to report on their experience and observations. Discussion questions can include:

1. What was the birthday celebration like for you?
2. What did you like?
3. What was uncomfortable?

Next, discuss the parts of the birthday celebration the family wishes to incorporate into their home life. Ask the family to consider the important ingredients needed to provide a positive and nurturing birthday celebration at home. Additionally, ask the family how they might incorporate their own family and cultural traditions to make these observances at home more meaningful.

This simple activity can provide the opportunity for a positive nurturing experience in session as well as the stimulus for families being more intentional in providing nurturing experiences in their family life.

Discussion

Many families observe children's birthdays as a part of their family tradition. Birthdays highlight the individual child's value to the family and provide an opportunity to surround the child with supportive family and friends. While there are cultural variations, birthdays include inviting people to attend, time for play and socializing, refreshments, and an exchange of gifts. These very simple steps reflect a much deeper pattern shared with important family rituals of many kinds (Doherty, 1999; Imber-Black & Roberts, 1998; Imber-Black, Roberts, & Whiting, 2003). These family traditions are how families affirm and sustain the connections between family members, providing reinforcement for attachment bonds as children get older.

Unless there is some specific cultural or religious prohibition for the family, including a birthday observance into family therapy can be a meaningful event for both the child and participating family members. Some families may have had a rich but now neglected tradition of observing birthdays, due to the stresses of change and family transitions such as death or divorce or due to disruption caused by the family coping with a house fire or some natural disaster such as a tornado or hurricane. Other families may have a history of less involvement and attention to the life and nurturing of family members, with a previous lack of interest in beginning or sustaining meaningful family traditions.

Birthday observances in family therapy can be a time of healing for birthdays missed, as well as the starting point for families to renew or begin a meaningful tradition that can enrich the life of the child and family. While this activity suggests a basic outline and materials, therapists are encouraged to adapt the activity to their treatment approach, the family's culture and existing traditions, and availability of materials and setting. For additional suggestions for developing family traditions for birthdays and other family events, see Cox (2003).

References

Cox, M. (2003). *The book of new family traditions: How to create great rituals for holidays and everyday.* Philadelphia: Running Press.

Doherty, W.J. (1999). *The intentional family: Simple rituals to strengthen family ties.* New York: Harper Paperbacks.

Imber-Black, E., & Roberts, J. (1998). *Rituals for our times: Celebrating, healing, and changing our lives and relationships.* New York: Jason Aronson.

Imber-Black, E., Roberts, J., & Whiting, R.A. (Eds.) (2003). *Rituals in families and family therapy (2nd ed.).* New York: W.W. Norton.

About The Author

John W. Seymour, PhD, LMFT, RPT-S, is an Associate Professor in Counseling at Minnesota State University, Mankato. He has been a family therapist and play therapist since 1978. He is a Registered Play Therapist Supervisor with the Association for Play Therapy and an Approved Supervisor with the American Association of Marriage and Family Therapists. Prior to teaching graduate family therapy and play therapy courses at the University, he worked in a variety of settings, including hospital, agency, and residential treatment.

Box of Memories
Source: Karen Freud

Goals
- Strengthen family communication skills
- Increase cohesion among family members

Materials
- White paper (one sheet for each family member)
- Drawing materials such as markers or colored pencils
- Acrylic or tempera paint and brushes
- Magazine photos, decorative embellishments, and other collage materials
- Glue
- A cardboard box with a lid

Advance Preparation
Arrange a flat space for the art activity. Place the art materials near the flat surface so all family members can easily reach them.

Description
Each family member receives one sheet of paper and uses the drawing materials to draw a picture of a positive memory of something they have done together as a family.

When the drawings are complete, the family members use the art materials provided and work together to decorate the outside of the cardboard box. They can paint it, glue magazine photos and other decorative items onto it, and so on.

The members are then invited to talk about the memories they have chosen to depict in their drawings. Process questions can include:

1. What made the event special?
2. What is it like for you when you are doing something fun together as a family?
3. What else would you like to do together as a family?
4. When you were decorating the box, did you all agree on how to decorate it? If not, how were disagreements handled?
5. What was it like to work together to decorate the box?

All the images are then placed in the box and covered with the lid. Families have the option of taking their memory box home. They can refer to it as needed and may add more drawings or magazine photo collages. They can also include trinkets and photographs.

Discussion
This activity serves to strengthen family ties by focusing on the positive aspects of the family. Sharing stories about the various memories fosters open communication. Decorating the box together encourages open communication, compromise, and respect for each other's choices and decisions.

Linesch (1993) notes that in addition to self-expression, the art therapy process allows for "interpersonal communication and relationship building" for family members. Linesch further explains that "a dependence on words can prevent individuals (and families) from finding the opportunities for invigorating their conversation styles. The art process can offer a means for liberating bound and redundant interpersonal styles that make relationships stale and rigid." A further benefit to using art therapy with families is that the art process is "a creative and productive endeavor; as such, it promotes a sense of self and accomplishment."

Reference
Linesch, D. (1993). *Art therapy with families in crisis.* New York: Brunner/Mazel.

About The Author
Karen Freud, BA, A.T., received her training at the Toronto Art Therapy Institute. She is based in Toronto and currently conducts individual and group art therapy sessions and workshops for various community organizations. Her experience includes working with children and adults, and she has worked in a variety of settings that include mental health agencies, long-term care facilities and private practice.

© Karen Freud

Building Together – Understanding Together
Source: Linda E. Homeyer

Goals
- Increase ability to understand the perspective of other family members
- Increase empathy between family members
- Identify communication styles within the family
- Build a common experience through which family members jointly work to build effective relationship skills

Materials
- Sandtray half-filled with sand
- Variety of small toys or figurines representing different categories such as people, animals, plants, buildings, vehicles, etc.

Advance Preparation
Check the sandtray to ensure there are no hidden objects in the tray and smooth out the sand to create a neutral, flat surface. Check to see that the small toys or figurines are organized to allow easy access by clients. (For further information on how to organize the sandtray materials, see Homeyer & Sweeney, 2010.)

Description
Note: This activity is for one parent and an adolescent.

This semi-directive, joint sandtray creation is used to identify interaction deficits and areas of empathy (or lack thereof) between a parent and an adolescent.

With the family dyad in the sandtray therapy room, invite both to stand around the sandtray (standing helps them engage more easily and assists them in starting to build, as they are already in an "active" mode). Then explain the activity as follows:

"Here is a tray of sand and a collection of objects. Please build a scene in the sand of how your week has gone. You can use as many or as few of the objects as you like. I would like you each to work in your own section of the tray (therapist makes a dividing line in the sand with her/his hand, dividing the sandtray into two equal-sized sections). Once you are done, please have a seat and we'll wait until you both are done before talking about what you have created."

While the parent and teenager are building their individual scenes it is critical to observe the individual process and interaction between them, for example: Are either of them totally focused on their own creation to the exclusion of being aware of the other? Does one intrude into the physical or emotional space of the other? Do they respect the sandtray space of the other? Do they "take" space from the other? Openly or covertly? Be sure to be aware not only of what is being created in the sandtray but also of the body language of the builders.

Once both have completed their individual sections of the tray, pull chairs up close to the tray and invite them to share their creations. The therapist can say, "First, please share with us what you have created. We will wait to ask questions until you have told us about it." As each share, be sure to observe the other person's reactions.

Possible prompts while each person shares his/her own scene in the sand include:

1. How do you feel about having shared your scene?
2. I noticed as you built the tray, you seemed (hurried, indecisive, frustrated, distracted). Please tell me more about what you were experiencing during the making of your tray.
3. Where are you in the scene (if not clearly stated)?

Once the individual scenes are shared, begin to encourage active responses and feedback between the parent and the adolescent:

1. Mom/Dad, how did you feel as you saw your teenager's scene and heard him/her talk about it?
2. I noticed, Mom/Dad/teen, that you had a hard time staying on your side of the tray. Can you tell us more about what was going on with you?
3. What is similar/different about your scenes?
4. What helped improve your communication today?
5. What hindered more open and honest communication today?
6. What did you learn about each other through this activity?
7. What was the biggest stressor in each other's life this week, as shown in the sandtray?
8. What was the biggest area of happiness/pleasure/accomplishment in each other's life this week, as shown in the sandtray?

As the discussion continues, allow them to move or add/delete items in their sandtray scenes, should they desire to do so. This reflects the more dynamic side of life as opposed to the static side.

During the discussion, the therapist models reflecting feelings and expressing empathy. The therapist comments on what is enhancing or interfering with communication.

Discussion

Once family members become disengaged from each other, it becomes increasingly difficult for them to be aware of life events and perceptions of each others' worlds.

This can be particularly the case for adolescents and parents, as adolescents work through their developmental stage of breaking away from parental controls. Additionally, parents often have expectations of what their teenager's lives "should" be like and fall out of touch with the reality of their teens' experiences.

Building together in the sandtray allows the therapist insight into how much each pays attention to the other. Some parents are so disengaged with their teen, and so self-absorbed, that they may not be aware of what the teen is building until discussion time (or vice versa). Others may be too involved with their teen to the point of assisting him/her in building the scene and/or adding items to or removing them from the teen's scene.

Modeling the expression of empathy and reflecting feelings is the first step toward assisting the family dyad in learning to do the same. Inviting each to share with the other is key. Observing the communication style provides the therapist with ample information to help the dyad set goals for improving how they communicate.

The natural development of symbols and metaphors that occur in sandtray therapy may also help to develop a common language for the dyad in future therapy sessions. This adds to the richness of the interaction and enhances the valuing of each other through a common, shared experience.

Reference
Homeyer, L.E., & Sweeney, D. (2010). Sandtray therapy: A practical manual. New York: Routledge.

About The Author
Linda E. Homeyer, PhD, LPCS, RPT-S, is a Professor of Professional Counseling at Texas State University. She teaches play therapy and sandtray therapy, and she provides clinical supervision. She also teaches internationally and writes extensively. Many of her works have been translated into Korean, Spanish, Russian, and Chinese. Her latest work is a second edition (revised and expanded) of Sandtray Therapy: A Practical Manual, co-authored with Dr. Daniel Sweeney.

Chains of Change
Source: Sara Michelle Mennen

Goals
- Reduce children's behavioral problems
- Increase parents' understanding of the principles of effective parenting and behavior modification
- Increase parents' targeted praise of their children
- Increase the rate of positive verbal comments and pleasurable exchanges between family members
- Reestablish the parental hierarchy

Materials
- Construction paper
- Tape
- Scissors

Description
Explain to the family that this activity will help the child improve his/her behavior, for example, his/her verbal and physical aggression. The family works together, with the therapist's help, to create the paper chain. The directions are as follows:

1. Fold each piece of construction paper in thirds so that each strip is approximately 3" by 11" in length.
2. Cut each paper into strips, cutting along the lines that were formed when folding. Cut out 9 to 12 strips.
3. Fashion the first strip into a circle and tape the ends together.
4. Pick up a second strip of paper and thread it through the middle of the first circle, then tape the ends together to begin the formation of the paper chain.
5. Work together to complete the rest of the paper chain.

The parent should be coached to allow the child to take the lead in creating the paper chain, so the child gains mastery and ownership over the project. The parent can verbally praise the child's efforts as he/she completes the paper chain.

Once the paper chain has been created, the therapist explains the rules of the activity as follows:

1. When the child wants something changed (such as a younger sibling to move) she/he will first ASK the other person in a respectful way to do the task or make the change.
2. After asking the person to change the behavior (if the person does not respond by making the change) the child will tear off one link from the paper chain.

3. After the link of the chain has been torn, the child will go to the parent/guardian and give it to that person, explaining what happened.
4. The parent/guardian will take the link of the chain from the child and verbally reinforce the child's behavior for making a request instead of being aggressive. The parent/guardian will then take care of the situation that needed to be managed and talk with the child about how it was helpful that he/she came to the adult.
5. The parent will keep all the links that have been removed from the chain to reinforce the child's understanding that he/she can control aggressive behavior and has done so on several occasions.
6. A reward can be given after the child has removed each of the links from the chain.

The child and parent can practice the steps in the session by role-playing a common scenario, for example, the child's sibling changes the channel while the child is watching a favorite television show.

If appropriate, each child in the family can create his/her own paper chain. The parents and/or guardian could also make his/her own chain to model the activity and to reinforce the steps, process, and positive behavior.

Discussion
All too often, children do not learn effective ways to control their behavior and/or emotions when they do not get what they want. Thus, they react in an inappropriate way such as yelling, hitting, kicking, or throwing objects. At times, this behavior is reinforced through negative attention and so the cycle continues. The Chains of Change activity helps the child refrain from engaging in verbal or physical aggression, and provides the parent with opportunities to praise the child for demonstrating appropriate behavior. Furthermore, this activity helps the caregiver reestablish the parental hierarchy. By keeping the links, the child can receive further positive verbal reinforcement for "working hard" to control his/her behavior. The child can bring these links to the therapist for further reinforcement.

About The Author
Sara Michelle Mennen, MS, NCC, LPC, LAMFT, RPT, is a Registered Play Therapist in Minnesota. Currently, she is working at a community mental health agency with children and adults. Her specific areas of clinical interest include play therapy strategies, Dialectical Behavior Therapy (DBT) strategies for both adolescents and adults, and actively working with the community to integrate services.

Closing Time
Source: Steve Harvey

Goals
- Increase the rate of positive verbal communication from parent to child using the actual play events from the session
- Increase the child's ability to smoothly transition from one activity to another
- Create story metaphors with the parent and child that describe their interactions
- Increase the frequency of positive interactions between parents and the child

Materials
- Assortment of age-appropriate toys and games
- Age-appropriate dress-up clothing (optional)
- Paper
- Coloring materials such as markers or crayons
- Binder

Advance Preparation
This technique takes place over several sessions. A variety of toys and games are required. Generally, toys or games that promote family interaction are preferred, such as large scarves, large pillows, and drawing material. It is also appropriate to use dress-up clothes that encourage imaginative expression, that can be used in a variety of different ways, and that can be changed to match the interactions of the family.

Description
This activity is designed to take place toward the end of a family-oriented play session with parents and children after the therapist has made mention of the approaching time for the session to stop. The storytelling is meant to be used for families with children in their preschool and early primary years (4–7). Older children (8–11) can be engaged through modifying the story by giving it a more complex narrative and more fully developed characters.

The story is introduced after the announcement that the session will need to close, for example, the therapist says, "The play time will end once I count from ten back to one." Then with each number the therapist takes the role of a storyteller/narrator and retells what happened during the play interactions one step at a time in the order that they occurred, starting with "ten."

For example, if the mother and her five-year-old son began the session drawing together and then played a tug of war, the therapist as the narrator begins by saying, "Ten...the boy and his mom were drawing happily together. Nine...the boy drew all over the paper in a wild way. Eight...then the mom and boy picked up the stretchy rope and started to pull it between them. Seven...the boy and his mom laughed and then....Six...they were pretending to be mad when they were pulling. Five...but they really weren't mad and they each had a turn at pulling the rope." The therapist continues counting until he/she reaches the number one, continuing to name each event until the ending is reached. Then he/she says, "One ... and then they got ready to stop playing and they did."

In the early sessions, the narrative of the story follows the actions the parent and child have actually done during their play. The child (or children) is described as the boy or the girl. The story then proceeds with one small piece of activity being verbally presented with each number until the therapist reaches one. At this point, the session ends and the family prepares to leave.

The therapist clearly chooses the events from the session to be emphasized and retold in a positive way. The storytelling stays very close to the actual interactions when the activity is initially introduced. After a few sessions the therapist begins to indentify emotional content and themes and is careful to reframe the actions as occurring in a helpful parent–child interaction. Positive emotional interactions, especially clear nonverbal communication such as smiles and a parent's gesture of comforting the child with a touch or a hug, are given emphasis in the storytelling. In the example above in which the child and parent are engaged in a tug of war, any smiling or playful expression would be mentioned using a reference such as "the argument full of smiles."

Once the family members have become familiar with the narration as an ending activity, the therapist can begin leaving out some of the numbered steps and ask different family members to provide the narration for that part. For example, the therapist could say, "Six...and then, what do you think the next part is (asking the child or parent)?" The goal is for the family members to develop a story version of their play session with minimal help from the therapist, who coaches them in a friendly manner on how to identify the important themes from the session as metaphors.

At this point, material can be added to the dramatic recounting. Family members can choose a name for the character that represents them, and they can add thematic elaborations and plot development as they become more comfortable with their own storytelling. For example, in one dramatic play session a child enacted a kitten finding a home. The therapist suggested that the child retell the story beginning with the kitten discovering a place to live, and developing the story from there. It is important that the therapist keep the emerging stories focused on the family's play session by linking their stories to the actual interactions that took place in the session and that have personal relevance for them.

Once the parent and child develop their own story material, the therapist can help them draw the major parts of the story. These drawings are used to make a book with written parts as well as drawings. The drawings can be compiled in a binder. The book is to be taken home and used as part of homework established to address therapeutic goals. Using the drawings in the binder as a bedtime story can be particularly effective for children having difficulties with sleeping.

Discussion

Troubled families who attend therapy often have difficulties communicating in a positive way. Play interactions can lack the creative and imaginative aspects that seem so natural in children in more functional families. This is especially true during transition times when the child may become frustrated.

This activity combines storytelling with drawing and is designed to use the actual interactions from a parent–child play session as the starting point for developing a mutual storytelling exercise. The therapist as narrator can help to model the use of imaginative verbal expressions. Story metaphors and themes can then be introduced as a way to describe important emotional interactions as well as convey more positive themes.

The play aspects of this activity are used to help parents communicate in a more positive manner with their child even as they are trying to address immediate conflict, such as small arguments that may come up at the end of a play session. The use of drawing to elaborate the story can help family members extend this imaginative activity together. The book development is an effective way for families to bring these activities into the home.

This activity was developed to help children and their parents play together in an active and constructive way. This method can help the therapist address both the presenting concerns as well as the family relationships (Harvey, 2006).

Reference

Harvey, S.A. (2006). Dynamic play therapy. In C.E. Schaefer and H. Kaduson (Eds.), *Contemporary play therapy*. New York: Guilford.

About The Author

Steve Harvey, PhD, RPT-S, BC-DMT, is a Licensed Psychologist in the United States and is registered as a Psychologist with clinical and educational scopes of practice in New Zealand. He is a Registered Play Therapist Supervisor and a Board Certified Dance Movement Therapist. He is currently the Consultant Psychologist for the Child and Adolescent Mental Health Service for the Taranaki District Health Board in New Plymouth, New Zealand. He helped pioneer the use of Play Therapy approaches with families and has written several professional chapters and articles in the field published in *The International Journal of Play Therapy, Contemporary Play Therapy, Play Diagnosis and Assessment*, and *Blending Play Therapy with Cognitive Behavioral Therapy: Evidence-Based and other Effective Treatment Techniques*. He has presented and consulted extensively internationally on topics related to the use of family play in the evaluation and treatment of attachment and psychological trauma in children.

© Steve Harvey

Creating a Better World for Our Child
Source: Theresa Fraser

Goals
- Establish a safe and open therapeutic environment
- Encourage parents to identify common values, hopes, and goals
- Identify how parents can support their child and each other in working toward specific family goals
- Set goals to be addressed in treatment

Materials
- Sandtray half-filled with sand
- Variety of miniature objects or figurines representing different categories such as people (various ages, races, abilities, and occupations), animals (pets, farm, and wild), vehicles, plants, and things from nature (rocks, shells), furniture/household objects, buildings, fantasy figures
- Paper
- Pen (one for each parent)
- Camera

Description
Note: Three sessions are required for the completion of this activity, and it is intended for parents and one child.

Session One (Session with the Child)
The child is invited to build a world in the sandtray. The six phases are consistent with the Sandtray-Worldplay Method developed by De Domenico (1995):

1. Introduction to the medium
   The therapist shows the builder the tray, sand, water, and miniature objects and invites him/her to use these to create whatever he/she would like in the sandtray.

2. Free and spontaneous playing/building
   When the playing begins, the therapist does not initiate interaction either verbally or nonverbally. All play throughout this phase is viewed as being interconnected.

3. Builder experiencing phase
   The builder finishes at which time he/she may say "I am done." The therapist encourages the builder to look at the world and invites him/her to make any changes desired. If the builder speaks, the therapist (witness)

111

mirrors what is stated to support the experience rather than initiate any builder–witness interaction. This supports De Domenico's (1995) thesis that "the world confronts the maker."

4. Client–therapist joint experiencing phase
    The therapist (witness) asks the builder to take her/him into the builder's world. The therapist sits on the same side as the builder to view the world from his/her perspective. The therapist can ask questions such as "Who in this world knows everyone else?" "Where in this world do the animals feel safe?" The questions should be focused on increasing the builder's experience of his/her world.

5. Reflecting phase
    When the builder and the therapist "come out" of the world, the therapist asks the builder what the title of this world would be if it were a story, or what the message of the world might be for the builder or for all who see it. De Domenico (1995) writes, "Work is done around discovering practical ways of applying the world's teachings to the daily life of the client."

6. Photographing phase
    The builder is invited to photograph his/her world.

At the end of the session, ask the child if the picture of his/her world can be shared with the parents when they come for their therapy session. The world is photographed and, if possible, left to stand until the parent session occurs. If it is decided that the world will not stay in place, the therapist dismantles it after the builder has left and after the therapist has had the opportunity to reflect on the world and the client's experience of it.

Session Two (Session with the Parents)
During this session, the parents are shown the world (or the photograph of the world) built by their child and each parent is invited to choose two items from the child's world to place into the empty sandtray. They are then invited to add additional objects or figures and to work together to build the kind of world they would want for their child. More specifically, they are asked to build a world that reflects the ideal family for their child, the sorts of relationships (family, extended family, friends, etc.) they want their child to have, the activities they want their child to participate in, the community supports they believe would be helpful for their child, and so on. The parents are asked to build without talking to the therapist or to each other.

The therapist stays in the room and observes. When both parents feel that they are finished, they are each invited to share what was built and what they experienced while building it. Both are encouraged to listen to each other without interrupting or asking questions.

When both have taken the other parent and therapist on a tour, the therapist may reflect or wonder about specific areas of the world. This provides everyone with the opportunity to get to know this world more closely. This portion of the session is known as the client–therapist joint experiencing phase.

During the reflecting phase, the therapist invites the parents to reflect on what common themes or variant themes emerged. The therapist can comment on these themes. It may be appropriate at this point to discuss how images from the child's world were included in the parent's joint world.

To facilitate further exploration and discussion, ask the following questions:

1. Describe the ideal family you envision for your child.
2. Describe the parent–child and sibling relationships, interactions, and dynamics that exist in this ideal world.
3. Discuss the relationships outside of your immediate family that you want for your child, for example, extended family, friends, community supports.
4. What activities would you like your child to participate in and why?
5. What elements do you share or agree on in your vision of an ideal world for your child?
6. What changes need to happen in order to create this better world for your child?
7. What can each of you do to create a better world for your child?
8. How can therapy help you create this better world?

Both parents are then asked to write a joint letter to their child identifying what their hopes and dreams are for the world that they want their child to grow up in. They are invited to take photographs of their joint world using a camera or a cell phone to add to these letters.

Prepare the parents for the following session in which they will share the letter with their child.

Session Three (Session with the Parents and the Child)
Have the parents read their letter to the child. Discuss the letter and the child's reactions to the letter. Then identify goals for future treatment sessions.

Discussion
This activity can be very powerful for the family. Asking the parents to study the child's sandtray helps them to explore the issues that the child is experiencing from a more objective vantage point.

This activity can help parents to think about the hopes and dreams they have for their child and the role they each will take in order to optimize the creation of that world. Additionally, it helps them identify necessary supports and interventions collaboratively.

The creation of the letter honors their parenting roles and the aspirations that each of them holds for their child.

Reference
De Domenico, G.S. (1995). *Sandtray-worldplay: A comprehensive guide to the use of sandtray in psychotherapeutic and transformational settings*. Oakland, CA: Vision Quest Images.

About The Author
Theresa Fraser, MA, CYW, CPT, works with children, youth, and families. She is a founding Clinician/Manager of Clinical Services at a Children's Mental Health Agency. In 2009 she published the book *Billy Had to Move* to help children deal with the foster care experience. She has provided workshops internationally to foster care providers about the challenges of daily service provision for children who have experienced trauma and attachment disruptions. She is a part-time instructor at Humber and Mohawk Colleges. She is a Certified Play Therapist and the President of the Canadian Association for Child and Play Therapy.

The Doves and the Hunter

Source: Transcribed by Susan Perrow from a traditional Indian tale

Goals
- Increase awareness that each family member has a part to play in making things better
- Initiate discussion to identify ways that family members can work together toward a common goal

Materials
- The story "The Doves and the Hunter" (included)
- Doves, mouse, and hunter puppet outlines (included)
- Scissors
- Tape
- String
- Two Popsicle sticks
- Rice (approximately one spoonful) or small bits of paper
- One piece of netting or muslin (about 15" x 15")
- Earth colored cloth or a large sheet of paper (optional)
- Potted plant or vase with greenery (optional)
- Clay or Playdough (optional)
- Paper
- Marker

Advance Preparation
Note: The steps below can be completed by the therapist prior to the session, or the family can assist in the creation of the puppets and the scenery.

Prepare the puppets as follows: Photocopy the sheet with the doves, mouse, and hunter, ideally onto card stock for extra durability. Make multiple copies. Cut out the mouse, hunter, and enough doves so there is a flock of doves and so each family member can play at least one role in the puppet show. Tape each dove onto a string. Tape the mouse and the hunter onto Popsicle sticks.

The following scene and props are recommended for the puppet show, but are not required as the family can enact the puppet show without these items. Cover the table with earth-colored cloth (or color a sheet of paper to make it look like the earth). Have a vase of greenery or a potted plant to represent the tree on one side, with some rice (or bits of paper for rice) sprinkled under the tree. Create a small hill out of clay for the mouse's home and place it on the other side.

Description

Read or tell the story "The Doves and the Hunter" (Perrow, 2008) to the family.

Next, retell the story as a puppet play. The family members can be the puppeteers as they sit behind the table or around the rug on the floor, moving the puppets while the therapist reads the story. This facilitates participation of all family members and maintains their interest in the story. To help the selection process, write the names of each puppet on separate pieces of paper, fold them, and have each family member select one piece of paper. Alternatively, the therapist can be more purposeful in assigning the puppets to the different puppeteers. Depending on the family size, some members may need to work more than one puppet.

If there is time (or in the next session), repeat the puppet play, changing the choice of puppeteers.

Active discussion among the family is discouraged during the first puppet play (this will give each puppeteer time to absorb the full meaning of the story), but conversation could be encouraged during any repeat plays.

After the puppet play, facilitate a discussion by asking the following process questions:

1. How did it feel to play the part of the hunter, or one of the birds, or the mouse? (The therapist may wish to expand on feelings or issues disclosed by the family members.)
2. Which part did you like playing best? Which part did you like the least?
3. What new information did you learn about working together?

Discussion

In many traditional cultures, throughout human history, wise "elders" have used metaphors and stories in their role as mentors and guides for their communities. Using "wisdom" tales to guide and manage behavior, they have tapped into children's and adults' imaginative reality and reached them in positive and pro-active ways. This example of a therapeutic story encourages a revival of the use of metaphor and storytelling for guiding and transforming challenging behaviors and situations.

For this situation, working with metaphor and storytelling can help shift the focus of "blame" in a family conflict to the realization that each family member has a part to play in making things better. Involving the family members in performing the story as a puppet show can help to strengthen the experience and the transformation.

When using a story to heal such a challenging behavior or situation, the goal is not to make "bad" behavior "good"; rather, it is about bringing the behavior or situation back into wholeness/balance. The story is not intended to moralize or to induce guilt – this point cannot be stressed enough! The objective is to simply reflect what is happening and, through the story's metaphors and journey, provide an acceptable means of dealing with the behavior/situation and/or finding a realistic resolution.

The use of metaphor is a vital ingredient in therapeutic story work. Metaphors help build the imaginative connection for the listener. An integral part of the story's journey, metaphors often play both the negative roles (the obstacles, tempters, and temptations that help to pull the behavior or situation out of balance – in this case, the "hunter" and the "net") and the positive roles (the helpers or guides that lead the behavior/situation back to wholeness or balance – in this case, the "dove leader" and the "mouse").

The therapist can use the observations of the puppeteers and the discussion following the story to assess styles of interaction and attitudes, and to intervene therapeutically to address issues raised by the family.

Reference
Perrow, S. (2008). *Healing stories for challenging behaviour.* London: Hawthorn.

About The Author
Susan Perrow, M.Ed., has 30 years of experience in teaching, counseling, and storytelling. After completing her master's degree on a cross-cultural study of storytelling in teacher training, she set up a 150-hour module on storytelling at Southern Cross University in Australia. Since 1995, she has worked in Teacher Training and Parent Education in Australia, Africa, Europe, and Asia, specializing in storytelling, therapeutic story writing, and creative discipline.

The Doves and the Hunter
Story

Transcribed by Susan Perrow from a traditional Indian tale, 2008

One morning, a flock of doves was flying across the land in search of food. Suddenly, the leader of the doves saw some white grains of rice scattered on the ground under a banyan tree. He flew down towards the rice, with his flock following behind. Overjoyed at their good luck, they alighted on the ground.

The hungry doves started picking the grains, but within minutes they found their feet trapped in a net spread by a hunter. The next moment, they looked up from their trap and saw the hunter coming toward them. He was carrying a big club in his hand. The doves were sure that their time of living would soon be over.

But the leader of the doves was very wise and very brave. He spoke to his flock. "Listen to me, my fellow doves. We are surely in serious trouble, but we need not lose hope. I have an idea. We can still get away unharmed if we all fly upwards together, carrying the net with us. We are small creatures and separately we can do little. But together we can easily lift the net and fly away with it."

The doves were not sure of this idea but, in fact, they had no choice. So, each one picked up a part of the net with its beak. Then they all flapped their wings and rose together away from the tree and high in to the air. The hunter watched helplessly as the doves made their escape.

When they had flown a safe distance, the leader said to the rest of the doves, "Half our troubles are over. But we are still not out of danger. We cannot pull our feet out of the net. I have a friend, a little mouse, who lives in a hole at the foot of the next hill. Perhaps he can gnaw at the net with his sharp little teeth and set us free."

The doves welcomed yet another good idea from their leader and off they flew to the place where the mouse lived. They landed on the ground in front of the mouse's home. "What is the matter, my friend? You look worried," the little mouse enquired of the leader of the doves. "Can I help you in any way?"

"As you can see, we have been caught in this net," said the leader. "We have managed to fly together and bring it so far. Can you please help us now and set us free?"

"I can indeed," said the mouse and got down to doing his work. With his sharp teeth, he slowly chewed the cords of the net to pieces. One by one, all the doves were set free.

The doves thanked the mouse for his help. "You are most welcome," he said.

They also thanked their leader for saving them from an almost certain death. They were proud of such a wise dove that had taught them how to face problems by being united in strength. With a song of joy in their hearts, they flew up together and across the open blue sky.

© Susan Perrow

The Doves and the Hunter
Puppet Outlines

The Doves and the Hunter
Puppet Outlines

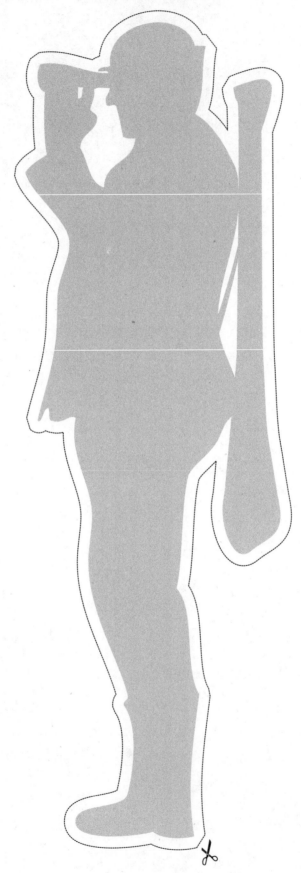

Dream-enacting with a Family
Source: Deborah Armstrong Hickey

Goals
- Help family members be empathic and attuned with the child who directs this activity
- Increase family members ability to follow the lead of the child who directs this activity
- Increase the child's ability to vocally tell family members what he/she needs from them

Materials
- Yarn or masking tape
- Dramatic play materials such as scarves, swords, objects that make sounds, including musical instruments, and playhouses (optional)
- Craft supplies to make masks, costumes, and scenery (optional)

Advance Preparation
Place yarn or masking tape around a large area where the "dream reenactment" will take place.

Description
Note: This activity requires at least 90 minutes and can be completed in one long session or over two sessions.

Explain to the family that our dreams involve an experience in which we can solve problems more easily, express who we are from the heart, and do anything we want to do, even if it is very scary or different than what we would normally do. Then ask the child to direct a play about a dream that he/she has had, and let the child know that he/she can change the dream if they want to. If the child agrees, the parents and other members of the family are instructed that the child is the director and that they are to follow the child's directions and pretty much do, say, and feel whatever the child directs them to do.

The steps of the activity are as follows:

1. The child identifies the title of his/her dream then describes two or three feelings that he/she had in the dream and who and what (things) were noticed in the dream. He/she then describes the dream as if it were happening "right now" while the therapist transcribes the telling.
2. The family is instructed not to ask questions, interpret, or say anything while the child is telling the dream, when he/she has finished, or at anytime afterward.

3. The child will then decide who will play whom in the dream; this includes choosing someone to play him/herself since he/she will be the director and not one of the actors, as well as choosing individuals to play the objects or things that might be important.

4. The necessary props and the room will be prepared, including placing yarn or masking tape around the space where the "dream reenactment" will take place.

5. The child will direct everyone to do, say, and feel what he/she wants them to do in each part of the dream that is reenacted (usually children's dreams are short enough to do the entire dream, but sometimes choosing one or two parts is sufficient). The dream may be enacted once, twice, or even three times until the child is satisfied with how it is done.

6. The child can change the dream's ending to a more preferable one if he/she wants to do that.

7. Family members are instructed to do, say, and feel exactly what the child directs them to do without any questions.

After the dream reenactment is completed, the family comes outside the "dream space" and the process is discussed. The following questions can guide the discussion:

(To the child/director):
1. What was this like for you?
2. What did you like best?
3. Was there anything you did not like or wish was different?
4. What are some of the feelings that you had while directing the enactment?

(To the family members/actors):
1. What was this like for you?
2. What did you like best?
3. Was there anything you did not like or wish was different?
4. What are some of the feelings that you had while playing the characters or objects in the enactment?

Ensure that the family does not discuss or interpret the dream itself.

Discussion

Dreaming holds certain characteristics that allow creativity, authenticity, and emotionally charged issues to enter into our consciousness. Children, particularly those who are younger, experience dreams that are frightening more often than other groups, and dreams are a reliable source for discovering what is in their minds and hearts. This activity is designed for families where the parents are experiencing challenges empathizing and feeling attuned with their child. For a short period of time, and with the therapist present, a little of what lies deep in the heart of the child can be explored. The parents not only discover more about what lies within the child's heart but also experience what it is like to be there, dwell there, and what feelings their child may be experiencing.

For the child, it is an opportunity to direct his/her parents as they embody and experience some of what lies inside of him/her. It also gives the child a chance to reenact a dream that might be scary or frustrating. As a director/observer, the child gets to see something of what lies inside of him/her from the outside (i.e., outside looking in), and this may help him/her to gain mastery and control over the material as well.

Dreams are highly personal and this activity should only be used when the therapist is confident that the parents and family members will hold this dream in confidence, and respect how very personal and tender the material may be to the child. If the child has sustained a trauma and is dreaming about it, caution and discernment should be used, though the activity is not absolutely contraindicated because of this possibility.

Therapists who engage families in this activity are best prepared when they have engaged in some dreamwork of their own and have referred to the ethical guidelines of the International Association for the Study of Dreams. This exercise is not for the purpose of interpreting or analyzing dreams and, in fact, this should be avoided during this activity.

This activity rests comfortably within the landscape of experiential family therapy, as informed by Satir and Baldwin (1983). It is also consistent with the theory and practices of Filial family therapy (1969). Experiential family therapy seeks to promote awareness and self-expression and unlock deeper levels of connection and communication between family members. These deep levels of communication, accompanied by the freedom to be oneself and openly relate to others, are considered to be the foundations of well-being. Filial family therapy engages parents in the role of treatment providers by using non-directive play therapy principles. It has been found to effectively reduce symptoms in children and increase parents' empathy with what their children are feeling.

References

Bleandonu, G. (2006). *What do children dream?* London: Free Association Press.

Foulkes, D. (1999). *Children's dreaming and the development of consciousness.* Cambridge, MA: Harvard University Press.

Guerney Jr., B.G. (1969). Filial therapy: Description and rationale. In B.G. Guerney Jr. (Ed.), *Psycho-therapeutic agents: New roles for nonprofessionals, parents and teachers.* New York: Holt, Rinehart and Winston.

International Association for the Study of Dreams. *http://www.asdreams.org/*

Satir, V., & Baldwin, M. (1983). *Satir step by step: A guide to creating change in families.* Palo Alto, CA: Science and Behavior Books.

Siegel, A., & Bulkeley, K. (1998). *Dreamcatching: Every parent's guide to exploring and understanding children's dreams and nightmares.* New York: Three Rivers Press.

About The Author

Deborah Armstrong Hickey, PhD, LMFT, RPT-S, has been licensed as a Marriage and Family Therapist specializing in expressive and play therapies for over 30 years. She has conducted research on dreams, has been a board member with the International Association for the Study of Dreams, and has been working with her own dreams for over 40 years. She is a core faculty member with Capella University in the Marriage and Family Therapy Counselor Education Program and maintains a private practice, The Mindgarden, in Greenville, South Carolina.

Exploding Balloons
Source: Lauren Snailham

Goals
- Learn, practice, and implement appropriate strategies for expressing anger
- Identify how holding anger inside can lead to problems

Materials
- Balloons (two for each participant and therapist)
- Large sheet of paper
- Tape
- Marker
- Safety glasses

Advance Preparation
Tape the sheet of paper to a wall.

Description
Provide each family member with a balloon. (It is also advised to have each family member put on a pair of safety glasses to avoid injury when the balloons explode.) Then ask them to think about a time when they felt angry. (Tell them they are to think about the angry situation but they are *not* to talk about their angry feelings at this point.) Ask them to blow the angry feeling into their balloons. Have them think about another time when they felt angry and ask them to blow *that* angry feeling into their balloons. This is repeated using a variety of situations that they can think of as they each continue blowing into their balloons.

Eventually the balloons will explode. Invite the family to say why they think the balloons exploded. Ask:

1. What happens when you hold onto angry feelings for too long?
2. How does it make you act?

Give each family member a second balloon and ask them to again think about a time when they felt angry and to start to blow the angry feelings into their balloons. Once the balloons have been filled a bit with air, have the family members stop and talk about their angry feelings. As they talk about their anger, have them release the air from the balloons a little at a time. Once this is done, ask the family members what is different about what they are doing this time. The therapist can help them see that if the balloon is filled with air that is then released, it will not explode.

125

Ask the family members what they can do to stop themselves from exploding when they feel angry. Write these coping strategies on the sheet of paper. If they are having difficulty thinking of ideas, offer suggestions such as the following:

1. Talk to someone about your feelings.
2. Slowly count backwards from 10.
3. Breathe in and out slowly until your body becomes relaxed.
4. Think about a happy memory.
5. Visualize a stop sign.

Once the list has been generated, have the family vote on their favorite coping strategy. Have the family members practice the strategy in the session to ensure they do it well. Then have the family use this strategy at home. To motivate the family, suggest that they have a contest to see who does the best job using the favorite coping strategy at appropriate times.

As an optional ending activity, read the book *The Angry Feeling* (Snailham, 2008).

Follow up in the next session. Ask the family the following questions:

1. Can you tell me about a time since the last session when you used the coping strategy to stop yourself from exploding when you felt angry?
2. Who did the best job managing their anger?
3. Were there any explosions and, if so, what stopped you from using the coping strategy?
4. What other strategy from the list would you like to try?
5. How can you help one another to prevent further explosions at home?

Discussion

Many families struggle to express their anger in appropriate ways. Some family members externalize their anger by becoming verbally or physically aggressive, while others internalize by withdrawing or isolating themselves. Neither of these coping styles is a healthy one. This technique provides an engaging way to help families understand the dangers of bottling up anger and how it can lead to destructive behavior or being left helpless and broken. They are further given the chance to see how useful it is to release anger as it starts to grow and how much better they (or the balloon) are able to cope.

This activity provides the family with a variety of anger management techniques that they can use at home and elsewhere. These skills can be used on a daily basis and will leave them feeling empowered and successful.

Reference
Snailham, L. (2008). *The angry feeling.* Kwa-Zulu Natal, South Africa: Self-Published.

About The Author
Lauren Snailham, MA Clinical Psychology, is a Clinical Psychologist in private practice in Durban, Kwa-Zulu Natal, South Africa. She provides assessment and treatment services to children, adolescents, and adults with a variety of psychological difficulties. She incorporates play therapy, psychotherapy, and parenting interventions in her clinical work. She has authored a set of therapeutic story books that focus on issues such as feelings, bullying, abuse, divorce, trauma, anxiety, anger, alcohol abuse, and loss. These books are used by therapists, parents, and teachers.

Family Jenga
Source: Nikole Jiggetts

Goals
- Implement new methods of effective communication between family members
- Learn to discuss volatile topics with reduced tension and conflict
- Increase the rate of positive verbal comments and pleasurable exchanges between family members

Materials
- Jenga game
- Index cards
- Markers
- Paper
- Pen

Advance Preparation
The therapist should have a clear understanding on how to play the Jenga game.

Description
Jenga is a stacking game that uses wooden building blocks, the object of which is to remove blocks from the lower portions of the stack and place them on the top without knocking over the wooden structure. When using it to enhance family relationships, the basic rules of the game are followed, and the therapist can add the following instructions:

The family should be seated in a circle or across from each other. Set up the Jenga tower between them. Discuss what the tower of blocks looks like or represents to them (the therapist can interject with statements such as "a strong structure" or "tight unit"). Then each member will take turns removing a block from the tower as the game is set up to play. As members remove a block they are to verbalize a negative statement they often hear from another member of their family; for example, "You can never do anything right" or "Go to your room, I can't deal with you right now." Members hold on to their blocks once they have finished verbalizing their statements. (The therapist will take notes as each member takes his/her turn.) The game will continue until the tower falls. Once the tower falls, members will take notice of all the blocks they have and reflect on how the blocks or "the negative statements" make them feel. (The therapist will take notes during this reflection and state how each block taken from the unit made it weaker until it fell apart, just as negative communication can weaken a family unit.)

The family then works together to build the Jenga tower back up. The family plays Jenga again, only this time, for each block members pull, they will state a positive statement about another participating family member; for example, "Mom, you make great meals" or "Sis, you are helpful with my homework." Once they make their statements, instead of holding on to the block, they will place the block on top of the tower. Once everyone has a turn, the therapist will stop the game for a moment and ask everyone to reflect on the tower. The therapist will explain that the bottom of the tower, where there are gaps, can represent negative communication and illustrates how negative communication can make the foundation of the relationship unstable. The top of the tower, however, is solid because members expressed positive statements which helped to build a stronger family unit. The family can continue to play until the tower falls or they can keep the tower as is and continue to share positive statements until each member has been given at least three positive statements. The members will write the positive statements on index cards and give them to the receiving member.

The activity can then be processed by asking the following questions:

1. How did each of you feel during the game when negative comments were made?
2. How did each of you feel during the game when positive comments were made?
3. What can be learned through this activity?

Discussion

This game can be played with family members to encourage open communication and playfulness. Because it is a game "with definite rules, expectations, and goals, it tends to minimize resistance, and thereby give families additional ways to interact" (Gil, 1994). Moreover, playing Family Jenga and taking turns sharing feelings and emotions allows each person to speak without being interrupted. Communication between family members can be heard more clearly in this structured setting.

This activity can help parents to be more insightful about their child's feelings. The stage can then be set for a more compassionate, empathetic environment where the family can communicate more openly and directly.

Families typically enjoy game play, and this activity creates a new emotional climate that facilitates cohesion among family members.

Reference
Gil, E. (1994). *Play in family therapy*. New York: Guilford.

About The Author
Nikole Jiggetts, MSW, LCSW, RPT, is a Social Worker at the National Counseling Group, INC., in Petersburg and Richmond, Virginia. She provides clinical supervision and practices Play Therapy in the home setting and in an outpatient setting. She provides monthly trainings on innovative interventions that are used in a home-based setting with children and families who have been diagnosed with mental health disorders.

Family Locogram
Source: Heather Venitucci and Jacob Gershoni

Goals
- Identify unspoken wants, needs, desires, and wishes of family members
- Increase open communication among family members
- Reveal unspoken or "hidden" feelings within the family unit
- Explore differentiation of self while remaining engaged with the family

Materials
- Paper
- Black marker
- Tape
- Sample sentence completions (included)

Advance Preparation
Write the following words, one word per sheet, on white or colored paper.

- Excitement	- Music
- Games	- Anxiety
- Movies	- Time together
- Hugs	- Television
- Anger	- Money
- Laughter	- Love
- Sadness	- Understanding
- Loneliness	- Respect
- Space	- Computer
- Privacy	- Encouragement
- Quiet	- Cleanliness
- Fun	- Death
- Arguments	- Compliments

Include a blank piece of paper so that family members have the opportunity to express words that are not represented.

Tape the words/papers around the room before the family arrives.

Prior to the session, decide on the issues to be explored with the family and prepare the sentence completions accordingly. Choose from the sentence completions included below or create ones that are appropriate to the family's situation.

Description

Explain the activity by saying, "I am going to read a sentence and the way that I would like you to answer is by standing next to the sign that expresses the best response for you."

Read one sentence at a time. As family members choose a sign, ask them to share information about the response they chose and why. If members are not ready for this level of sharing, have them write the words on a piece of paper and ask them to share as much as they are comfortable sharing. If all members opt not to share, facilitate a discussion about the reasons for the secrecy and ask the members what they need in order to feel safe opening up with their family.

Depending on the level of trust, offer the family members an opportunity to ask questions of their own.

The discussion can then focus on the following questions:

1. What was the best and the most difficult part about this activity?
2. Say something you learned about another family member. Did anything surprise you?
3. What similarities emerged? How did it feel when everyone responded in a similar way?
4. Were there any differences? How did it feel when you chose something different from the rest of the family?
5. What other words do you feel could have been presented?
6. Is there a word that you feel might be more or less important to you in six months, a year, five years?
7. What do you think was the purpose of this activity?

Discussion

This activity was adapted from a similar exercise developed by Romance (2003). The locogram can be used at all stages of work with families and can be used to facilitate discussion about general family issues or specific family topics such as illness, loss, divorce, the arrival of a newborn, stepfamily dynamics, school problems, and the effect that addiction, abuse, or trauma have on the family system.

The structure and boundaries presented through the locogram create a safe space for family members to explore difficult feelings, unspoken conflicts, wishes, desires, and needs. Each member is given the opportunity to share without interruption or critique. The key to the exercise is to encourage the value of open expression without the implication that the person is "wrong" or "bad," while emphasizing that all feelings within the family unit are important. This often leads to spontaneous family interactions as members practice active listening skills, patience while waiting for their turn to speak, and tolerating uncomfortable feelings. Often similarities and differences among family members are revealed and can create a sense of bonding. At the same time, uncomfortable feelings may reveal challenging behaviors, unhealthy communication patterns, conflict, areas of disconnect, and role assignments within the family unit.

The use of action in family therapy creates a sense of immediacy and facilitates a deeper level of spontaneous physical and emotional interaction throughout the exploration of family dynamics. "The therapist's directive to act is in the service of clarity and precision in the immediate here and now of a personal engagement. 'Show us,' 'Say it,' 'Explain to him,' 'Look at him,' 'Change roles and be him,' 'Express yourself without words,' and 'Stay with that feeling' are some of the injunctions that focus attention upon the full experience of self in the presence of others" (Farmer & Geller, 2003). Through this, family members learn the possibility of differentiation while remaining engaged in the family unit.

References

Romance, J. (2003). It takes two: Psychodrama techniques with straight and gay couples. In J. Gershoni (Ed.), *Psychodrama in the 21st century: Clinical and educational applications*. New York: Springer Publishing.

Farmer, C. & Geller, M. (2003). Applying psychodrama in the family systems therapy of Bowen. In J. Gershoni (Ed.), *Psychodrama in the 21st century: Clinical and educational applications*. New York: Springer Publishing.

About The Authors

Jacob Gershoni, LCSW, CGP, TEP, is a Psychotherapist certified by the American Group Psychodrama Association. He works with individuals, couples, and groups both in private practice and at the Psychodrama Training Institute in New York City, where he is a co-director. He is also on the staff of the Columbia Presbyterian Medical Center. A Trainer, Educator and Practitioner (TEP) certified by the American Association of Group Psychotherapy and Psychodrama, he offers training classes for group therapists and others interested in Action Methods in psychotherapy. He graduated from the Hebrew University in Jerusalem (1971) and the University of Michigan (1975). His postgraduate training has been in Family Therapy and Psychodrama. Since 1980, he has maintained an active affiliation with two counseling services for the Gay, Lesbian, Bi-sexual, and Transgender community in New York City: Identity House and the Institute for Human Identity. His employment history includes work at the Fred Finch Youth Center in Oakland, California, and at the Queens Child Guidance Center in New York City.

Heather Venitucci, MSW, received her Master of Social Work degree in 2010 from Hunter College School of Social Work, where she graduated with honors. While at

Hunter, she trained with Jacob Gershoni and Nan Nally-Seif at the Psychodrama Training Institute where she facilitated groups and worked with individuals and couples dealing with depression, anxiety, trauma, and addiction. Before graduate school, she used creative writing and role-play with inner-city school-age children to address issues of abuse, violence, depression, addiction, and family conflicts. From 2000 to 2005, Heather and her husband built a theater in New York City, where they housed their theater company, The Actor's Playground. In that time she worked with Broadway veterans such as Tony Award–Winner Norbert Leo Butz, and actors such as Sandy Duncan, Didi Conn (*Grease*), Katherine Narducci (*Soprano's*), and Julie Bowen (*Parenthood, Boston Legal, and Ed*). An early version of Heather's one-woman show, *Dad and Me* (the final version is titled *Father/Daughter*), was a finalist in *The Strawberry One-Act Festival* in 2006 where she was nominated as Best Actress and chosen to be part of the festival's publication of *The Best Plays From The Strawberry One-Act Festival: Volume 4*.

Family Locogram
Sample Sentence Completions

The most important thing about family is...

One thing I wish we had more of is...

One thing that we need is...

One thing that I want us to have is...

One thing that I don't care about is...

One thing I don't need is...

One thing that makes me happy is...

One thing that makes me upset is...

One thing I worry about is...

The best thing about our family is...

© Heather Venitucci and Jacob Gershoni

Family Orchestra
Source: Ken Gardner and Lorri Yasenik

Goals
- Increase nonverbal communication among family members
- Increase parent attunement
- Identify aspects of parent sensitivity and responsiveness to children's emotional needs/states

Materials
- Toy drum or percussion instrument (hand drum or tambourine)
- Eight index cards
- One die

Advance Preparation
Each index card should have the word "change" written on the front and a simple picture that shows the type of body percussion on the back of the card. Under the picture, the type of body percussion should be identified with words (see list below). The following eight forms of body percussion are used initially. More types can be included to add variety or increase the level of challenge.

Card #1: "Hand Clapping"
Card #2: "Foot Stomping"
Card #3: "Hand rubbing"
Card #4: "Cheek Popping"
Card #5: "Tongue Clicking"
Card #6: "Toe Tapping"
Card #7: "Shoulder Pats"
Card #8: "Whoo Whoo" (making sounds with your mouth like an owl)

Description
Prepare the parent to lead this activity by reviewing the family instructions (see below). The therapist should first demonstrate the eight types of body percussion and ask the parent to consider how he/she might "animate" or vary each type of body percussion to meet the developmental capacities of their children. (For families with very young children, consider using only four types of body percussion.) Emphasize that the parent may choose to extend or shorten rhythms, increase or decrease the volume or loudness, and speed up or slow down a rhythm to keep everyone involved.

Ask the parent to read aloud the following family instructions:

"We are first going to learn to make special sounds with different parts of our body. After we practice these sounds, we will learn to make short pieces of music that go along with the beat of this drum. To become a family orchestra, we need to copy the rhythm or beat played on the drum. The person with the drum is the leader or

135

the conductor; whoever has the drum gets to start a new beat or rhythm and the rest of us have to follow along closely."

Step #1:
"Let's look at the types of percussion sounds we get to make with our mouths or bodies. Everyone take a card and we will go around and demonstrate what kind of sound the card asks us to make."

Step #2:
"Now we are going to place all the cards back in the middle and mix them up."

Step #3:
"I am now going to pass around the drum, and everyone can have a short turn making a rhythm on the drum. I am going to start. I want you to notice if I am drumming loud or softly. Also notice if I am drumming slow, medium, or fast."

Step #4:
"Ok now that we have practiced, we will start to play together so we become an orchestra with different body percussion sounds. We will roll the dice, and whoever has the highest number gets to be the conductor or leader and will begin with one rhythm on the drum. The person sitting to the right of the leader gets to pick up a 'change card' from the middle and copy the rhythm with the type of body percussion that is shown on the card. Once they match the rhythm, they turn to the person on their right and pass the rhythm on to the next person. When the rhythm is passed to you please keep playing it until it goes all the way back to the leader. Everyone stops playing when the rhythm or beat returns to the leader."

Step #5:
"We had a chance to go around once. Now, we will pass the drum to the next person on the right of the first leader. That person gets to start a new beat or rhythm and pass it on to the person on their right. That person needs to pick up a new change card, and copy the new rhythm. The rest of us will have to copy the leader's beat or rhythm with the new body percussion sound."

This sequence continues until all family members have a chance to be the conductor.

Step #6:
"For the final round, we are going to mix up all of the change cards in the middle. One person will begin with a new drum beat and when it gets passed your way you pick one change card and match the rhythm with the body percussion sound for your card. Each person will pick a different card as we go around. Let's see what kind of orchestra sound we get now."

After the final round, facilitate discussion by asking the following questions:

1. What was the most fun part about the family orchestra?
2. What was it like to be the leader or conductor?
3. What change card did you like the best? Why?
4. If you could make a family beat or rhythm that represents your family, what would it sound like?
5. If you could add another instrument, which one would you pick? Who would be good at playing this instrument in your family orchestra?
6. When in your daily family life might you need to speed up or slow down your pace or rhythm?
7. How can you tell if others are in sync with you?

Discussion

This activity amplifies attunement behaviors as the parent, as well as other family members, must mirror and replay the actions of each other. It offers a rich opportunity to examine parent sensitivity and attunement, because the parent may need to support certain children or modify certain rhythms so that each child has an opportunity to participate meaningfully.

The process questions at the end of the orchestra game are designed to facilitate discussion among family members and provide a means for the parent to recognize individual contributions. The therapist also has an opportunity to comment on the ability of the family to "play" together. The therapist, in observing and tracking the process, should be prepared to comment on how family members watched, followed, or supported each other during the activity.

The therapist needs to be prepared to amplify or expand upon feelings and highlight for the parent ways in which the family's interactions communicate needs for recognition, comfort, safety, support, or reassurance.

About The Authors

Lorri Yasenik, MSW, RFM, CPT-S, RPT-S, and Ken Gardner, M.Sc., R.Psych, CPT-S, are the Co-Directors of the Rocky Mountain Play Therapy Institute. The Institute is an internationally recognized professional training program dedicated to offering relevant and experiential learning opportunities in child and play therapy. Lorri is a Certified/Registered Play Therapy Supervisor, a Clinical Social Worker, and a Registered Family Mediator who has been working with children and families in the areas of treatment of trauma, high conflict separation and divorce, and a range of situational and developmental issues during the course of her therapy career. Ken is a Clinical Psychologist and Certified Play Therapy Supervisor who specializes in the areas of learning/adjustment, children with development challenges, and achievement motivation. Lorri and Ken have extensive experience as consultants and trainers and regularly teach for college and university programs in the areas of play therapy, mediation, assessment, and counseling. They are the authors of the book, *Play Therapy Dimensions Model: A Decision Making Guide for Therapists.*

Family Sculpting with Puppets
Source: Darryl Haslam

Goals
- Gather information about the symbolic themes and structures in the family
- Identify the family interactional patterns that are contributing to the problematic behavior
- Increase open communication about volatile topics among family members
- Increase understanding and acceptance of other family members' perspectives

Materials
- At least 6 to 12 puppets (or stuffed animals) of varying themes and expressive styles (i.e., docile/playful vs. aggressive, common vs. mysterious/weird, etc.)

Description
Inform the family that they are going to participate in a fun family activity using puppets (or stuffed animals). The therapist explains to the family members the nature of the exercise, which is similar to the way that Satir (1972) set up her family sculpting. If young children are in the session, the therapist should explain the rules and goals of the activity at a developmentally appropriate level.

Examples of ways to explain the exercise include:

"I would like each person to take turns and pick a puppet that represents each member of your family, even if those members are not here, and place the puppet somewhere in this room. Puppets can be close together or far apart; some can be high or low, out in the open or hidden. Place the puppets in ways that show what things feel like in your family."

"I want you to make a 'sculpture' with these puppets that represent your family and that show how things feel for you in the family. Pretend that the puppets are sculptures that show a picture about your family to others. Choose puppets that represent each member of your family and place them somewhere in this room so that they represent how people are with each other in your family."

Explain to the family that there is "no right way of doing this" and that "any way you do it is okay in here." Also explain to the family that the rule is "that we accept the way each family member sees things. We are not allowed to debate, argue, or devalue what any member of this family does with this activity." The therapist can model this by showing enthusiasm and acceptance for what each member does in creating a family sculpture with the puppets.

After each person has sculpted the puppets, gather more information by asking questions such as:

1. What can you tell me about this scene you have created with these puppets?
2. What sort of feelings exists between them? Are any of them friends? Or do some fight? Are any scared of each other? Do any of them feel lonely or left out?

More specific questions may be asked by the therapist about particular aspects of the puppet sculpture, as long as he/she asks questions about the puppets themselves. This is not an appropriate time for the therapist to interpret the sculptures (connecting it to here and now), especially when the young children have created one. Instead, the therapist makes mental or written notes of things to come back to with the parents later on in the session or in a subsequent session.

After the activity, facilitate a family discussion by asking the following process questions:

1. What do you think about each of your creations?
2. What was it like for you as a family to do this activity?
3. What did you learn about each other while doing this activity?
4. What interested or surprised you the most about the puppet sculptures?

The therapist can ask specific interpretive questions about what he/she noticed in the exercise, either about the themes in the puppet sculptures or in the reactions observed by the family itself. In doing so, the therapist should take care to never make strongly opinionated or unequivocal comments about her/his observations or the meaning behind them.

Possible ways of discussing therapist hypotheses about these observations with older members, or to stimulate reflective responses from the family, may include:

1. I wonder what you thought about. . .
2. One thing I thought was interesting was when. . .
3. How are the puppet sculpture and the way you did the activity like your family in real life?

The discussion should remain explorative and supportive so that it bolsters a positive experience for the family.

Discussion

The use of puppets and related materials in therapeutic situations has been discussed in the literature as having unique evocative qualities that can be beneficial in both general clinical contexts with children (Broomfield, 1995; Irwin, 2002) and with families specifically (Ross, 2000). Sculpting has been noted in the literature during the burgeoning era of family therapy as an effective and dynamic family therapy intervention (Duhl, Kantor, & Duhl, 1973; Satir, 1972). Therefore, combining play-oriented materials like puppets with a dynamic intervention like family sculpting can provide a potentially powerful option in a therapist's treatment regimen.

The purpose of this activity is to help family members express their feelings and perceptions in a creative, multi-sensory and symbolic way. Young children often struggle with expressing their feelings to parents or other family members and play therapy builds a natural vehicle to help them do this. The other purpose is to display symbolic themes and structures in the family. Representations of family interactions such as closeness or distance, inclusion or exclusion, dominance or passiveness, and hostility or cooperativeness should be noted. Since the themes are expressed symbolically, the play helps buffer troubled emotions attached to the expressions and its indirect nature makes it safer for members to express themes more openly. Again, the therapist should take care to prevent any critical or accusatory comments being made of any member's creation. If this occurs, the therapist can process the influence of this damaging comment in the family and how it creates barriers to open expression and emotional closeness.

During the discussion phase, younger children may lose attention and drift mentally or physically. This is not unusual and should not be reined in strictly, as long as the therapist and parents can have a short conversation about a few insights that were obtained. It might be helpful to videotape the session so that the activity can be reviewed and processed in more depth with the family (or, if appropriate, just with the parents) at a later time.

References

Bromfield, R. (1995). The use of puppets in play therapy. *Child & Adolescent Social Work Journal*, 12(6), 435–444.

Duhl, F.J., Kantor, D., & Duhl, B.S. (1973). Learning, space and action in family therapy: A primer of sculpture. In D. Bloch (Ed.), *Techniques in family psychotherapy*. New York: Gruen & Stratton.

Irwin, Eleanor C. (2002). Using puppets for assessment. In C.E. Schaefer & D.M. Cangelosi (Eds.), *Play therapy techniques* (2nd ed.). New York: Jason Aronson.

Ross, P. (2000). The family puppet technique for assessing parent–child and family interaction patterns. In K. Gitlin-Weiner, A. Sandgrund, & C. Schaefer (Eds.), *Play diagnosis and assessment* (2nd ed.).Hoboken, NJ: John Wiley & Sons.

Satir, V. (1972). *Peoplemaking*. Palo Alto, CA: Science and Behavior Books.

About The Author

Darryl Haslam, PhD, LCSW, RPT, is an Assistant Professor in the School of Social Work at Missouri State University in Springfield, Missouri. He received a bachelor degree and a master of social work degree from Brigham Young University and his doctorate degree from Texas Tech University in Marriage and Family Therapy. He has over 15 years of clinical practice experience and has worked in various medical, mental health, military, and family violence settings. In addition, he has been a clinical supervisor for both social work and family therapist trainees. His greatest area of professional interest has remained the integration of play and family therapy methods. He has studied play therapy for over 14 years, receiving his certification as a Registered Play Therapist in 2003 from the Association for Play Therapy. He is in the process of obtaining his credentials as a Registered Play Therapist Supervisor. He has presented on play therapy in numerous local, regional, state, and national venues and has taught play therapy and family play therapy courses at the graduate level. He has authored several scholarly works in this subject area, including a chapter entitled "The Puppet Reflecting Team" in *The Couple and Family Therapist's Notebook* (Hertlein & Viers, 2005).

Family Spectrogram
Source: Heather Venitucci and Jacob Gershoni

Goals
- Build trust and cohesion among family members
- Identify the family interactional patterns that are contributing to the problematic behavior
- Reveal similarities and differences among family members

Materials
- Sample statements (included)

Advance Preparation
Prior to the session, decide on the issues to be explored with the family and prepare the statements accordingly. Choose from the sample statements included below or create ones that are appropriate to the family's situation.

Description
Note: This exercise should not be used when there is an open conflict within the family, but only when some work has been done around the conflict and there is a deeper sense of closeness between the family members.

Before beginning the activity, say to the family: "It is important that in this exercise we try our best to focus on ourselves and to avoid making comments about other family members' choices. It is important that we feel safe so we can share honestly and avoid criticism."

Next, walk across the room, from one end to the other, to indicate a spectrogram (or line) as you explain the exercise. In some cases, it may be useful to use objects, tape, rope, or scarves to represent the line.

Explain the activity as follows: "I would like you to imagine a line that stretches across the room representing a continuum, with each end representing two extremes, such as 'a lot' on one end and 'very little' on the other end. Throughout this exercise I will make two statements. I would like you to place yourself somewhere along this spectrum (or line) that represents your feeling in relation to the statements. For instance, this end [therapist walks to one side] represents 'I am very tired right now' and this end [therapist walks to the other end] represents 'I have a lot of energy right now.'"

Ask the family members to place themselves anywhere along the line that represents their feelings and then ask them to share. There are several options to choose from in relation to sharing:

1. Ask members to do the exercise in silence and to pay close attention to where they are in relation to other family members.
2. Ask members to share why they chose to stand in their place on the spectrum.
3. Ask members to share in pairs.
4. Ask members to share in pairs and then come back to the full group and share with one another. This encourages active listening and allows for members to express another family member's feelings. It is often fun, depending on the safety level among the family members, to ask them to "reverse roles with your partner and share from their point of view." This allows family members to step out of their roles and into the roles of others (the talkative daughter becomes the quiet mother or the feuding father and son reverse roles and find humor in "acting" like each other).

Process the activity by asking the following questions:

1. What similarities emerged? Any differences? What other similarities/differences do you notice in the family?
2. Is there anything you would like to ask or tell another family member as a result of what you learned about them today?
3. What do you think was the purpose of this activity?
4. What was it like for each of you to make your own choice in relation to sharing?
5. What was it like to communicate without words?
6. What would you like to explore with this exercise? Would anyone like to put out a statement/question?

Discussion

This activity was adapted from a similar exercise developed by Romance (2003). The spectrogram is a valuable tool at all stages of family therapy. It works as a check-in at the beginning of a session to allow family members to release pent up emotions from the day, while they warm up to one another through sharing. This facilitates family bonding and connection through the exploration of specific issues. At later stages of work, the spectrogram's structure offers safety when delving into deeper feelings about difficult issues such as divorce, loss, illness, addiction, and conflict. The option to stay silent eases anxieties and the structure alleviates fears associated with the pressure to "come up with something to say" throughout the process of ongoing family sessions.

The spectrogram reveals similarities and differences among family members and offers them the opportunity to communicate with one another visually, physically, and verbally, enforcing a sense of closeness among family members, while allowing

143

for individuation and personal choice. The spectrogram often uncovers subgroups and family dynamics within the family unit, which can act as a springboard for discussion about roles and relationships within the family system.

Feelings within families are often expressed through negative patterns of behavior that cause conflict. Painful interactions often leave members feeling misunderstood, neglected, or hurt. Through the spectrogram, members are encouraged to express difficult feelings in a healthy way, replacing old patterns, while offering a safe space to practice new ways of "being together." All members are given the opportunity to "speak" through action, giving silent members a "voice" and verbal members the chance to stay silent.

Moreno (1977) believed that "man developed his potential to the fullest only insofar as he interacted and truly communicated with other men.... [Moreno] further exclaimed that since we were wounded in interaction, that is where our healing should occur" (Lipman, 2003). The use of Moreno's action methods in family therapy offers members the opportunity to lay the foundation for deeper levels of trust, emotional expression, and healing through corrective family interactions.

References

Lipman, L. (2003). *The triadic system: Sociometry, psychodrama, and group psychotherapy.* In J. Gershoni (Ed.), *Psychodrama in the 21st century: Clinical and educational applications.* New York: Springer Publishing.

Moreno, J.L. (1977). *Psychodrama. Vol. 1.* Beacon, NY: Beacon House.

Romance, J. (2003). It takes two: Psychodrama techniques with straight and gay couples. In J. Gershoni (Ed.), *Psychodrama in the 21st century: Clinical and educational applications.* New York: Springer Publishing.

About The Authors

Jacob Gershoni, LCSW, CGP, TEP, is a Psychotherapist certified by the American Group Psychodrama Association. He works with individuals, couples, and groups both in private practice and at the Psychodrama Training Institute in New York City, where he is a co-director. He is also on the staff of the Columbia Presbyterian Medical Center. A Trainer, Educator and Practitioner (TEP) certified by the American Association of Group Psychotherapy and Psychodrama, he offers training classes for group therapists and others interested in Action Methods in psychotherapy. He graduated from the Hebrew University in Jerusalem (1971) and the University of Michigan (1975). His postgraduate training has been in Family Therapy and Psychodrama. Since 1980, he has maintained an active affiliation with two counseling services for the Gay, Lesbian, Bi-sexual, and Transgender community in New York City: Identity House and the Institute for Human Identity.

His employment history includes work at the Fred Finch Youth Center in Oakland, California, and at the Queens Child Guidance Center in New York City.

Heather Venitucci, MSW, received her Master of Social Work degree in 2010 from Hunter College School of Social Work, where she graduated with honors. While at Hunter, she trained with Jacob Gershoni and Nan Nally-Seif at the Psychodrama Training Institute where she facilitated groups and worked with individuals and couples dealing with depression, anxiety, trauma, and addiction. Before graduate school, she used creative writing and role-play with inner-city school-age children to address issues of abuse, violence, depression, addiction, and family conflicts. From 2000 to 2005, Heather and her husband built a theater in New York City, where they housed their theater company, The Actor's Playground. In that time she worked with Broadway veterans such as Tony Award–Winner Norbert Leo Butz, and actors such as Sandy Duncan, Didi Conn (*Grease)*, Katherine Narducci (*Soprano's*), and Julie Bowen (*Parenthood, Boston Legal, and Ed*). An early version of Heather's one-woman show, *Dad and Me* (the final version is titled *Father/Daughter*), was a finalist in *The Strawberry One-Act Festival* in 2006 where she was nominated as Best Actress and chosen to be part of the festival's publication of *The Best Plays From The Strawberry One-Act Festival: Volume 4.*

Family Spectrogram
Sample Statements

To support the beginning stages:

"I feel comfortable in the room right now – I feel uncomfortable in the room right now."

"I have a lot to say today – I have nothing to say today."

"I had a bad day today – I had a good day today."

To encourage open discussion about the therapy session:

"I like this room – I hate this room."

"I hate being here – I love being here."

"I feel this is good for us – I feel this is not good for us."

To address specific issues:

"I have a lot of feelings about separations [endings, divorce] – I have very few feelings about separations [endings, divorce]."

"Cancer [or enter another illness] makes me really angry – Cancer doesn't make me angry at all."

"I feel sad [mad, lonely, numb] when I think about [fill in the name of the family member not present or who passed away] – I don't feel sad [made, lonely, numb] when I think about [fill in the name].

Family-Structured Play
Source: Amber L. Brewer

Goals
- Increase the frequency of positive interactions between parents and children
- Parents to establish and enforce consistent rules and routines
- Reduce the children's behavioral problems

Materials
- Paper
- Markers
- Small candies
- Assortment of age-appropriate toys and games

Advance Preparation
This technique takes place over several sessions. For the first session, paper, markers, and a bag of small candies will be needed. A variety of toys and games will be required for the remaining sessions. Generally, toys or games that promote family interaction are preferred. Play materials such as bubbles, action figures, dolls/doll house, puppets, and board games are appropriate.

Description
Note: Several sessions are required for this activity.

Session 1

(1) *Getting Started:* Explain to the family that the next few sessions will be spent helping them learn how to get along while they have fun together. Tell them that they will be playing games of their choosing and, to help them not argue as much, the session will be devoted to coming up with some "Playroom Rules." For now, these rules will apply <u>only</u> to therapy sessions.

(2) *Identify Problematic Behaviors:* Ask the family to name things that could happen while they are playing together that could prevent them from having fun. Many families will try to focus only on child problematic behaviors, therefore, help the family create a list of problematic behaviors that could be shown by anyone in the family, including both parents and children. The list may consist of such problematic behaviors as name-calling, hitting, yelling, not participating, not sharing, and so on. Parent problematic behaviors might include controlling the play or not giving the child appropriate attention. Explore some of the reasons these behaviors are problematic (e.g., results in safety problems, angry feelings, or power struggles).

(3) *Rank the "Biggest" Problems:* Ask family members to identify the three

"biggest problems" on the list. Put a "1" next to the biggest problem, a "2" next to the second biggest problem, and so forth until the top 3 problems are in hierarchical order.

(4) *Brainstorm Consequences for Problematic Behavior:* Ask the family members if they know what consequences are. Explore why people give consequences for problem behaviors in different places (e.g., school, home, the community) and talk about how consequences are usually provided to keep others safe.

Invite the parents to lead a family discussion, generating ideas of possible consequences that might make it less likely the three biggest problems would happen in session during family playtime.

Prompt parents to ask the children for details on how the consequences could be implemented. For example, if time-out is suggested, have the family discuss possible location, length, or warnings given. If children choose not to help their parents make the rules, then the parents will choose the rules for them.

Put parents in charge of enforcing the consequences. Talk with the parents about how they might enforce the consequences in an appropriate way. Explore what would happen if a parent breaks the rules. Ask what strategies parents have tried when enforcing consequences before, what worked and what did not work. Discuss what tone of voice, physical proximity, use of physical touch, body language, or age-accommodations might be helpful. Describe examples of helpful strategies and ask the parents what they think about those ideas. Mention that there will be opportunities to evaluate and adjust the strategies during the activity.

(5) *Select the New Rules:* Help parents facilitate a family conversation about the consequences that will be used during the session. Instruct parents to obtain the children's feedback, but remind them that they will make the final decision. If two parents are present, both parents must agree on the rules.

(6) *Create an Official "Playroom Rules" Document:* The selected rules are written on a separate piece of paper, which will be posted on the wall for the remaining sessions.

(7) *Check Children's Understanding of the Rules:* Direct the parents to quiz the children on their understanding of the rules. Hypothetical (or "what if") situations are role-played. Children often enjoy pretending a parent broke one of the rules and getting to put the parent in time-out. Correct answers may be rewarded with small candies.

Session 2

(1) *Review the Rules:* Inform the family they will get to play for most of the session

148

that day. However, before they begin, ask the parents to help their children remember the Playroom Rules they made last session.

(2) *The Family Decides How to Structure Their Play:* Invite parents to talk to the children about how the family will decide what play activities they will do together that day. They will need to decide whether the parents or the children will choose the play activities, or whether they will take turns choosing.

(3) *The Family "Practices the Rules" While Doing Family Structured Play:* Tell the family they may now play together until the last 10 minutes of the session.

Parents are in charge of enforcing the playroom rules. Do not intervene unless someone might get hurt and parents fail to take protective action. If so, step in temporarily to keep the family safe. For example, if a child is engaging in risky behavior, direct parents to note the unsafe behavior and then offer suggestions on how to intervene. For example, "Mom, little Kammy is standing on that chair and I'm afraid she will fall. Can you stand by her to make sure she is safe?" Model the desired behavior if necessary. If a child hits or pushes another child and the parent does not intervene, say, "Uh oh, I see some hitting. Now what did you say should happen when there is hitting? Mom or Dad, what do you do now?"

Give the family five- and one-minute warnings before playtime ends.

(4) *Process the Session:* During the final 10 minutes of the session, discuss what family members liked and did not like during the playtime. Highlight positive interactions and process conflicts. Ask parents what worked and did not work in the way they enforced the consequences. Ask what changes the family could make to be safe and have a better experience next time.

Sessions 3-4

Continue Practicing the Rules While Doing Family-Structured Play: The next few sessions follow a format similar to session two, that is, the family reviews the rules and then does family-structured play until the final 10 minutes when conflicts and positive interactions that occurred during the session are discussed. Highlight growth that occurs across sessions, and introduce relationship-enhancing concepts such as compromise and mutual respect.

Sessions 5-6

Apply Lessons Learned to Homelife: When the family can manage conflict in session, invite them to regularly set aside 30 minutes in the week to have family playtime at home. Discuss how they can make this a successful experience. Ask the family what they have learned in session that can help them resolve conflicts at home.

Discussion

Family-structured play (FSP) is designed to strengthen attachment in families with preschool and school-aged children. The procedure helps families work together to organize family bonding activities and create a personalized contract for handling family conflict. FSP builds on the concept in Filial Therapy (Guerney, 1964) and Parent-Child Interaction Therapy (Eyberg, 1988) of teaching parents sensitive discipline strategies during periods of parent-child play; however, FSP is unique in that it goes beyond dyadic therapy to include whole families. Modifications to the procedure, such as varying the number of "practice" sessions, conducting FSP with one parent at a time, or having supplemental parent-only sessions may be needed to help families learn the desired skills.

When families initially start playing together in this activity, it is common for them to demonstrate higher levels of conflict. Most games involve some level of competition and have pre-established rules, and this can – at first – trigger some arguments and angry feelings. Over time, however, families usually learn the skills to handle the conflict more appropriately.

Family games with a mild to moderate level of competition give members the opportunity to practice being "good sports" and the art of losing gracefully. Members can also learn valuable life skills, such as turn-taking and respecting rules, which can help them in contexts outside the family as well. Through this activity, family members can discover that having fun together is more important than winning and that family rules are designed to help them be safe and get along. This often leads members to be less resistant to the rules and more focused on enjoying one another during family time.

References

Eyberg, S.M. (1988). Parent-child interaction therapy: Integration of traditional and behavioral concerns. *Child & Family Behavior Therapy, 10(1)*, 33-46.

Guerney Jr., B. (1964). Filial therapy: Description and rationale. *Journal of Consulting Psychology, 28(4)*, 304–310.

About The Author

Amber L. Brewer, PhD-ABD, LMFT, provides therapy at a counseling agency in Utah. She specializes in integrating play therapy techniques into family therapy to treat child-focused problems, and has presented on the subject at multiple national conferences. Her authorship includes article publications and a book review on such topics as attachment and therapy alliance, bereavement, and divorce.

Feeling Body Sculpting
Source: Trudy Post Sprunk

Goals
- Identify how each family member expresses feelings and the impact this has on others
- Identify the family interactional patterns that are contributing to the problematic behavior
- Implement new methods of effective communication among family members

Materials
- Two small open shallow containers
- Comfortable and Uncomfortable Feeling Words (included)
- Cardstock (optional)

Advance Preparation
Photocopy the Comfortable and Uncomfortable Feeling Words (preferably onto colored cardstock). Cut out each feeling word and place them in the containers. Place the "comfortable" feeling words in one container and the "uncomfortable" feeling words in the other container.

Description
Request that a parent or one of the older children be the first to pull a feeling word from the container that has the "comfortable" feelings and tell which feeling they chose. Ask the family member to describe a time when he/she has felt that way, e.g., happy. Next ask what he/she thinks would make each family member feel that way. Then guide the person who chose the feeling to ask each family member if he/she will permit body-sculpting. To do this, the person positions each family member's body in a way that demonstrates how he/she sees their body and facial expressions when they are experiencing the feeling that was selected. For example, if the son in the family selects the proud feeling word, he might say that his dad had a proud look when he received a good grade on a math test. He would then ask his dad if he could arrange his dad's body to demonstrate how it looked to him when he perceived his dad was feeling proud.

Continue this until the child has positioned each family member's body in the position that demonstrates how he/she sees that person's body and facial expression when they are expressing the selected feeling.

Upon completion, invite another family member to pull a feeling word and continue the process. Begin with the container that has the "comfortable" feelings, then proceed to the container that has the "uncomfortable" feelings, or alternate between the two containers.

It is important that every member of the family have an opportunity to participate in this process.

151

Discuss the experience by asking the following questions:

1. What was the easiest feeling to sculpt?
2. What was the hardest feeling to sculpt?
3. Which feelings are the most difficult to express/talk about in your family? What would make it easier to express/talk about these feelings with your family?
4. What did you learn through this activity in general? What did you learn about how feelings are expressed through body language? What did you learn about how one person's feelings affect others in the family?

Discussion

The purpose of this activity is to increase communication about feelings and the effect feelings have on family members. Through the use of body sculpting, family members are given the opportunity to nonverbally express themselves as well as learn how others interpret their body language. This is especially helpful for children who may not have the same vocabulary skills as their older siblings and parents.

Virginia Satir states, "Sculpting has value because it makes explicit what is going on. This picture is not to shame how bad people are but to help them see what is going on." She added, "I am bringing people in touch with the various ways they use themselves as well as how they can use themselves differently" (1964). Catherine Sori further emphasizes that family sculpture "is a form of psychodrama that allows family members to gain a deeper understanding of one another through reenactments of conflicts" (2006).

References
Satir, V. (1964). *Conjoint family therapy*. Palo Alto, CA: Science and Behavior Books, Inc.

Sori, C.F. (2006). *Engaging children in family therapy: Creative approaches to integrating theory and research in clinical practice*. New York: Routledge.

About The Author
Trudy Post Sprunk, LMFT-S, LPC-S, RPT-S, CPT-S, is a Licensed Marriage and Family Therapist and Supervisor who has been practicing psychotherapy since 1971. She has presented at international, national, and local conferences and has been interviewed on radio and television. She is certified as an EMDR Specialist and is a Registered Play Therapist Supervisor. She is past-president of the Association for Play Therapy and president and co-founder of the Georgia Association for Play Therapy.

Feeling Body Sculpting
Comfortable Feelings

Happy	**Excited**	**Proud**
Relieved	**Enthusiastic**	**Relaxed**
Brave	**Smart**	**Thankful**
Important	**Hopeful**	**Loved**

© Trudy Post Sprunk

153

Feeling Body Sculpting
Uncomfortable Feelings

Sad	**Angry**	**Scared**
Nervous	**Guilty**	**Jealous**
Bored	**Disappointed**	**Embarrassed**
Tired	**Hurt**	**Frustrated**

© Trudy Post Sprunk

Feelings Checkers
Source: Shannon Culy

Goals
- Increase open communication about feelings among family members
- Implement new methods of effective communication between family members
- Share feelings that underlie conflict within the family

Materials
- Feelings Checkers Game Board (included)
- Checkers Board Game red and black game pieces (the tokens)

Advance Preparation
Photocopy the Feelings Checkers Game Board. This can be copied onto cardstock and laminated for extra durability.

Description
Two family members can play against one another, or the family can be divided into teams.

Feelings Checkers is similar to the regular Checkers Board Game and the same game rules apply. Players can move one square, diagonally-forward on the game board. Players can also "capture" other's tokens by "jumping" over the other player's token into an empty space. A move can include jumping over two of the other player's tokens, resulting in a double jump. Once the player is "captured," his/her game piece is removed from the board. When the player reaches the other side of the board, the token can be flipped and be considered a "king," which can move forward or backwards on the board.

Players choose a color for their tokens and place all 12 tokens on the white squares with feeling words (Shy, Thankful, Angry, Surprised, etc.) written on them. Decide who goes first and each player takes turns moving on the game board trying to "capture" the other player's tokens. When a player moves to another "Feelings Square," he/she has to identify a time when he/she experienced that feeling. For example, for the feeling "Jealous," a response could be, "I was jealous when my brother got lots of presents on his birthday." The therapist can provide encouragement, praise, or validation to the family members during this process.

Upon completion of the game, the therapist can explore issues further by asking the following questions:

1. What is something you learned about a family member through this game?
2. What was the hardest feeling to talk about?
3. What feeling(s) do you think should be added to the game board?

Variations of the game:

- Definitions: Players can take turns providing a definition of the feeling, for example: Brave: being courageous when facing something difficult.
- Role-Play: Players can take turns role-playing a situation when they experienced a particular feeling.
- Body Language and Facial Expression: Players can show what his/her body/face would look like when he/she experiences a particular feeling.

Discussion

At times, it can be hard for families to discuss thoughts and feelings; it is often easier for family members to communicate more openly through games. The aim of this activity is to help family members identify and express a variety of feeling states. The game "can be an effective tool to encourage communication about emotions. Because the game has rules, children tend to follow directions, speak and listen at appointed times, and generally cooperate with the process" (Gil, 1994).

The family can take the game home to play as a way to encourage them to openly express their feelings. As Gil suggests, when children are upset and incommunicative, parents can bring out the game and engage the child in play. In this way, "parents and children can communicate and use the game as a buffer when verbal communication is difficult. The game can diffuse potential arguments, and assist children to release pent-up emotions" (Gil, 1994).

Reference
Gil, E. (1994). *Play in family therapy*. New York: Guilford.

About The Author
Shannon Culy, BSW, RSW, has been employed with Mental Health-Child and Youth Services in Estevan, Saskatchewan, since 2001. She provides individual, family, and group counseling to children, youth, and parents with diverse mental health needs. As part of her work, she writes a monthly newsletter addressing some of these mental health needs. She is an active member of several professional committees.

Feelings Checkers

Happy		Ashamed				Happy	
	Thankful		Bored		Scared		Lonely
Lonely		Scared				Proud	
	Sorry		Brave		Worried		Jealous
Shy		Jealous				Loving	
	Proud		Worried		Excited		Ashamed
Angry		Frustrated				Bored	
	Excited		Loving		Guilty		Sorry
Surprised		Guilty					Confident

Feelings Hide and Seek
Source: Sueann Kenney-Noziska

Goals
- Provide a safe environment for family members to verbalize and discuss their feelings
- Increase open communication regarding various emotional states
- Strengthen family relationships through direct communication

Materials
- Index cards with various feelings written on them
- Tape
- Prizes such as stickers or small individually wrapped candies (optional)

Advance Preparation
Prior to the session, write various feeling words on index cards such as happy, sad, angry, scared, jealous, guilty, brave, excited, etc. For durability, cards can be printed on card stock and laminated. If prizes or candies are being included in the game, then a smiley face can be drawn on several of the cards.

Using tape, the index cards are hidden around the room at varying levels of difficulty. For families with younger children, the cards will be hidden in obvious places. For families with older children, the cards can be hidden in more secretive places.

Description
This technique is a therapeutic version of the popular childhood game hide-and-seek. However, instead of people hiding, the therapist has hidden cards with various feeling words on them.

The therapist explains that in many situations, people ignore their feelings and keep them hidden instead of dealing with them. Even though this may seem effective, "hidden" feelings still exist and continue to bother the person until the feelings are brought out into the open and addressed.

In this game, feelings start out hidden and, through the course of hide-and-seek, are found and discussed. During the intervention, family members take turns finding the hidden feeling cards and processing a time they experienced the feeling written on the card.

If the optional cards with smiley face are used, players who find one of these cards discuss a feeling of their choice and then receive a prize such as a sticker or a small candy.

At the end of the game, process the activity by asking the following questions:

1. What was the easiest feeling to discuss?
2. What was the hardest feeling to discuss?
3. Is it better to hide or talk about your feelings and why?
4. Who is the easiest person in the family for you to talk to about your feelings and why?
5. Who is the hardest person for you to talk to about your feelings and why?
6. How do you think your family can make communication about feelings better or easier?
7. What did you learn from this game?

Discussion

The family system provides a unique forum for facilitating the development of healthy, direct communication. This intervention targets communication within the family by providing an opportunity for the family to directly identify, communicate, and process their emotions. Some families lack the language to communicate about emotions. This activity helps build and expand the family's emotional vocabulary and fosters a family environment conducive to healthy emotional expression. For families who avoid discussing distressing emotions, this technique can facilitate emotional expression of "hidden" feelings. Parents can model healthy emotional expression and direct communication. In addition, this intervention can lay the foundation for family members to provide emotional support for one another.

As feelings are chosen for the intervention, the therapist can prescriptively select emotions according to the family's presenting problem, issues, or treatment goals. The emotions identified and processed can be common emotions to support family communication around feelings in general or geared toward a specific topic such as divorce, death, or abuse.

As stated in the "Description" section, cards with a smiley face can be hidden along with the feeling cards. Players who find one of these cards select a treat, sticker, or other small prize and discuss a feeling of their choice. Although this is an optional element, the prospect of "winning" something during the course of the activity may lower defenses and incorporates an additional element of playfulness to the technique.

Throughout the activity, normalize and validate the emotions discussed by the family. As an optional component, coping skills to manage emotional distress can be identified and discussed.

Reference

Kenney-Noziska, S. (2008). *Techniques-techniques-techniques: Play-based activities for children, adolescents, and families*. West Conshohocken, PA: Infinity Publishing.

About The Author

Sueann Kenney-Noziska, MSW, LISW, RPT-S, is a Licensed Independent Social Worker and Registered Play Therapist Supervisor specializing in using play therapy in clinical practice with children, adolescents, and families. She is an accomplished author, instructor of play therapy, guest lecturer, and internationally recognized speaker who has trained thousands of professionals. She is founder and President of Play Therapy Corner, Inc., is actively involved in the play therapy community, and is author of the book *Techniques-Techniques-Techniques: Play-Based Activities for Children, Adolescents, and Families.*

Five Important Things
Source: Trudy Post Sprunk

Goals
- Increase open communication among family members
- Identify verbally what is important to each family member
- Increase understanding and awareness of needs

Materials
- Pencils
- Five Important Things Worksheet (included)
- Two small containers

Advance Preparation
Arrange seating so that each can write privately on a flat surface. Make a copy of the worksheet for each family member, and cut each worksheet.

Description
Explain to the family that they will each be silently listing things that are important to themselves (Part A) and to another person in the family (Part B).

After each family member completes the first section (Part A), ask him/her to put it into a container. Then after each family member has completed the second section (Part B), place it into the second container.

Next, the therapist pulls one of the strips from the container and reads the first word on the strip out loud. For example, the therapist pulls a strip prepared by a 10-year-old boy, in a family with three children, who wrote the following five things:

1. Puppy
2. Computer
3. Friends
4. Recess
5. Dessert

The therapist reads the first item on the list, "Puppy." The family then attempts to guess who wrote it. The 10-year-old who actually wrote it pretends that he did not write it and suggests that another family member wrote it…perhaps his sister.

Once the family has determined that puppy was written by the 10-year-old, the therapist checks puppy off the list of five and returns the paper to the container.

The therapist then pulls a paper that was completed by another family member and repeats the process.

When the therapist pulls a Part B strip he/she says, for example, "Mom wrote that she thinks sports are most important to someone. Who is that person?" In this scenario, the family tries to guess who it is that Mom believes this could be.

A discussion of each family member's responses during this activity is encouraged. During the discussion, the therapist may request clarification, explore feelings, and so on.

After the activity, process by asking the following questions:

1. What did this game reveal about who you know best/least in your family?
2. What did you like best about this game?
3. What do you think was the purpose of this game?

Discussion

This technique provides family members the opportunity to increase communication by discussing those things in life that are important to them. The family is engaged in determining how well they know each other, as well as providing information to others.

The therapist serves as a guide in helping to increase open communication about beliefs and needs. The activity allows each person to express him/herself and learn about others in the family.

About The Author

Trudy Post Sprunk, LMFT-S, LPC-S, RPT-S, CPT-S, is a Licensed Marriage and Family Therapist and Supervisor who has been practicing psychotherapy since 1971. She has presented at international, national, and local conferences and has been interviewed on radio and television. She is certified as an EMDR Specialist and is a Registered Play Therapist Supervisor. She is past-president of the Association for Play Therapy and president and co-founder of the Georgia Association for Play Therapy.

Five Important Things
Worksheet

Your name_____

Part A: List 5 things that are most important to you:

1_____

2_____

3_____

4_____

5_____

==

Cut here

Your name_____

Part B: List 5 things that you think are most important to_____
                                                        (Other family member)

1_____

2_____

3_____

4_____

5_____

Follow the Big Leader
Source: Steve Harvey

Goals
- Learn how to respond to children with more sensitivity
- Establish appropriate rules and limits
- Increase physical attunement between parent and child

Materials
- A video for recording the session (optional)
- Assortment of age-appropriate toys and games

Advance Preparation
A variety of toys and games should be set up for this activity. Generally, toys or materials that engage the parent and child in interactive play are preferred, such as large scarves, large pillows, drums and other musical instruments, dress-up clothes, action figures, dolls, and drawing material.

Description
This activity is based on the game, Follow The Leader. In this version, the role of who decides the leader of game action and when the leadership changes is determined by the parent only, while the child plays the game either as a Little Leader or as a follower as directed by the parent. The parent also continues to play the game in any of the roles they determine to be best.

Clarify the roles below:

The Big Leader (played by the parent): The parent in this role has two responsibilities-to play the game as well as to choose who is to be the leader and when the change of leadership occurs.

The Little Leader: Initiates actions for the players to follow.

Followers: Copies the actions that are initiated by the Little Leader.

The Little Leader initiates an action and it is expected that the followers will copy that action to the best of their ability. As the game proceeds, the Big Leader (the parent) has several choices to make and is free to assign the role of the Little Leader to another family member, simply to allow the children to continue, or take on the role of the Little Leader themselves.

While Follow the Leader can certainly involve physical action, it is more about copying and turn taking and can make use of any number of play actions and props from musical instruments to dress up costumes. The game requires the leader to use actions that are challenging for him/her and are also interesting to the other players. The followers likewise must have the play skills to copy the leader while also being engaged.

The purpose of having the parent in the decision making role of the Big Leader allows for the game action to become a metaphor for a parent's use of various leadership styles. The therapist observes the game action to notice the communicative process of game action, particularly how the parent's actions and decisions about leadership impact the nature of the play actions. Some interesting observations that the therapist can note are when the parent is too overbearing in their choices of who should be the leader, or alternatively the parent who can not assert themselves to control the game when it is necessary. The parent's performance of this role becomes the material for discussion with the therapist after the game is over.

After the game, the therapist and parent can discuss how the parent was able to provide structure as well as to encourage the child's playful expression. Directed questions can add focus to important parenting issues. These questions include:

1. How did it feel to be in the role of the Big Leader?
2. How did it feel to be in the role of the follower?
3. In what ways were you able to provide structure and limits for your child?
4. What strategies did you use to make this fun for your child?
5. When can these strategies be used at home?
6. What do you think might prevent you from using this? How will you address those constraints?

Additionally, the therapist can use specific interactions from the game in the discussion. It is especially helpful to point out interactive moments when things went well.

Discussion
Parenting often requires competing abilities to understand children as well as provide limits. This activity can be used as an experiential task to help parents learn and practice this kind of leadership style.

To be successful, the parent has to be observant of the child's interests and intentions in the immediate moment, especially as expressed in the child's physical and nonverbal communication. The Big Leader requires the parent to be a participant/observer within their child's play action. The child's reactions to the game can provide immediate feedback on the parent's ability to use these principles. The result of a good balance is for the game to proceed in a playful manner that has intrinsic interest for the child and a parent showing the flexibility to adjust to the needs of the moment.

The theoretical background involving physical play among families and how such activities can be more developed is presented more fully elsewhere (Harvey, 2000, 2003, 2006).

If it is possible, it is helpful to video record the session so it can be viewed later with the parent for the purposes of exploring dynamics that emerged during the game using the actual episodes from the game.

References

Harvey, S.A. (2000). Dynamic play approaches in the observation of family relationships. In K. Gitlin-Weiner, A. Sandgrund, & C. E. Schaefer (Eds.), *Play diagnosis and assessment.* New York: Wiley & Sons.

Harvey, S.A. (2003). Dynamic play therapy with an adoptive family struggling with issues of grief, loss, and adjustment. In D. Wiener & L. Oxford (Eds.), *Action therapy with families and groups.* Washington, DC: American Psychological Association Books.

Harvey, S.A. (2006). Dynamic play therapy. In C.E. Schaefer and H. Kaduson (Eds.), *Contemporary play therapy.* New York: Guilford Publications.

About The Author

Steve Harvey, PhD, RPT-S, BC-DMT, is a Licensed Psychologist in the United States and is registered as a Psychologist with clinical and educational scopes of practice in New Zealand. He is a Registered Play Therapist Supervisor and a Board Certified Dance Movement Therapist. He is currently the Consultant Psychologist for the Child and Adolescent Mental Health Service for the Taranaki District Health Board in New Plymouth, New Zealand. He helped pioneer the use of Play Therapy approaches with families and has written several professional chapters and articles in the field published in *The International Journal of Play Therapy, Contemporary Play Therapy, Play Diagnosis and Assessment*, and *Blending Play Therapy with Cognitive Behavioural Therapy: Evidence-Based and other Effective Treatment Techniques.* He has presented and consulted extensively internationally on topics related to the use of family play in the evaluation and treatment of attachment and psychological trauma in children

Garden of Birds
Source: Susan Perrow

Goals
- Increase awareness of the importance of listening to others
- Encourage respect for other points-of-view

Materials
- Story "Garden of Birds" (included)
- Songbird outlines (included)
- Crayons or pencils
- Scissors
- Wooden sticks (such as Popsicle sticks)
- Tape

Advance Preparation
The following scene and props are recommended for the puppet show, but are not required as the family can enact the puppet show without these items. Cover the table with earth-colored cloth (or color a sheet of paper to make it look like the earth). Have some vases of greenery or some potted plants to represent the trees in the garden. Alternatively, use a rug on the floor for family members to sit around.

Description
Have the family cut out the birds, color them in, and tape them onto wooden sticks.

Read or tell the story "Garden of Birds" (Perrow, 2008) to the family. Retell the story as a puppet play several times, each time rotating the turn of the "main" songbird among the family members. This facilitates all members' participation and maintains their interest in the story.

Active discussion among the family is discouraged during the puppet plays as this will give each puppeteer time to absorb the full power of the story. However, active music-making – for example, singing or humming or whistling – could definitely be encouraged (if the therapist thinks this could be appropriate and if family members feel comfortable with this).

After every family member has had a turn as the "main" songbird, facilitate a discussion by asking the following process questions:

1. How did it feel to be the "main" songbird in the beginning of the story?
2. How did it feel to be the "main" songbird at the end of the story?
3. How did it feel to be one of the other birds in the garden?
4. What new information did you learn about working together?

Discussion

Working with Therapeutic Stories: Using the definition for healing, *bring into balance, become sound or whole*, therapeutic stories for challenging behaviors or situations are stories that help the process of bringing an out-of-balance behavior or situation back into wholeness or balance.

When using a therapeutic story to heal the challenging situation of family members "not listening to each other," it is not a question of "bad" behavior made "good." It is about trying to bring the behavior or situation back into wholeness or balance – in this case, from "not listening" to "listening and respecting other points of view."

Metaphors, Journey, and Story Props: The use of metaphor is a vital ingredient in therapeutic story work. In the story, "Garden of Birds" the bird metaphors are used to help build the imaginative connection for the listener. The journey is the formative part of the therapeutic story construction. An eventful journey is a way to build the "tension" as the story evolves and can lead the plot into and through the behavior "imbalance" (e.g., the "dominating songbird") and out again to a wholesome, pro-active resolution.

Metaphors can be strengthened by the use of story puppets in the telling of the story –for example, the different birds in the garden. Involving the family members in both making the birds and performing the story as a puppet show can help to strengthen the experience and the transformation.

The therapist can use the observations of the puppeteers and the discussion following the story to assess styles of interaction and attitudes, and to intervene therapeutically to address issues raised by the family.

Reference

Perrow, S. (2008).*Healing stories for challenging behaviour*. London: Hawthorn.

About The Author

Susan Perrow, M.Ed., has 30 years of experience in teaching, counseling, and storytelling. After completing her master's degree on a cross-cultural study of storytelling in teacher training, she set up a 150-hour module on storytelling at Southern Cross University in Australia. Since 1995, she has worked in Teacher Training and Parent Education in Australia, Africa, Europe, and Asia, specializing in storytelling, therapeutic story writing, and creative discipline.

Garden of Birds

Story by Susan Perrow, 2008

Once upon a time there was a bird that sang so beautifully she filled the garden with her bird song from morning to night. Many other birds lived in this garden but they weren't able to sing over the top of the beautiful songbird. Even if they tried to sing, their sounds just seemed to disappear into nowhere. The songbird filled the air and the garden with her nonstop singing and there was no room for any other songs. If the other birds wanted to practice their singing, they would have to fly out of the garden and high up into the mountains where there was no competition.

One day, however, the beautiful songbird grew very sick and was not able to sing any more. She rested in her nest, day after day. The garden around her was very quiet, and each day when the birds returned from the mountains they wondered what had happened.

One by one, the other birds began to stay behind in the garden and take turns singing. Soon the garden was filled with the sound of many birds with many different songs.

The sick bird was very surprised to listen to so many other birds – all their songs were very different and very beautiful. She had never heard anything like this before. The more she lay in her nest and listened to the new sounds the stronger she grew. The singing was helping to heal her.

Soon the songbird was feeling better and she was able to sing once more. But she decided to only sing every so often and not all the time. This way she was able to enjoy the songs of the other birds. She was also learning so many new bird sounds by listening to the others, and over time her own singing became richer and better because of this.

As time passed, this garden became well known for its beautiful bird songs and its rich variety of bird sounds. People came from far and wide to spend time here to walk, sit, and listen. Some even found healing in such a wonderful place.

Note: The story can be modified with a male as the dominant songbird.

© Susan Perrow

Garden of Birds
Songbird Outlines

Hurt Hearts and Healing Hands
Source: Betty Bedard Bidwell and Brenda Lee Garratt

Goals
- Identify strengths of individual family members and the family as a whole
- Increase open communication about painful life experiences among family members
- Verbalize an increased sense of mastery over trauma symptoms

Materials
- Several pieces of poster board in a variety of colors
- Several sheets of large construction paper in a variety of colors
- Package of construction paper (9" X 12") in a variety of colors
- Scissors
- Glue sticks
- Markers or colored pencils

Advance Preparation
Place the materials on a flat surface that can be easily reached by everyone.

Description

Part 1: Acknowledging the Hurts
After the family members are comfortably seated around the table, present them with the different colors of poster board. Instruct them as a family unit to choose a color that represents safety for them. Remove the extra sheets from the table. Then ask the family to choose one large sheet of construction paper. Explain that this sheet will represent their family hurts. Remove the extra sheets of paper. Each family member then chooses a sheet of 9" X 12" construction paper in his/her favorite color. The heart each person cuts out will represent his/her individual hurts. Once their individual hearts are cut out they will divide them into 4 sections. Each section will contain three phrases or words of their choosing that express 1. What scares them? (first section) 2. What makes them mad? (2nd section) 3.What makes them sad? (3rd section) 4.What are they worried about? (4th section). Have each family member share his/her individual hurt heart with the family. Allow time for discussion. Process questions could include but should not be limited to:

1. What was it like to share your hurt heart with your family?
2. What similarities/differences did you notice among the other hurt hearts?
3. How can sharing your feelings with your family help you and your family as a whole?

171

Once all family members have participated, a large family hurt heart is cut out (from the previously chosen sheet of construction paper) and glued in the center of the sheet of colored poster board that represents safety. Then all family members glue their own hurt hearts onto the sheet representing safety, placing them around the large family hurt heart so that it remains visible. Divide the large heart into four sections.

Once this has been completed, each family member chooses one hurt from their individual heart and writes it onto each of the four sections of the family heart that corresponds to the individual's divisions of hurt.

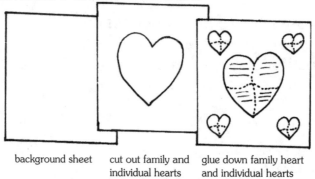

background sheet   cut out family and   glue down family heart
               individual hearts   and individual hearts

Part Two: The Healing Process

Family members each choose two sheets of 9" X 12" construction paper in their favorite colors and cut out tracings of their left and right hands. On the right hand, they write five things they need from their family to heal their hurts. On the left hand, they write five things they have to give to the family to help heal the family hurts. Process this phase of the activity by asking family members to each share what they have written.

Process questions could include but should not be limited to:

1. What can others in your family do to help you with your hurts?
2. What can you do for your family to help them with their hurts?
3. How will you feel once you have received help and support from your family?

Next, have family members glue their two cut-out hands (place glue only on the wrist area) in close proximity to the family heart in an area of their choosing. The family heart is now supported by the family members' healing hands both visually and through the shared experience.

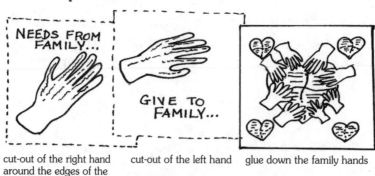

cut-out of the right hand   cut-out of the left hand   glue down the family hands
around the edges of the
family heart

Discussion

Hurt is an emotion that runs deep and is not always easy to share after a family experiences a difficult event. Expressing the emotion requires that each member acknowledge how he/she has felt it individually and how the hurt has affected the family unit. Often, the hurt is so overwhelming that family members turn away from their strengths and isolate themselves from the very supports and strengths they had previously shared and relied on within their family.

According to Malchiodi (2003), Rubin (2005), and Dr. Bedard Bidwell, family art therapy enhances communication between family members through the process and content created by the art activity. The activity offers the family a cooperative way to communicate by using their own creative potential to problem-solve, acquire and give empathy, and to support each other through changes in behavior.

This activity allows all of the family members to express their thoughts and feelings surrounding their hurt and the loss they are presently experiencing. Once again, the individual family members can begin to heal within the supportive system they have relied upon in the past and experience less isolation while doing so, alleviating the stress brought on by fear, anger, sadness and worry about themselves and their family.

References

Malchiodi, C.A. (2003). *Handbook of art therapy*. New York: Guilford Press.

Rubin J.A. (2005). *Child art therapy*. New York: Wiley & Sons.

About the Authors

Betty Bedard Bid well, PhD, ATBC, OATR-S., PTR, CPTR-S, CTC-S, is a Registered Art and Play Therapist Supervisor and a Trauma & Loss Consultant Supervisor. She was the 2001 recipient of the Trauma & Loss Consultant Supervisor of the Year Award and the 2001 Premier's Award in Applied Arts: Community Services. She was one of the co-founders of the Art Therapy Program at the University of Western Ontario and was the founder and developer as well as the first program coordinator of the Canadian Association for Child and Play Therapy (CACPT) Play Therapy Certificate Program where she continues as an instructor. She has presented workshops across Canada and in the United States. She edited and co-authored the books, *Hand in Hand One-Practical Application of Art and Play Therapy* and *Hand in Hand Two-Art and Play Therapist Treasure Chest*, and is published in numerous journals. She is also a Compassion Fatigue Trainer, Resiliency Trainer, and Life Skills Coach Trainer. In recent years, she has become an Animal Assisted Therapist and now uses pets as part of her therapeutic approach. She has also become a trained holistic health provider within her private practice. She has been the owner/operator of Betamarsh Incorporated, a residential and foster care agency, since 1981, and since that time has also been a treatment foster parent.

Brenda Lee Garratt, T.A.T.I. Intern, A.O.C.A.D., E.C.E., is completing the Art Therapy Program offered by the Toronto Art Therapy Association. She is completing a student practicum at Betamarsh Inc. in Goderich, Ontario, under the supervision of Dr. Betty Bedard Bidwell. She is a member of both the Canadian Art Therapy Association and the Ontario Art Therapy Association. In addition to her professional studies, she teaches drawing and painting workshops.

We would like to acknowledge the therapeutic work of Wanda Sawicki (for the hands idea) and Dr. William Steele (for the trauma terminology "mad-sad-scared"). Their expertise and knowledge have allowed us as therapists to further develop successful family techniques that are both supportive and healing.

Hut! Hut! Hike!
Source: Katherine M. Hertlein

Goals
- Define specifics about what needs to change in the child's behavior
- Track goals achieved in therapy
- Create a token economy
- Reduce the child's behavioral problems

Materials
- Football field diagram (included)
- Construction or colored paper
- Markers
- Post-it® Notes and/or note cards

Advance Preparation
Photocopy and enlarge the football field diagram, or recreate through a word processing program such as Microsoft Word, or create by hand on construction paper.

Description
This intervention is to assist children or families track their success in attaining their goals. It is designed for children who are at the age when they can understand making progress toward reaching their goals (generally between the ages of 5 and 11). It can also be used with multiple members of a family who are trying to reach the same goal.

The therapist works with the family to identify the goal to be addressed in treatment. The therapist can either keep the word "Touchdown" as the goal or change the word to the goal identified by the family. The therapist explains that the football field will help the child keep track of his/her progress in reaching the goal. Each time that the child makes progress or achieves a step, he/she can move the game piece to a new yard line. The therapist asks the family to identify a reward once the "Touchdown" is reached. This reward must be something that is manageable to the person who is providing the reward. Some children may prefer a financial reward; others may prefer quality time with Mom and Dad or a similar activity.

The therapist and family discuss the steps that would lead to that goal and apply a step to each of the yard markers. The therapist and family write each of the steps on the note cards. The yard markers can be (1) independent steps to achieve a goal, or (2) relate to the frequency of a behavior. For example, Julia might ask that her son, Nathan, go through the week of school without being disciplined by his teacher for being disruptive in class. On the Post-it® Notes, the family writes

175

"Monday," "Tuesday," and so on through to the final day of the week, which is "Touchdown: Friday." Alternatively, the therapist and family can elect to make each yard marker a particular task leading up to an overall goal. If Julia brings Nathan to treatment to address his bedtime tantrums, for example, then each yard marker would describe a certain task in preparation for bedtime. For example: the 40-yard marker is for "Taking a Bath"; the 30-yard marker for "Brushing Teeth," and so on.

Once the steps toward goal completion are described on the Post-it® Notes, the therapist and family can decorate the field with the markers and determine how to attach the Post-it® Notes to the field. The Post-its® can be attached to the bottom of the page underneath each yard marker to display a certain step. In this way, the field can be reused for different goals. If the family is unconcerned about reusing the field, the Post-its® do not have to be used; instead, each of the goals can be written in marker on the field in between the yard lines.

After generating the football field and the appropriate yard markers, the therapist can ask the following questions:

1. Who is the quarterback/person calling the plays?
2. Who/what are blockers that prevent you from going down the field?
3. Who is the coach and how can the coach be helpful?
4. Is there a referee? If so, who?
5. What are some of the plays/strategies that work best?

The therapist then works with the child or family to create a game piece to move throughout the field, such as a football, a helmet, or another symbol. This can be created with the construction paper or colored paper and can be affixed to the field to indicate how the child's progress is coming along. If there are multiple members of the family working toward the same goal, they can develop their own game pieces. If it is a goal for the whole family and each member can participate in working through the steps, the family can determine what one game piece would best represent all of them. The family can also develop a team name, a mascot, and a cheer!

Discussion

This intervention provides a playful opportunity for family members to interact with one another and participate in the child's attempts to reach his/her goals, or to participate together in a joint attempt to reach the goal. It helps a family to keep track of the goal and increases the likelihood of the child or family members reaching the goal through the implementation of a token economy. While there should be a reward for achieving a "Touchdown," the therapist may also decide it is valuable to provide incentives along the way at each yard marker.

The intervention uses the metaphor of football to visualize and evaluate progress in achieving goals. There are circumstances in which the football metaphor will not suit a particular child or family. In those cases, the therapist may choose to use another field, like soccer. In such cases, the word "Touchdown" can be replaced with the word "Goal."

About The Author

Katherine M. Hertlein, PhD, LMFT, is an Associate Professor in the Department of Marriage and Family Therapy at the University of Nevada-Las Vegas. She received her Master's Degree in Marriage and Family Therapy from Purdue University Calumet and her doctorate degree in Marriage and Family Therapy from Virginia Tech. She is a member of the American Association for Marriage and Family Therapy, the Association for Play Therapy, and the America Association for Sexuality Educators, Counselors, and Therapists. She formerly served as president of the Nevada Association for Play Therapy. She has published 50 articles and book chapters and five books, including *The Therapist's Notebook for Family Healthcare* and *The Couple and Family Therapist's Notebook*.

Hut! Hut! Hike!
Football Field Diagram

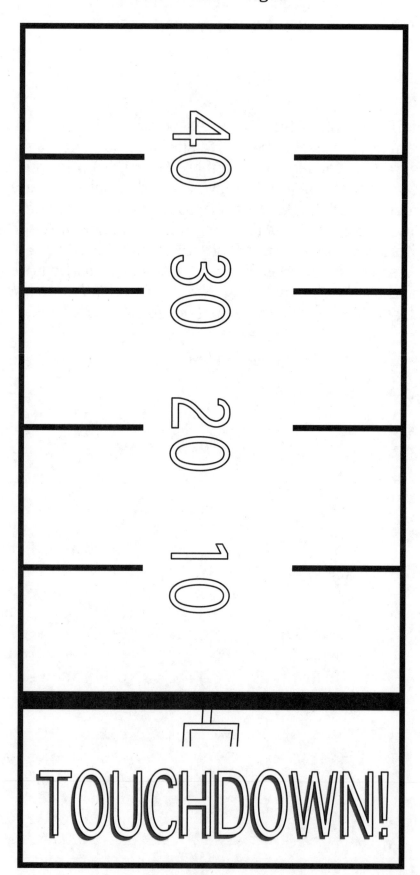

Land of No Rules
Source: Theresa Fraser

Goals
- Assess dynamics and interactions within the family, particularly rules, roles, and hierarchy
- Establish and enforce appropriate rules within the family
- Encourage parents to increase their understanding of their children's worldviews
- Increase family members' ability to communicate their needs

Materials
- Every Family Is a Kingdom Questionnaire (included)
- Paper
- Pencils
- Markers
- Camera

Additional Materials for the Sandtray Version
- Sandtray half-filled with sand
- Variety of miniature objects or figurines representing different categories such as people (various ages, races, abilities, and occupations), animals (pets, farm, and wild), vehicles, plants and things from nature (rocks and shells), furniture/ household objects, buildings and fantasy figures. Make sure there is a King and Queen figurine.

Description
Note: This activity requires at least two sessions.

Complete the Every Family Is a Kingdom Questionnaire with the family. If the sandtray version is being used, the family can respond to the questions verbally, as well as illustrate their responses by creating a picture in the sand using the miniatures provided.

In the following session, divide the family into two dyads. (The children should be teamed up with the parent whose relationship can benefit from one-to-one time. The dyad portion of the activity also ensures that quiet children have the opportunity to express their feelings and views. If there is only one parent, then have the whole family work together rather than dividing the family.)

The family is asked to imagine a Land of No Rules. Each dyad is instructed to draw a picture together (or create a scene in the sandtray) that illustrates their Land of No Rules. Each dyad can decide how, what, when, and where the Land of No Rules operates. This picture can be a positive description of how the Land of No

Rules is viewed or it can be a negative description. This is up to each small group of family members. Next, each dyad creates a story about their Land of No Rules. The parent in each dyad is asked to write down the story that is created. This is especially important for dyads where children have difficulty honoring the authority of their parents. (The therapist needs to be clear about this small group leadership role when explaining the directions.) Then the dyads come together to share their pictures and stories.

If the small groups do not bring up the negative possibilities of what happens in places where there are no rules, the therapist can ask questions such as:

1. What is it like in this Land of No Rules?
2. How safe do the children and adults feel if everyone around them does whatever they want?
3. What happens when nobody is in charge?
4. What problems arise when there are no rules?
5. How do parents feel when they may not know where their children are or what they are doing?

A discussion should follow about what the general rules need to be so that all the citizens in this land benefit equally. The family can create a new story or end their former stories with this new unifying information.

The final part of this session is when the family identifies the rules that are appropriate in their home. One of the parents can list these rules on a sheet of paper.

The family is then invited to create a new drawing (or picture in the sand) illustrating The Land of Important Rules. That is, this drawing illustrates the rules that need to be in place at home for the safety and well-being of all family members and describes who sets and enforces them, the consequences when rules are broken, and so on.

Take a photograph of the mural or the sandtray for the family (as well as for the clinical record).

Discussion

This activity is appropriate with a family who is struggling with rules and roles. It is also helpful for a family for whom one of the treatment goals is to support a healthy parent–child relationship, particularly when there may be ongoing conflict between the parent/child dyad.

Through storytelling and drawing (or sandtray), family members gain a better understanding of each other's views of the family, the rules and need for structure, and individual feelings of safety. Often, these approaches provide a way to externalize this discussion in a way that provides more clarity to the entire family about individual family members' views and experiences. As Harvey (2008) contends, "A basic assumption is that families have the creative ability to address their conflicts in a naturalistic manner and that they can and do use play in their ongoing day-to-day life to both problem solve and resolve their basic emotional conflicts."

When using the sandtray as a method of expression, De Domenico (1995) suggests that one method a therapist can use is to "assign a topic, an experience or an interaction to be worked on during the session."

The dyad portion of the activity can enhance the parent–child relationship. Additionally, the dyad experience provides a venue for the quiet child to voice his/her ideas that are then repeated when the activity is presented to the larger group. Problem-solving and communication among family members is also enhanced through this activity. Combs and Freedman (1998) write, "We interact with family members one at a time, inviting the others present to serve as an audience," which, they argue, "makes family relationships more visible" by helping members "hear instead of defend." That said, "family functioning cannot be fully understood by simply understanding each of the individual family members or subgroups" (Miller et al., 2000). Hence, it is important that the whole family comes together to create the alternative Land of Important Rules as an ending to this experience.

References

Combs, G., & Freedman, J. (1998).Tellings and retellings. *Journal of Marital and Family Therapy*, *24*, 405–408.

De Domenico, G.S. (1995). *Sandtray-worldplay: A comprehensive guide to the use of sandtray in psychotherapeutic and transformational settings*. Oakland, CA: Vision Quest Images.

Harvey, S. (2008). An initial look at the outcomes for dynamic play therapy. *International Journal of Play Therapy*, *17*(2), 86–101.

Miller, I., Ryan, C., Keitner, G., Bishop, D., & Epstein, N. (2000). The McMaster approach to families: Theory, assessment, treatment and research. *Journal of Family Therapy*, *22(2)*, 168. Retrieved June 7, 2010 from Academic Search Premier database.

About The Author

Theresa Fraser, MA, CYW, CPT, works with children, youth, and families. She is a founding Clinician/Manager of Clinical Services at a Children's Mental Health

Agency. In 2009 she published the book *Billy Had to Move* to help children deal with the foster care experience. She has provided workshops internationally to foster care providers about the challenges of daily service provision for children who have experienced trauma and attachment disruptions. She is a part-time instructor at Humber and Mohawk Colleges. She is a Certified Play Therapist and the President of the Canadian Association for Child and Play Therapy.

© Theresa Fraser

Every Family Is a Kingdom
Questionnaire

Each family is like a Kingdom. Answer the following questions about the Kingdom in which you currently live.

1. Who are the citizens of this Kingdom?

2. Who are the King and/or Queen of this Kingdom? (This individual usually makes the final decisions about matters of importance. How do you know that this individual is the King or the Queen?

3. What are the laws of the land? How does this Kingdom maintain the laws of the land? Are all citizens expected to follow the same laws?

4. What are the consequences or punishments imposed when citizens break the law? Are consequences or punishments forgotten once given? Do consequences or punishments match the crimes of the citizens or are they too easy or too harsh?

5. How do the King / Queen share news with the citizens? How do citizens share information with the King / Queen? If citizens are upset in the Kingdom, do the King / Queen know? Is it easy or difficult to talk to the King / Queen? Are citizens comfortable telling the King / Queen how they feel? How do the King / Queen usually react?

6. What do citizens do for fun in this Kingdom?

7. Who helps to make sure that all the citizens have shelter, food, clothes, ways to play, and so on? Is there always enough food for all citizens? What happens in the Kingdom if some citizens do not want to share food with other citizens?

8. Are there any dangers in this Kingdom? If so, what are the dangers? Are the citizens protected from this danger and, if yes, how are they protected – do they protect themselves or are there others who are in charge of protecting the citizens?

9. How do citizens contribute to making this Kingdom a happy and safe place to live? Who shares their gifts willingly with other citizens? Who helps to keep the peace? Is there a troublemaker in the Kingdom? Is there a joker in the Kingdom? What other roles do citizens take on?

10. What three words best describe this Kingdom?

© Theresa Fraser

Let It Rip!
Source: Sheri Eggleton

Goals
- Increase awareness of anger triggers
- Verbalize anger while involved in a cathartic activity
- Implement appropriate ways of expressing anger
- Increase the frequency of positive interactions among family members

Materials
- Paper towels
- Paper towel roll
- Glue
- Water
- Cup
- Paint brushes
- Shoebox
- Paint
- Assorted colors of tissue paper and magazines (optional)
- Garbage bag or newspapers
- Paper
- Pens or pencils

Advance Preparation
Arrange a flat surface for the activity so that each person has easy access to the materials. Cover the work area with a garbage bag or newspapers to prepare the space for messy activity.

Pour some glue into a cup and add some water to create a thinner consistency. Arrange the art supplies and glue on or near the flat surface so that they can be easily reached by all family members.

Description
Note: Two sessions are required to complete this activity.

Begin by talking about anger, normalizing that this is something that everyone experiences. Correct any misconceptions that anger is a bad emotion, and reinforce that anger, like all other feelings, is okay and can even be helpful, as long as it is expressed in a way that does not hurt oneself or others. Introduce the activity by saying, "Today I'm going to teach you how you can use your own personal power to turn anger into something useful."

Discuss how there are varying degrees of anger. Demonstrate how the paper towel roll can be used to measure the amount of anger experienced by giving the following instructions to the family: "Think of a time when you felt angry. If you felt a *little* angry, unroll a little bit of paper. If you felt *really* angry, then unroll lots of paper." Family members can take turns. Allow them to use as much paper as needed to reflect the intensity of their anger. Validate the experience with comments such as "Wow! I can see that you felt really angry about that!"

For older children, introduce additional feeling words along the anger continuum, such as irritated and enraged, thereby helping them to develop a more advanced feelings vocabulary.

The family members are then invited to take turns tearing their paper into smaller pieces. Ask open-ended questions to encourage discussion of the experience in more detail. During this "tearing and sharing," the therapist responds empathically. The family can then be asked about other things that have made them feel angry, repeating the process above for each. When the family has finished tearing the paper, the pieces of torn paper are gathered together. The therapist chooses one piece of paper and compares the size of the anger at the beginning of the activity to its size at the end, emphasizing how talking about the anger has reduced its size and intensity.

Next, bring out the shoebox and explain, "I would like you to use the torn up pieces of anger to decorate this box, which will be used to hold things that you can use to calm yourself when you are angry." It is helpful to have a box already completed, as this will provide the family with a sense of structure and direction, while still allowing for flexibility. Have the family members use a decoupage technique by using the brushes and glue to apply the torn paper to the sides of the box. Point out how the layers of paper will add to the strength of the box. As an optional step, have different colors of tissue paper and old magazines available that can also be used for creating the decoupage. Allow the creation to dry until the next meeting.

Introduce the box at the next session, and invite the family members to feel how much stronger it has been made by the layers of paper. Use this as a concrete example of how talking about angry feelings is a great strength and an important coping skill. Invite the family to use the art supplies to paint and/or decorate their box. Then, assist the family in brainstorming a list of things that they can do to calm themselves when they are angry. Some examples may include taking deep breaths, thinking of a happy memory, slowly counting backwards from ten, etc. Write each calming strategy down on a separate piece of paper and place it in the box.

Process the activity by asking questions such as:

1. What do you think was the purpose of this activity?

2. Tell about something you learned about yourself and your family through this activity.
3. Which strategy do you think would help you the most to calm down when you feel angry?

At the end of the session, again point out the strength of the box and how strong the family members are for talking about their angry feelings. Also, acknowledge the creativity used in decorating the box and how this will help them to "create" their own ways of expressing anger safely.

In addition to creating a calming box, there are other ways that anger can be transformed, allowing the activity to be adapted to the needs and experiences of clients. Other possible variations may include:

Safety shield: Use decoupage to apply paper pieces onto a shield and to decorate the reverse side with pictures of things that help the family members to feel safe and protected.

Mask Making: Use decoupage to apply paper pieces onto a mask and use it to discuss the more vulnerable feelings that often underlie anger (i.e., hurt, fear) as well as what others see versus what is hidden.

Discussion

This activity provides a therapeutic opportunity for family members to express anger in a controlled way, while having their feelings validated by a caring adult. It provides a cathartic release of anger while simultaneously connecting kinesthetic activity with the verbalization of feelings. This play and art activity enables clients to channel and express their anger effectively. A key factor in therapy "is the need and ability to discharge and then channel difficult feelings into artistic expression. Continued use of this sharing of potential space in art and therapy fosters the growing relationship between parent and child" (Parashak, 2008).

During the process, the therapist's role is to offer encouragement and validation and to bear witness to feelings expressed so that anger is experienced as both safe and manageable. Caregivers are invited to learn and practice the anger management skills along with their children so that they are better able to model the skills at home. Caregivers will feel empowered in their ability to help their children, increasing the likelihood that the strategies learned will be generalized. This activity also reframes anger management as a family issue, rather than an individual issue.

This activity provides a visual illustration of how talking about angry feelings makes these feelings appear smaller and more manageable. It also empowers clients to take control of their anger in a way that reaffirms their personal strength and power.

By having the family decorate one box together, the therapist can assess the family's ability to tolerate closeness and the family's need for boundaries. Working collaboratively on the box also builds family cohesion.

It is important that the family leave the session with a feeling that their anger has been contained and controlled. Once members have physically released their anger, they will be calmer and better able to use anger management tools.

Reference
Parashak, S.T. (2008). Object relations and attachment theory: Creativity of mother and child in the single parent family. In C. Kerr, J. Hoshino, et al. (Eds.), *Family art therapy: Foundations of theory and practice*. New York: Routledge.

About The Author
Sheri Eggleton, BA, is employed by Niagara Child and Youth Services as a member of a multidisciplinary team in the Early Assessment Support and Intervention Program, which provides mental health assessment and individualized treatment to families with children aged 0–6. As well, she currently works as a Family Support Worker for Community Living–Welland/Pelham, providing respite and in-home supports to children with developmental disabilities. She has a Bachelor of Arts degree from Brock University and has completed the Play Therapy Certificate Program offered through the Canadian Association for Child and Play Therapy.

Love Bug
Source: Megan Cowan

Goals
- Implement new methods of effective communication between family members
- Reduce conflict within the family

Materials
- Paper
- Markers

Advance Preparation
Arrange a flat drawing space for each family member. It is important that the sheets of paper are not in direct eyesight of each other.

Description
Distribute paper and markers to each family member. Say, "I am going to describe a love bug. I would like you to draw the bug as described. It is important that you do not look at each other's drawings, or speak to each other, or ask questions during the drawing part of this activity."

Read the description below to the family. As the description is read aloud, have each member draw their own love bug:

1. The bug is round.
2. The bug has eight (8) legs, grouped in pairs, with four (4) legs on each side. In one of the pairs, one (1) leg is longer than the other.
3. The bug has two (2) eyes.
4. The bug has two (2) squiggly antennae.
5. The bug has two (2) pea-pod shaped wings.
6. The bug has spots on its wings.
7. The bug has a triangular tail.
8. The bug has two (2) feelers on each foot.
9. The bug has a round mouth.
10. The bug laid five (5) eggs.

Once everyone is finished drawing, have each family member hold up their drawing so everyone else can see it. Notice some of the similarities and differences between the drawings. Facilitate discussion by asking the following process questions:

1. If everyone in the family heard the same description of the love bug, why is everyone's picture different?
2. Can you each think of a time in your family when there was a

misunderstanding or conflict because the same information was heard and understood differently by different family members?

3. If each of you hear and process information differently, how can you use this information in your family to help you get along better?

4. What new information did you learn about your family?

Brainstorm with the family ways of communicating that are healthy and unhealthy. Examples of healthy ways of communicating include using respectful language, using words instead of actions, and telling others what you are feeling. Examples of unhealthy ways include yelling, swearing, hitting, and not listening to each other when someone is speaking.

Discussion

Miscommunication in families can be a major factor in family arguments. This activity can provide a fun way for the therapist to introduce the concept of listening and processing information in different ways. The fact that each family member hears the same information but produces a different drawing can be a starting point for discussion around communication styles in the family. Once parents are encouraged to see that their child may not be ignoring them but, in fact, is processing the information in a different way, it may help them to speak to their child in a different, more supportive manner.

About The Author

Megan Cowan, MSW, RSW, is a Social Worker and Play Therapist Intern in Toronto. She works at a Children's Mental Health Centre in Toronto as a Child and Family Therapist and maintains a small private practice. She has completed the Play Therapy Certificate Program through the Canadian Association for Child and Play Therapy.

Make Your Own Board Game
Source: Rebecca Fischer

Goals
- Implement new methods of effective communication between family members
- Increase the rate of positive verbal comments and pleasurable exchanges between family members
- Achieve the desire and ability to laugh and have fun together

Materials
- Poster board
- Markers
- Decorative supplies such as glitter, paint, felt, etc.
- Playing pieces such as pennies
- Dice or construction paper

Advance Preparation
Prior to the session, the therapist should have an idea of what specific theme and rules will be built into the game to serve as a starting point if the family initially needs help. For example, a family who has been working on anger management may create a board game where they have to answer questions regarding the safe expression of anger in order to advance in the game. Similarly, a family who has been learning coping skills may draw cards that require the players to brainstorm coping skills for specific situations. The therapist can prepare as much or as little of the materials in advance as he/she believes is appropriate for the family and the situation.

Description
Several sessions should have occurred prior to the game creation in order to establish rapport and assess the family. The therapist should assess the gross and fine motor skills of the children, as well as their language abilities. The family's main presenting problem should also be determined.

The therapist and family can work together to create a board game that reflects the presenting problems being worked on in therapy. The parents and children should jointly agree on the format and rules for the game. Encourage the children to make the choices and the parents to support and contribute. The family may want to model the rules after those of their own favorite board game. Families may choose to reward the "winner" of the game with something special, such as a choice of a special dinner or family activity. Alternatively, families may choose to create games that require the entire family to work collaboratively, that is, either the whole family wins or the whole family loses.

In creating the game, the therapist can ask the family to consider the following:

1. The theme of the game, i.e., anger management.
2. The format for the game, that is, a circular or winding path, connected boxes, etc.
3. Advancement of the players, for example, rolling a dice or drawing a card.
4. If drawing a card for advancement is being used, then discuss the content of the cards such as questions, activities, etc.
5. The rules of the game, for example, the number of players, who goes first, rewards, or consequences.
6. Determine if there will be a winner of the game and, if so, how do players win the game.
7. The skills and abilities needed to play the game (it should be tailored so the youngest member in the family can participate but it should also be of interest to older children in the family).

During the game construction period, the therapist should facilitate participation of all family members and help each person in the family feel successful and take ownership for his/her specific contribution to the game. The family can draw the format of the game on the poster board, such as a winding or circular path. The therapist might suggest that this be drawn in pencil first and then traced over with marker. The therapist can join the family in coloring, cutting, creating, and so on, and act as a model for the family in their interaction with one another.

After the game is created, the family should play the game. The therapist can play along and facilitate positive interaction. If problems arise, the therapist can engage the family in problem-solving.

After playing the game, the therapist can ask the family questions such as:

1. How did it feel to work together to create this game?
2. What positive contributions did each person make to the game?
3. Give examples of positive interactions that were displayed during the activity such as cooperation, positive communication, and adhering to rules.
4. How can the skills you used to progress in the game be carried over into real life?

The family can then take the game home to play so they can continue to work on the issues outside of the therapy session.

The game can be played in future sessions and modified as new situations or issues arise.

Discussion

The purpose of the family creating the game is twofold. First, the family is reinforcing whatever skills they have been working on in therapy through a new medium. Many families might never have had an opportunity to discuss the problems that they are dealing with in a manner such as the one that the game facilitates. To continue to facilitate these goals, the therapist can encourage the family to continue to create new questions for the game, or the therapist can provide new questions at various intervals. Second, through the game creation, the family is working together toward a positive goal. They must communicate to reach the goal of a completed game. Each family member will need to take an active role and each will likely need to use many positive communication skills to give their input and get input from others. Should unforeseen problems arise with the rules of the game, these problems can be discussed and a mutually acceptable solution reached by the family, leading to additional opportunities to practice communication and problem-solving.

The therapist should use all stages of the game creation and game play to help the family work on treatment goals. The therapeutic process is the key element in this activity in helping the family to cooperate, communicate, and problem solve.

Modifications can be made to the game rules for each family's situation. For example, a family who is working on the use of consistent discipline with younger children may have a game with statements such as, "You pick up your toys the first time your parents ask. No time out for you! Move ahead two spaces!" The repetition of cards with statements such as these, rather than problem-solving questions, may be especially beneficial for families with young children.

Playing the game at home will encourage the family to continue to share their newfound skills and reinforce continued communication. Additionally, it will encourage generalization of these skills to the home environment.

About The Author

Rebecca Fischer, PhD, received her doctorate degree from the University of Toledo. She has worked with children, adolescents, and families in both inpatient and outpatient settings. She currently works in private practice as a Psychology Postdoctoral Trainee and is working toward psychology licensure in the state of Ohio.

Mapping
Source: Steve Harvey

Goals
- Increase communication about difficult behaviours and parent–child conflict
- Encourage parents and children to use joint problem-solving
- Use play to increase positive interactions
- Develop metaphors to address conflict

Materials
- Sheets of large butcher paper
- Markers or crayons
- Magazines to cut out pictures and other material for collages

Description
This activity can be used with children or adolescents of any age. Parents are included in the role of helpers. The task of drawing a map and adding storytelling can be made more complex for older participants.

The beginning step involves the child/adolescent drawing a map that has an identified starting and ending place on the paper. An initial step to increase the complexity of making the map is for the child to scribble over the paper with his/her eyes closed. The child is then asked to find the beginning and ending places within the scribble and make the pathway(s) of the map pass through the scribble to connect the two positions. The child can be challenged to add several pathways or roads, some of which have maze-like blind endings, to make the path to the end point more difficult to find.

The therapist then reframes the drawing as a map through the problems that the child or family has presented, the beginning point indicating the start of therapy and the end place as a future time when these real problems will be solved. The child is then asked to identify where the problems might be along the pathways and where the child believes he/she is on the road toward the problems being resolved. The parent is then included in these discussions using the map. At this point, the therapist can help the parent and child label the parts of the map that represent the real problems. For example, a specific point of the drawing can be labeled as being "mad land" if a presenting problem includes expressions of anger, while another point can become "nightmare land" and so on.

The basic map activity can then be elaborated by having the child or the child and parent use art expression to extend the basic outline. Each place on the map can be fully developed as well as the problem points. Such elaborations can include using large pieces of paper so that each part of the map can be fully developed (the points, the alternative pathways, etc.) by using various colors. Other media, such as pictures cut out from magazines, can be used to create a collage.

Another very helpful way to develop the map is to add storytelling to the activity. This is a useful way to adapt the activity for families with older children. In this step, the therapist asks the mapmaker to tell a fairytale in which they cast themselves as an animal on a journey. In the tale, the child is asked to identify the most dangerous parts of the map and find an ally. The child (with the parent's help) tells the story of going on the journey as indicated by the map/drawing. The therapist can help the teller use both a storytelling as well as a drawing medium to lead the story into more dramatic episodes. However, the therapist keeps the solution end point somehow within the action. For example, if the child has presented with anxiety, the therapist might have the child choose to tell about an animal finding his way through the caves of fear while the parent becomes an ally who provides guidance and light to the end point of safety.

The parent(s) are invited to participate in the drawing/storytelling section once the child has developed the initial outline of the joint story/map. The parent is coached to help the child find his/her way along the map using the narrative and art production in collaboration with the child. At this stage the therapist helps link the themes and metaphors of the journey to the process of therapy. Most often the parent is cast as the ally in the story.

The story can be extended to an action mode as well in which elements of the map and story can be developed into dramatic activities to be completed in the therapy room. In this part of the activity, the parent is clearly cast as the child's helper to complete the journey through the dangerous problem points along the way. This dramatic adaptation is described in more detail elsewhere (Harvey, 2005).

Discussion

Often when children and adolescents are referred for mental health treatment with their families, they are confused about their emotional life. They may have difficulty verbalizing their feelings and generating play or other expressions that reflect their inner state. In this regard, children and families have little understanding of what mental health intervention is or how to use such intervention to actively address their life problems.

The child–parent activity of mapping and using the map to develop a story as a clear metaphor about the problems that brought them to therapy can address this issue. In this activity, playful creative expression is built from concrete real life issues. The mapping/storytelling has an educational component to it in that children and their parents use the drawing of a map to represent a process of change initially using real life events. Any creative elaborations using the map and storytelling are explained as a way the parent and child can participate in joint problem-solving.

The theoretical background involving metaphor-making with families and how such activities can be more fully developed is presented more fully elsewhere (Harvey, 2003, 2005, 2006).

References

Harvey, S.A. (2003). Dynamic play therapy with an adoptive family struggling with issues of grief, loss, and adjustment. In D. Wiener & L. Oxford (Eds.), *Action therapy with families and groups*. Washington, DC: American Psychological Association Books.

Harvey, S.A. (2005). Stories from the islands: Drama therapy with bullies and their victims. In A.M. Weber & C. Haen (Eds.), *Clinical applications of drama therapy in child and adolescent treatment*. New York: Brunner-Routledge.

Harvey, S.A. (2006). Dynamic play therapy. In C.E. Schaefer & H. Kaduson (Eds.), *Contemporary play therapy*. New York: Guilford.

About The Author

Steve Harvey, PhD, RPT-S, BC-DMT, is a Licensed Psychologist in the United States and is registered as a Psychologist with clinical and educational scopes of practice in New Zealand. He is a Registered Play Therapist Supervisor and a Board Certified Dance Movement Therapist. He is currently the Consultant Psychologist for the Child and Adolescent Mental Health Service for the Taranaki District Health Board in New Plymouth, New Zealand. He helped pioneer the use of Play Therapy approaches with families and has written several professional chapters and articles in the field published in *The International Journal of Play Therapy, Contemporary Play Therapy, Play Diagnosis and Assessment*, and *Blending Play Therapy with Cognitive Behavioral Therapy: Evidence-Based and other Effective Treatment Techniques*. He has presented and consulted extensively internationally on topics related to the use of family play in the evaluation and treatment of attachment and psychological trauma in children.

Messages in Art
Source: Lori Gill

Goals
- Increase open communication in the family
- Implement new methods of effective communication between family members
- Share feelings that underlie conflict within the family

Materials
- Paper
- Assorted drawing mediums, such as markers, crayons, pastels, charcoal, paint, etc.
- Collage materials
- Glue and tape
- Scissors
- Art and other materials that could be used to symbolize different emotions, such as cotton balls, wire, bubble wrap, feathers, buttons, rocks, pipe cleaners, string, Popsicle sticks, tissue paper, felt, straws, Band-Aids, stickers, etc.

Description
Introduce the activity by explaining that sometimes it can be difficult to verbally express thoughts and feelings. Expressions through art can be a helpful way to release and communicate feelings. Ask each person to "choose a family member with whom you would like to communicate or share a message. Take a few minutes to think about what that message might be."

Introduce a visualization exercise to help the clients think metaphorically. For example, "Close your eyes and think about the feeling of anger. If anger had a tactile feeling (a touch), what would it be? Would it be soft like a pom-pom or prickly like wire? What would the structure be like – heavy and solid like a rock, or light and flimsy like a feather? If you could visually see the anger, what do you think it would look like? Would it have a particular color, shape, or size?" This serves as a primer to help the family visualize their emotions in a sensory manner.

Next, have the members use the art supplies provided to create their message. Once completed, ask members to explain their messages and the meaning of the materials they selected. They can share their messages with the person it is intended for either on their own or with the support of the therapist.

Process the activity by asking the following questions:

1. What was it like to communicate your message through art?
2. How did you feel during the message creation and message delivery part of this activity?

3. How did it feel to receive the message from your family member?
4. What did you learn through this activity about ways to communicate with your family about your thoughts and feelings?

Discussion

Many difficulties in family relationships result from a lack of communication. Feelings that are left unexpressed can be harmful to the individual as well as to others involved. This activity facilitates the identification and release of emotions through an arts medium. Communicating through art can be less threatening and allows family members to share feelings at a pace that is more comfortable.

Families who do not communicate well can find an alternative way to do so through this expressive activity. The art creation often reveals important issues that can be both seen and discussed. As Klorer (2000) suggests, "Art can be a very powerful tool, eliciting a multitude of repressed or unconscious feelings."

Reference

Klorer, P.G. (2000). *Expressive therapy with troubled children*. New York: Jason Aronson.

About The Author

Lori Gill, BA (SDS), CYW, is a Certified Counselor and Trauma Specialist who has been working with children, youth, and their families since 1999. She has a multi-disciplinary degree in Social Development Studies (Social Work, Psychology, and Sociology); diplomas in Social Work and Child and Youth Work; and certificates in Counseling Skills for Human Services and Criminal Psychology. She is currently completing her master's degree in Counseling Psychology. She has experience working within various professional organizations that specialize in child and youth counseling. She maintains a private practice, offering art and play-focused counseling. In addition to her full-time career as a Certified Counselor, she also presents at public speaking events and workshops and teaches at a local college.

Modified Scribble
Source: Trudy Post Sprunk

Goals
- Increase the family's ability to work toward a goal as a team
- Increase family cohesion
- Increase the frequency of pleasurable exchanges between family members
- Assess family relationships and dynamics

Materials
- White poster board
- Washable markers, a different color for each participant
- Blindfold or pillowcase to be used as a blindfold (optional)

Advance Preparation
Place the poster board on a flat, smooth space such as a table or floor. Ensure all family members can easily reach and see the poster board.

Description
Each family member chooses a different color marker.

The first participant closes his/her eyes and creates a scribble for three seconds (a blindfold may be helpful for some participants).

The second participant, using another color marker, starts his/her scribble where the first scribble ended (again with eyes closed or blindfolded). It is important to take turns and wait patiently for a turn.

This process continues until each family member has created three scribbles.

Upon completion, the entire family participates as a "team" looking for pictures that were created by their scribbles. During this time the therapist writes the list of words the family uses to describe the pictures the family finds in their joint scribble picture.

Next, ask the family to create a story using this list of words. Ask that the story have a beginning, middle, and end. After the story is completed, ask the family to give it a title.

The following tips and probes can be helpful when processing the activity:

1. How did you feel during the scribble part of the activity?
2. What was it like when you tried to present your ideas?

3. What was it like to work together as a family to create the story?
4. How is the story similar and different to your own lives?

Discussion

Scribbling with one's eyes closed decreases opportunities for competition, perfection, and the ability to control one another. Coloring blindfolded adds an element of play to the activity, and play tends to decrease defensiveness.

Creating a story (using the words that describe the objects seen in the scribble creation) is most likely a new experience, which may create feelings of vulnerability in family members. During this time, the therapist can observe how the family copes with stress, that is, do they support each other? Does one take control? Does one distract the other? Was one family member ignored? Did allies join forces? These observations and any others could be processed during the session.

D.W. Winnicott developed the Squiggle Technique for use with families in 1971. She asks the child to select a favorite squiggle and create a story about it. This technique provides a valuable engagement and assessment tool. Similarly, the Modified Scribble can be used to engage family members and assess family dynamics.

Narrative stories serve as a verbal projective technique in which the clients tell about their inner world through story-making. White (2005) wrote that narrative therapy is the client's expressions of their experiences. When a family hears their co-created story, they may choose to create changes in the future.

References

Winnicott, D.W. (1971). *Therapeutic consultations in child psychiatry*. New York: Basic Books.

White, M. (2005). *An outline of narrative therapy*. Available at www.massey.ac.nz.

About The Author

Trudy Post Sprunk, LMFT-S, LPC-S, RPT-S, CPT-S, is a Licensed Marriage and Family Therapist and Supervisor who has been practicing psychotherapy since 1971. She has presented at international, national, and local conferences and has been interviewed on radio and television. She is certified as an EMDR Specialist and is a Registered Play Therapist Supervisor. She is past-president of the Association for Play Therapy and president and co-founder of the Georgia Association for Play Therapy.

Mr. Opposite Man/Miss Opposite Lady
Source: Steve Harvey

Goals
- Reduce the child's oppositional behavior
- Increase communication about difficult behaviours and parent–child conflict
- Develop an activity to address ongoing negative interactions more productively

Materials
- Large piece of paper
- Tape
- Marker
- Play props that can encourage imagination in several ways (e.g., large scarves, stretchy bands, costume hats, large pillows)

Advance Preparation
Tape the paper to the wall and use it to create a score sheet.

Description
This activity is designed for children in their mid-primary years whose oppositional behaviours cause difficulties with their parents. At least initially, the game is played by one parent and the child in a dyad. However, other family members can take on roles such as Scorekeeper or Judge. The activity is presented in a competitive format in which the parent and child are trying to win by earning more points.

The roles for this game are verbally presented to the family and cast prior to start. The roles include:

1. Mr. Opposite Man (for boys) or Miss Opposite Lady (for girls)
2. Challenger
3. Score Keeper
4. Judge
5. Game Master (The therapist)

The game starts as the child takes on the role of Mr. Opposite Man (or Miss Opposite Lady) and the parent takes on the role of Challenger. The competition proceeds as the parent presents the child with a command such as "stand up." The child responds by trying to perform an action that is the opposite of what is being asked. For example, the child might sit down.

If the Judge agrees that the child has performed the opposite of the command, the child earns a point. However, the parent earns a point if the child is judged to complete an action that has the intention of the command. In this case, the parent would get the point if the child actually did stand up.

The roles are reversed after a pre-determined number of turns (e.g., five turns). The number can vary to increase the game's complexity. The Score Keeper keeps track of each of the players winning points using the scoreboard taped to the wall.

As the players learn to play the game with more confidence, the therapist, as the Game Master, encourages the players to use more complexity and creativity in their challenges as well as their responses. For example, challenges can include multiple requests such as "walk backward, screaming, with your eyes closed." An opposite response to this could be running forward through the room, miming the scream, while keeping eyes open. The therapist is free to coach the parent and the child to express actions creatively.

As the players become still more practiced, the game's complexity can be increased even more by adding challenges that have no clear opposite response and the Judge is faced with making more subjective choices about who the winner is.

Complexity can be added with the use of props. For example, the challenger might ask Mr. Opposite Man to hide in the pillows or become a wizard. These challenges offer a more dramatic form of action such that the opposite response would have to involve using the props to enact "not hiding" – perhaps by building a house with the pillows to come out of or using the scarves to become a witch rather than a wizard.

Discussion

Parents and children can develop communication patterns that decrease their ability to solve their emotionally related problems. Such patterns usually include negative comments and reactions to each other. In this situation, both the parent as well as the child become responsive to each other's expressed frustration and anger rather than engage in any reasonable problem-solving or understanding of the conflict. This can be particularly true when parents confront their child's opposition. Unfortunately, in these situations, the parent and child create a patterned way of interacting that produces negative feelings that prevent more productive communications from occurring. In short, no one "wins" and each member of the interaction is left feeling helpless. Unfortunately, such interactions are often repeated and can affect the family in a negative way.

This game is set up to make use of these repeated patterns by asking that both parent and child turn their interactions into a playful game. The competitive yet playful element is used to produce more positive feelings between the parent and the child.

The resulting game performances can lead to an experience of shared playfulness and can be very helpful in changing the way a child's opposition has been approached in the family. This game is meant to be used within a wider family intervention. Such interventions have been presented more fully elsewhere (Harvey 2003, 2006).

References
Harvey, S.A. (2003). Dynamic play therapy with an adoptive family struggling with issues of grief, loss, and adjustment. In D. Wiener & L. Oxford (Eds.), *Action therapy with families and groups*. Washington, DC: American Psychological Association Books.

Harvey, S.A. (2006). Dynamic play therapy. In C.E. Schaefer & H. Kaduson (Eds.), *Contemporary play therapy*. New York: Guilford.

About The Author
Steve Harvey, PhD, RPT-S, BC-DMT, is a Licensed Psychologist in the United States and is registered as a Psychologist with clinical and educational scopes of practice in New Zealand. He is a Registered Play Therapist Supervisor and a Board Certified Dance Movement Therapist. He is currently the Consultant Psychologist for the Child and Adolescent Mental Health Service for the Taranaki District Health Board in New Plymouth, New Zealand. He helped pioneer the use of Play Therapy approaches with families and has written several professional chapters and articles in the field published in *The International Journal of Play Therapy, Contemporary Play Therapy, Play Diagnosis and Assessment*, and *Blending Play Therapy with Cognitive Behavioral Therapy: Evidence-Based and other Effective Treatment Techniques*. He has presented and consulted extensively internationally on topics related to the use of family play in the evaluation and treatment of attachment and psychological trauma in children.

My Story
Sources: Rajeswari Natrajan-Tyagi and Nilufer Kafescioglu

Goals
- Increase the rate of pleasurable exchanges between family members through the process of co-creating stories
- Parents to provide their child with positive, nurturing messages

Materials
- Folders
- Labels
- Colored paper
- Markers
- Decorative craft items
- Hole punching machine
- Story outline (included)

Description
Note: This activity is for parents and one child.

Introduce the activity by stating to the child, "Do you like stories? Today you are going to write a story about yourself and your family."

Provide the child with the supplies needed to create his/her story and allow him/her to select one folder, a label, and several pieces of colored paper. Parents can use the suggested story outline to guide their child in creating his/her story. Encourage parents to co-create the stories with their child and suggest alternative interpretations to any narrative that may be disempowering the child. For example, if the child describes a bad day he/she had as he/she was teased by friends for falling off the swing, the parent can try to strengthen an alternative plot where the child handled the teasing in an appropriate way. Parents can also be encouraged to identify and label their child's feelings and emotions and validate them. This in turn can help the child cope with problems and empower him/her to use alternative problem-solving skills.

During this activity, the therapist can observe how parents interact with their child and identify problematic interaction patterns. The therapist can also prompt the parents to provide positive, nurturing messages to their child during the story-creation phase of the activity.

Depending on the developmental stage of the child, parents can help their child write the story on colored paper and pick out a name for the story. Encourage parents to let their child decorate and illustrate the pages that are finished. These pages can then be filed in the folder. Explain to the family that this storybook can be a never-ending storybook and new chapters can be added continuously.

It is important to stress to the parents that the activity is designed to encourage positive parent–child interaction and that their interaction is more important than completing the task of creating the folder.

Encourage parents to make it a ritual to read this story aloud to their child periodically.

Discussion

Stories shape the meaning of people's lives (Freeman, Epston, & Lobovits, 1997). The literature suggests that stories about oneself and about the family boost the parent–child connection and children's self-esteem (Dilallo, 2006; Shellenbarger, 2005). This activity provides an opportunity for parents and children to co-construct a story about the child and his/her family. Through this process, the parent–child relationship is enhanced. Additionally, parents can suggest alternative plots to their children that can empower them and give a different perspective if their childrens' stories about themselves are problem-saturated (Freeman, Epston, & Lobovits, 1997).

References

Dilallo, M.E. (2006). The family represented: Mother-and-father-child co-constructed narratives about families. Dissertation Abstracts International, 66, 10-B.

Freeman, J., Epston, D., & Lobovits, D. (1997). *Playful approaches to serious problems*. New York: W.W. Norton.

Schellenbarger, S. (2005). The power of myth: The benefits of sharing family stories of hard times. *Wall Street Journal*.

About The Authors

Rajeswari Natrajan-Tyagi, PhD, LMFT, is an Assistant Professor in the Marriage and Family Therapy Program at Alliant International University in Irvine, California. She has her master's degree in Social Work from Madras School of Social Work in Chennai, India, and a master's and doctoral degree in Marriage and Family Therapy from Purdue University, Indiana. Her clinical interests are working with culturally diverse populations and with children. Her research interests are in the areas of immigration, cross-cultural training, systemic training, self-of-therapist issues, cultural competency, and qualitative process research methodologies. She has authored several publications and has presented at local, national, and international conferences.

Nilufer Kafescioglu, PhD, is an Assistant Professor of Psychology at Dogus University in Istanbul, Turkey. She received her bachelor degree in Psychology at Ege University in Turkey, her master's degree in Clinical Psychology at the University of Indianapolis, and her doctoral degree in Marriage and Family Therapy at Purdue University, Indiana. She has been providing psychotherapy to children, families, and couples in diverse settings. She has authored publications on topics such as violence prevention programs, cross-cultural research on attachment theory, multicultural supervision, and couples coping with chronic illness. She has presented at numerous local, national, and international conferences.

My Story
Sample Outline

Chapter 1: About Me
1. My name and age:
2. What I look like:
3. What I like to do the most:
4. Some of my favorite foods:
5. To fall asleep I like to...
6. When I feel bad I like to...
7. I am especially good at...
8. What Mom/Dad like best about me:

Chapter 2: My Family
1. People in my family:
2. When I am with Mom I like to...
3. When I am with Dad I like to...
4. With my brothers and sisters I like to...
5. With my grandparents I like to...
6. My best times with my family have been when we...

Chapter 3: The Day I Was Born
1. Date, time, and place I was born:
2. How Mom/Dad felt when they held me for the very first time:
3. How I got my name:

Chapter 4: When I was a Baby
1. What I was like as a baby:
2. First words:
3. Foods I loved, foods I hated:
4. Some of Mom and Dad's favorite memories of me as a baby:

Chapter 5: My Favorite Day Ever
Chapter 6: One of My Worst Days Ever
Chapter 7: Our Best Time as a Family
Chapter 8: My Proudest Moment

© Rajeswari Natrajan-Tyagi and Nilufer Kafescioglu

Nighttime Protection Potion
Source: Jennifer Olmstead

Goals
- Establish a nurturing interaction between child and parent at bedtime
- Implement a concrete tool to cope with sleep difficulties and nightmares
- Increase feelings of safety and security

Materials
- Colored paper
- Marker
- Small transparent plastic container with lid or small transparent spray bottle
- Cinnamon
- Clove
- Vanilla extract
- Multi-colored glitter
- Water

Advance Preparation
Copy the poem below onto colored paper:

> *A good night's sleep bring to me,*
> *Happy dreams may I see.*
> *From all that darkness brings to scare,*
> *Keep me safe and in your care.*

Description
Begin by facilitating a discussion about the sleep difficulties and nightmares the child is experiencing. Explain that it is normal for everyone to have bad dreams. Next, explain to the parents and the child that they are going to work together to create a Nighttime Protection Potion that the child will put beside his/her bed to help scare away bad dreams.

Have the parents and the child add the ingredients below to a plastic container. As each item is added to the container, explain what each represents:

Cinnamon – To bring luck
Clove – To relax and soothe
Vanilla extract – To bring sweet dreams
Red – To help "stop" the bad dreams
Pink – To surround you with love
Blue – To bring calm and happiness
Green – To keep you strong and healthy
Gold – To bring spiritual and/or cultural protection
Water – To cleanse and wash away the "scary"

Once all the items are mixed, have the parent read the poem to the child.

An alternative to mixing the ingredients in a plastic container is to mix them in a small spray bottle. The parent and child can "spray" the bedtime area to add a "layer of protection." (Note: Ensure that the nozzle is on "spray" to prevent any glitter from being sprayed.)

The family can establish a bedtime ritual that involves several steps. For example, (1) the child shakes the potion while thinking of a sweet dream; (2) the parent reads the poem to the child; (3) hugs and kisses are exchanged. The family can modify this bedtime ritual as desired.

The following questions guide the processing component of this intervention:

1. How did you feel while you were working together to create the Nighttime Protection Potion?
2. In what ways can this potion be helpful?
3. Why is it important to establish a bedtime ritual?
4. (To parents) Why is it important for you to be a part of the bedtime ritual?

Discussion

Many children experience sleep difficulties as a result of nightmares, separation anxiety, or developmentally appropriate fears. This nighttime potion allows for a concrete and tactile portrayal of protection. It also gives the child a sense of control because it allows him/her to use the potion whenever he/she feels the need.

A more nurturing relationship between parent and child is established by having them create the potion together, and then having the parent read the poem to the child. Creating a consistent routine at bedtime is an additional element that brings the child a sense of comfort.

About The Author

Jennifer Olmstead, LMSW, RPT, C-ACYFSW, CAAC, is a Licensed Social Worker, Registered Play Therapist, Certified Advanced Child, Youth and Family Social Worker and Certified Advanced Addiction Counselor in Sault Ste. Marie, Michigan. She has worked in the field of human services since 1994 and is currently the clinical supervisor for Behavioral Health Services with the Sault Ste. Marie Tribe of Chippewa Indians. She has worked within the domestic violence, court, child welfare, community mental health, and health care systems.

© Jennifer Olmstead

Piece of the Pie
Source: Jennifer Olmstead

Goals
- Increase self-awareness of how much time is devoted to different areas in life
- Identify priorities in life and discuss how to make adjustments so more time is spent doing what is important
- Increase open communication among family members
- Increase family cohesion

Materials
- 4 paper plates for each participant
- Paper
- Writing materials
- Scissors
- Tape or glue

Description
Explain how life is busy because it is full of commitments, tasks, responsibilities, and so on. How do we "slice this out"? Provide each family member with a sheet of paper and a pen or pencil, and have them list on the sheet of paper all the different things that they spend their time doing (e.g., school or job, homework, enjoyable time with family members, arguing with family members, spending time with friends, cooking, chores, errands, exercising, eating, sleeping, arguing, nagging, listening to music, watching television, playing on the computer, extracurricular activities or hobbies, bathing and personal care, etc.). Then have the members use one of the paper plates to "cut their pie pieces" into sizes that represent how much time they actually spend (not what they wish they would spend) on each of the areas they listed. For example, "school" may be a very large piece, while "spending time with Mom" is a very small piece. On each pie piece that is cut out, have them identify which area it represents.

Once all the pieces are cut out, have them glue (or tape) their pie pieces onto another paper plate. As they place each piece, talk and process each one.

Then ask them, "If you could change your pie pieces to be the shapes you would like them to be, what would they look like?" Have them repeat the exercise with them cutting out the pie pieces to be the shapes they would like them to be. For example, a child may reduce their "homework" pie piece but increase the piece of "time spent with Mom."

Explore ways that the family could accomplish the changes. This could include using coping skills to reduce their time in negative activities (family arguments) and increase their time in positive activities (exercise, quality family time, etc.).

Discuss areas that are important, for example school and homework, and some of the reasons these areas are important, and generate ideas for "balancing" responsibilities with fun.

The following questions can guide the discussion:

1. What piece of the pie is most important to you?
2. What priorities do you have in common with one another?
3. What ideas do you have for finding more time to do the things that are important to you?
4. If there are disagreements about how to divide your time, how can you negotiate so everybody's needs are met?

Discussion

This activity helps participants to visually see how much time they are spending on different areas, how they wish their pie pieces could look, and, most importantly, learning ways that they can change their pie pieces. This is powerful for parents because it allows them to better understand their child's needs while at the same time assessing their own. The therapist can help family members discuss ways to increase quality family time, which leads to enhanced cohesion.

This activity can help clients to categorize their responsibilities, develop time management skills, and negotiate family disagreements.

About The Author

Jennifer Olmstead, LMSW, RPT, C-ACYFSW, CAAC, is a Licensed Social Worker, Registered Play Therapist, Certified Advanced Child, Youth and Family Social Worker and Certified Advanced Addiction Counselor in Sault Ste. Marie, Michigan. She has worked in the field of human services since 1994 and is currently the clinical supervisor for Behavioral Health Services with the Sault Ste. Marie Tribe of Chippewa Indians. She has worked within the domestic violence, court, child welfare, community mental health, and health care systems.

Pulled From a Hat
Source: Karen Freud

Goals
- Increase positive interaction within the family
- Increase cohesion among family members
- Implement new methods of effective communication between family members

Materials
- Drawing Directives (included)
- Paper or 10-15 index cards
- Scissors
- A hat (or other container large enough to hold the index cards)
- Large sheet of white paper
- Drawing materials such as markers or colored pencils

Advance Preparation
Copy the Drawing Directives and cut out each one, or copy each directive onto a separate index card. Place the directives in a hat.

Arrange a flat space for the large sheet of paper so that each person has easy access. Arrange the drawing materials near the flat surface so all family members can easily reach them.

Description
Tell the family that they are going to work together to make one picture according to specific instructions that they will pick out of a hat.

The family members sit together around the sheet of paper. One at a time, the members choose one index card from the hat and follow the directive. They may use any color they choose and they may use any part of the paper. When done, the member passes the hat to the person sitting to his/her left.

This continues until the family unanimously agrees that the drawing is complete. Members are asked if they would like to add anything to their drawing such as more lines, shapes, color, or images. Encourage the participants to decide together.

The family is then asked to identify the images in their drawing and to tell a story together about their drawing. The story must have a beginning, a middle, and an end, and each family member must contribute to the story.

Then lead the family in a discussion about the drawing. Discussion questions might include:

211

1. Was it easy or difficult to follow the instructions?
2. Was it easy or difficult to wait for your turn?
3. What is your favorite part of the story?
4. What was it like to work together as a family on the drawing and the story?

In addition to asking the above questions, it is important to address any issues that may have arisen during the process. For example, the family might have experienced a situation in which a parent or sibling drew on an area that another child had wanted to use. Or some family members might have taken more time than others to finish their turn, causing the others to feel impatient. The parents may have been tempted to make a decision for their child rather than allowing the child to make an independent choice about how to follow the directive.

Discussion

This activity enhances positive behavior within the family such as following rules, taking turns, and working together toward a common task. It also helps family members gain insight into how their choices and behaviors affect others, such as whether or not to follow the rules. The activity provides everyone in the family with the opportunity to exercise independent decision-making and emphasizes how each person's role is important. Discussions about the drawing, such as deciding when it is complete and/or telling a story about their drawing, can help the family develop their communication skills.

There are many benefits to using art in family therapy sessions. As Malchiodi (2005) writes, "Art therapy provides the client with an opportunity to externalize his or her thoughts and feelings through visual images. Making an image, whether a drawing, a painting, or a sculpture, is an experience of visual thinking and can be an additional source of information for both client and therapist...Art expression offers a tangible and lasting product that provides a valuable component to therapy...a drawing or painting can be looked at, referred to, and talked about immediately or in a later session."

Reference
Malchiodi, C.A. (2005). *Expressive therapies*. New York: Guilford.

About The Author
Karen Freud, BA, A.T., received her training at the Toronto Art Therapy Institute. She is based in Toronto and currently conducts individual and group art therapy sessions and workshops for various community organizations. Her experience includes working with children and adults, and she has worked in a variety of settings that include mental health agencies, long-term care facilities, and private practice.

© Karen Freud

Pulled From a Hat
Drawing Directives

Draw a straight line

Draw three dots

Draw a circle

Draw a square

Draw a squiggle

Draw a box

Draw a number

Draw an animal

Draw a person

Draw a tree

Draw a house

Draw a road

Draw water

Draw a mountain

Puppet Movie
Source: Amber L. Brewer

Goals
- Educate family members about interactional cycles
- Identify feelings underlying behaviors in problematic cycles
- Increase open communication about feelings
- Learn, practice, and implement conflict resolution skills
- Increase positive interaction between family members

Materials
- Puppets (ready-made or create one using paper lunch sacks and markers)
- Feelings chart (ready-made or create one)
- Remote control (ready-made or create one with cardboard and markers)
- Movie Map Worksheet (included)

Description
This activity is designed for parent-child or sibling dyads who experience ongoing conflict. The technique is used after the dyad expresses a desire to decrease its quarrelling.

Ask the two family members to pretend that they have been hired to make a puppet movie of their life. Help them think of a name for this movie. Then, invite the members to choose a puppet to play their part in the movie. If puppets are not available, members can make their own puppets out of paper lunch sacks and markers. Bring a remote control from home or create one out of cardboard and markers. Explain that the remote control will be used to play, pause, rewind, or fast-forward through the movie.

Next, inform the family members that they will use the puppets to act out two scenes from the movie. In the first scene, they will depict a time when they were getting along well. The second scene will portray a time they were NOT getting along. Give the family members a few minutes to decide which events they will act out.

"Play" Scene 1
Press "play" on the remote control to start Scene 1. Use verbal cues, hand motions, or sound effects to convey which buttons are being pressed. After the scene has played out, have the clients point to the emotion pictures on a feelings chart that best show how they felt during the event. Compliment the puppets on their use of positive social skills in this scene.

"Play" Scene 2
Next, press "play" (using the appropriate verbal cues) and watch the second scene.

If family members are reluctant to act out the scene, have them switch roles and play the part of the other person. This can decrease resistance and offer insights into clients' perceptions of the other family members.

Use the Worksheet to Process Scene 2

Show the Movie Map Worksheet to the clients. Write their names on the lines for Person A and Person B.

Explain that families often behave in patterns, called cycles, which are repeated over and over. It may be helpful to talk about the water cycle (evaporation, condensation, precipitation) as an example of what a cycle is. In a person-to-person cycle, both people influence each other's feelings and behavior. Tell the clients you would like to "re-play" the second scene to help them understand their cycle when they argue.

"Rewind" the movie to the beginning of Scene 2. Ask the members to use the feelings chart to indicate what emotions they had just before the argument started. Discuss why they felt these particular feelings.

Press "play" and watch the second scene again until the first person's behavior in the sequence is completed (e.g., Person A makes a request of Person B). "Pause" the scene immediately after this behavior. Discuss what behavior this puppet showed and write it down after the "B" in the first box of the Worksheet under Person A.

Ask the puppet playing Person A what led him/her to do this behavior (i.e., what was he/she trying to accomplish?). Write down Person A's thoughts and feelings in the first box. Then, ask Person B's puppet to use the feelings chart to identify his/her emotional reaction to Person A's behaviors. Ask the puppet why he/she felt these particular feelings. Write down Person B's thoughts and feelings on the Worksheet.

Press "play" again to continue the scene. "Pause" the scene directly after watching Person B's behavioral response to Person A's actions (e.g., Person B denies Person A's request). Write the behavior on the worksheet. Ask Person B's puppet what he/she was trying to accomplish through the behavior. Then ask Person A's puppet how he/she felt in response to Person B's behavior.

Repeat this pattern of questioning until Scene 2 ends. "Pause" the movie after each behavioral exchange and document the clients' thoughts, feelings, and behaviors as indicated on the Worksheet. More than one copy of the Worksheet may be needed to document the full sequence.

Process the End Result

When the "re-play" of Scene 2 is completed, ask the members' puppets how they felt after the argument ended. Then, ask the members what they think about how the puppets handled the conflict and what it was like for them to act out the scene with the puppets. Ask whether (and how) they wished the scene had gone differently.

Identify the Cycle

Review the Movie Map Worksheet with the clients. Discuss which of their behaviors in Scene 2 are typically repeated in arguments about other topics (e.g., homework, chores, shopping). Write down the typical behaviors on the back of the Worksheet in a cycle diagram (i.e., circle with arrows). Explain that this pattern is their cycle.

Explore Alternative Responses

Discuss the meaning of compromise. Help members identify the steps people use to "work out" a compromise. Ask how the puppets could have used these steps to resolve their differences in Scene 2.

Look over the cycle diagram again and ask members to identify places in the cycle that are good for compromising. Talk about key phrases for starting the compromise process, such as "Let's work something out." It may be helpful to ask when it is time to take a break or have a cool-off period. Discuss what an appropriate break would "look like" and how they could initiate it.

Role Play a New Ending

Invite the family members to make a new movie, called "What If...," in which the puppet characters act out a happier ending to the story.

Process the Activity

Discuss the members' experiences of what it was like to do different parts of the activity (i.e., using puppets to make the movie, role-playing a new ending). Explore how family members felt during the activity, whether they were surprised by anything, and what seemed most helpful.

Discussion

The Family Puppet Movie is generally appropriate for children aged eight and up as it requires the ability to communicate verbally, sustain attention, and think logically. Because the pacing may vary with each family, the technique may take more than one session to complete.

This activity incorporates several developmentally sensitive components, including puppets, role-play, and familiar life experiences, to help children learn abstract psychological concepts such as interactional cycles and mutual problem-solving. Puppets are useful tools in family therapy because they help diffuse anxiety, increase child engagement, and symbolically communicate members' views of themselves and others. The role-playing provides concrete interactional material that can be referred to later for assessment and intervention (Gil, 1994; Gitlin-Weiner, Sandgrund, & Schaefer, 2000).

The Family Puppet Movie was designed with a cognitive-behavioral and systems theory framework in mind. However, this protocol can be used within a variety of family therapy models because many such models are based on the concept of interactional cycles. This activity helps family members understand the connection between their thoughts, feelings, and behaviors, as well as the effect of their behavior on others. Finally, the Movie Map helps members identify interactional crossroads that can move them away from relationally damaging exchanges.

References

Gil, E. (1994). *Play in family therapy.* New York: Guilford.

Gitlin-Weiner, K., Sandgrund, A., & Schaefer, C. (2000). *Play diagnosis and assessment* (2nd ed). New York: John Wiley & Sons.

About The Author

Amber L. Brewer, PhD-ABD, LMFT, provides therapy at a counseling agency in Utah. She specializes in integrating play therapy techniques into family therapy to treat child-focused problems and has presented on the subject at multiple national conferences. Her authorship includes published articles and a book review on such topics as attachment and therapy alliance, bereavement, and divorce.

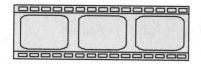

Puppet Movie
Movie Map

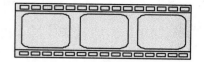

Person A   **Person B**

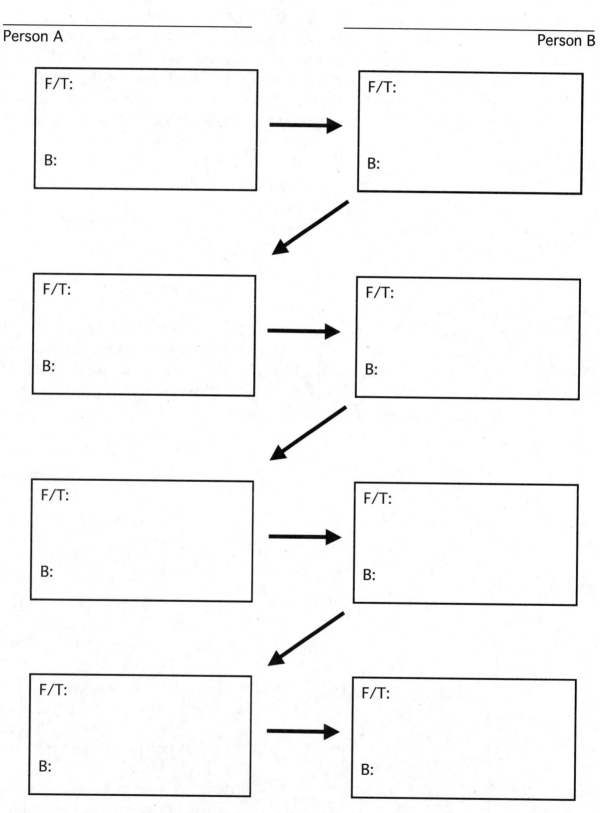

NOTE: F = Feelings   T = Thoughts   B=Behaviors

Red Light, Green Light...A New Light
Source: Angela Siu

Goals
- Increase feelings vocabulary
- Increase awareness of visual cues in relation to expression of feelings
- Increase open communication in the family
- Increase cohesion among family members

Materials
- Masking tape

Advance Preparation
A large space is needed for this activity. Create a starting line at one end of the room by marking a line on the floor with masking tape (about 20 feet away from the stop light). Consider creating two starting lines: one that is closer to the stop light for the children, and one that is farther back for the parents.

Description
The present intervention is a modified version of the traditional game "Red Light, Green Light." The therapist provides an explanation of the game as follows:

The therapist plays the "stop light" and the family members try to touch his or her back. The family members take their positions at their starting lines. The stop light (therapist) faces away from the family members and says "green light." At this point, the family members have to move toward the stoplight. At any point, the stop light may say "red light!" and turn around to face the family members. If any of the family members are caught moving after this has occurred, they are out. Play resumes when the stop light turns back around and says "green light." The stop light wins if all the family members are out before anyone is able to touch him/her. Otherwise, the first player to touch the stop light wins the game and earns the right to be the stop light for the next round of the game. Players are cautioned not to run or walk too fast because, when the stop light says red light, it will be difficult to stop.

A modified version is then played as follows: The therapist shouts out a "feeling" word when he/she faces away from the family. The members must demonstrate nonverbally (with facial expressions and body gestures) the meaning of these words. For example, when the word "happy" is called out, the members are expected to demonstrate actions such as showing a smiling face, arms in the air, and so on. After counting from one to three, the therapist turns around facing the family. He/she will then comment on the gestures each one is showing. Each family member can then tell of a time when they experienced that particular feeling. Any player who does not demonstrate or talk about the given feeling is sent back to the starting point. The game continues with the family members walking closer and closer to the therapist. The winner is the first person who reaches the therapist and touches his/her back.

This activity can be further elaborated to incorporate a more interactive element. For example, when the therapist turns to face the members, they are expected to demonstrate, in pairs, certain kinds of feelings. For example, hugging to illustrate a "loving family," or staring angrily at each other to show an "angry family." Ways of coping with emotions can be discussed.

After several rounds of the game have been played, process the activity by asking questions such as:

1. What did you enjoy most about the game?
2. Which feeling was the hardest to demonstrate or talk about?
3. What was it like to play a game together as a family?
4. What else can you do together as a family that would be enjoyable for everyone?
5. How was the interaction with your family just now different from how you relate with your family members at home? Why?
6. What were some special things you noticed about your family members while you were playing the game?

Discussion

Difficulties in emotional expression may be a driving force for families entering therapy. For instance, families often attend therapy to deal with a child's oppositional behavior. The child's negative behavior may be related to his/her having difficulty with verbal expression. Family therapy can help the child and the parents to express feelings openly and directly. This modified version of "Red Light, Green Light" facilitates the healthy expression of feelings.

The game encourages playful interaction among family members. Through the use of game play, the family is provided with an opportunity to "laugh and enjoy time together. Generating this laughter may prove to be the most therapeutic aspect of our work with families" (Revell, 1997).

The game can also be used as an assessment tool to evaluate the family's ability to allow emotional expression as well as their capacity to enjoy playing together.

Reference
Revell, B. (1997). Using play and art therapy to work with families. In B. Bedard-Bidwell (Ed.), *Hand in hand: A practical application of art and play therapy*. London, ON: Thames River Publishing.

About The Author

Angela Siu, PhD, RegPsychol. (Clin.), CPsyAssoc, CPT, CTT, has experience conducting assessments of and counseling for children and families in Hong Kong and Canada. She is currently working as an Assistant Professor in the Department of Educational Psychology at the Chinese University of Hong Kong. Her research areas include children with special needs, social and emotional needs among children, and creative arts therapies.

© Angela Siu

Royal Family
Source: Angela M. Cavett

Goals
- Establish an appropriate parent–child hierarchy with the parent fulfilling the leadership role
- Define the specifics about what needs to change in the child's behavior
- Encourage parents to establish consistent house rules and regulations
- Reduce the children's behavioral problems
- Increase the rate of positive verbal comments and pleasurable exchanges between family members

Materials
- A template of a crown (purchased or made) to make a king's crown, a queen's crown, a princess's crown, a prince's crown
- Paper
- Scissors
- Crayons, markers, or colored pencils
- Dress-up clothes that include royal robes, staffs, or scepters (optional)
- Decorative jewels or stickers

Advance Preparation
Purchase or create a template of a crown, and make a crown for each family member.

Description
The child and parents are asked to identify the Queen and King (or other parent constellation that represents the child's family) and each is given a crown to design. Each Princess or Prince is then identified and given a crown to design as well. The royal family members are crowned. It is important to process why it is necessary for the parents to be the most powerful members of the royalty. That is, in order for the child to be a Princess or Prince, his/her parents must be the King and Queen. The royal family is then asked to identify behaviors or styles of interaction that befit their royal status. For example, a "good" King or Queen sets appropriate laws of the land (rules), enforces the rules, and administers fair consequences or punishments. A "good" Prince or Princess is respectful of the King and Queen and abides by their rules.

The parents, child, and therapist then discuss the behaviors of each family member that show appropriate and inappropriate royal behavior. The therapist can ask questions to facilitate this discussion, for example:

1. Are the King and Queen nice or mean most of the time?
2. Are the King and Queen calm most of the time or do they yell a lot?
3. Do the King and Queen set and enforce appropriate laws of the land (rules)?
4. Do the King and Queen administer fair consequences or punishments?
5. Do the Prince and Princess listen to the King and Queen?
6. Do the Prince and Princess follow the rules? If not, which rules do they most often disobey?

Following this discussion, three behavioral problems that relate to the inappropriate roles and behaviors in the family are identified. Treatment goals are then defined that are based on the behavioral problems. (The therapist should ensure that the treatment goals identify areas of change for both the parents and the children.) The family and therapist discuss how the behavior that is desired is consistent with being King, Queen, Prince, or Princess. The goals are written on a "royal scroll" that the family takes home to guide interventions and to document progress toward reaching these goals. For example, a Prince listens to and complies with parental commands, which are, after all, "royal commands" from the King and Queen.

The family chooses one goal written on the royal scroll to work on that week (if appropriate, the therapist can guide the family in identifying one goal for the parents and one for the child).

It is helpful to teach parents how to focus on and attend to their children's positive behaviors and how to appropriately praise their children.

Circles are lightly drawn on the crown to be filled in with jewels as the child meets his/her goals. Each week the child and parent discuss whether or not the target goals were met and whether or not to add "jewels" to the crown. The family and therapist check-in on the royalty from week to week. Behavior is discussed within the metaphor of the royal family and the child and parents are encouraged to continue learning how to practice royal behavior.

The therapist is identified as the "Royal Advisor" who is in charge of helping the child and parents to make the behavioral changes.

Discussion

Structural family therapy (SFT) is primarily concerned with the order in which family members interact with one another. Of great interest to structural family therapists are the universal rules governing family organization, such as the power hierarchy between parents and children (Minuchin, 1974). At times children have a significant amount of power and control in the family. This can lead to inappropriate patterns of interaction, roles, power structure, and so on (Hoshino, 2008). Creative techniques and metaphorical interventions, such as The Royal Family, can help shift the hierarchical relationship of the members within a subsystem. This activity helps the parental subsystem to take on a position of leadership in the family by adopting the roles of King and Queen. Children adopt the roles of Prince and Princess. When family members take on these roles, they learn appropriate behaviors that befit their "royal" status.

This activity helps the King and Queen (the parents) to establish and enforce appropriate rules, which in turn decreases the Prince's and Princess' (the children's) inappropriate behaviors. A behavioral component, adding jewels to the crowns, allows the positive behavior to be reinforced.

The family therapist plays a significant role in facilitating changes in the family system. By taking on the role of "Royal Advisor," the therapist *joins* with the family and leads them toward more functional patterns.

References

Hoshino, J. (2008). Structural family art therapy. In C. Kerr et al. (Eds.), *Family art therapy: Foundations of theory and practice*. New York: Routledge.

Minuchin, S. (1974). *Families and family therapy*. Cambridge, MA: Harvard University Press.

About The Author

Angela M. Cavett, PhD, LP, RPT-S, is a Psychologist in private practice providing evaluation and therapy to children, adolescents, and families. She is an adjunct faculty member at the University of North Dakota in the Department of Counseling Psychology. She is a Registered Play Therapist Supervisor and provides training and supervision related to child psychopathology and treatment, including play therapy. She is the author of *Structured Play-Based Interventions for Engaging Children and Adolescents in Therapy* (2010).

Sculpture Musical Chairs
Source: Shirley U. Lindemann

Goals
- Identify social interaction skills among family members
- Identify and understand how each family member is perceived by other members of the family
- Increase communication through safe non-judgmental artistic expression

Materials
- Clay or Playdough
- White paper
- Markers
- CD of relaxation music
- CD player

Advance Preparation
Arrange chairs around a table so that each family member can take a seat. Ensure that each family member has space at the table to create a small sculpture. It is also important that family members are able to move easily around the table from chair to chair.

Place paper and markers around the table.

Description
Ask family members to each take a seat at the table. Explain the game of musical chairs. This will be the basis of this activity. Provide family members with the same amount of clay or Playdough and ask them to each create a sculpture of him/herself. Play relaxation music during the activity until the sculptures (including the additions) are completed.

Once this first task is complete, ask members to move to the sculpture to their immediate right. Then ask them to change that sculpture to symbolize something they like or appreciate about the family member who created it. (The change can be adding a symbol or it can be altering the sculpture, for example, carving a smile into the face of the sculpture.) This continues until each member has had the opportunity to work on each sculpture. Everyone then goes back to their initial seats in front of their sculptures.

Prompt the family members to look at their sculptures and to notice the additions made by the other family members. They can ask questions about the additions made by each participant. The owners of the sculptures are asked to tell each family member how they feel about the changes/additions made to their sculptures.

Facilitate a discussion by asking questions such as:

1. How did you feel while working on your sculptures?
2. How did you feel when making additions to the other sculptures?
3. What was communicated nonverbally through this activity?
4. How did it feel to receive appreciations from others in your family?
5. Did you see anything on other family members' sculptures that you would like to address?
6. When taking a look at your sculptures, what features do you especially like and why?
7. If your sculptures could talk, what would they say to the other sculptures?

Discussion

This art intervention is of special value to a family who has difficulty communicating with each other on a non-judgmental level. Focusing on the positive additions to the sculptures promotes positive feelings within the family, making them more open to addressing salient issues. The fact that each family member has an equal chance to make a contribution opens up a sense of acceptance and thereafter channels of communication.

It is advisable to start with making only positive additions to each sculpture in this session to establish a protective and safe setting in which participants can open up. In a follow-up session, introduce the option of adding areas of improvement as well to each sculpture. It is advised, however, to carefully assess the relationships between members before moving on to this more challenging intervention.

Clay or Playdough can change the affective response in a person, and it gives clients more freedom to express themselves while reducing avoidance and resistance. On a scale of one to ten (one being the least controllable and ten the most controllable), clay ranks as number one on Landgarten's list (Landgarten, 1991). Modeling clay gives clients multiple ways of interacting emotionally with one another. Playdough or clay offers an undefined consistency, making this form of nonverbal communication extremely effective.

Reference

Landgarten, H.B. (1987). *Family art therapy: A clinical guide and casebook.* New York: Routledge.

About The Author

Shirley U. Lindemann, C.A.C.T., S.R.S.P., is a professional member of the Ontario Art Therapy Association. She is a member of the Association for Psychotherapists in Germany and of the American Art Therapy Association. She graduated from college in Social Pedagogy and Early Childhood Education and went on to study Social Pedagogy at a university in Germany. She received her training and certificate as an Art and Creative Therapist at the Federal German Institute for Therapy, EREW, in 1995. She has been working in the field of psychiatric institutional care since 1989 and has led many workshops in art therapy for psychologists and social workers. She has also published several articles on art therapy. She has worked as an Art and Creative Therapist in private practice in Germany, Belgium, the Netherlands, and Canada.

© Shirley U. Lindemann

Self-Image
Sources: Rajeswari Natrajan-Tyagiand and Nilufer Kafescioglu

Goals
- Increase the rate of positive verbal comments and pleasurable exchanges between family members
- Increase children's awareness of their physical selves and their personal characteristics through drawing, naming, and talking about their characteristics
- Increase children's awareness of affective reactions to their characteristics through a dialogue with the parent/caregiver focusing on emotions when talking about the drawing

Materials
- Large roll of paper
- Markers
- Scissors
- Decorative craft items
- Glue

Advance Preparation
Arrange the therapy space so that the roll of paper can be spread out on the floor.

Description
Note: This activity involves one parent and one child.

Explain to the family that they will be participating in an art activity together. Tell them that the child will be creating a picture of him/herself and that the parent will help. Later, the parent will create a picture of him/herself and the child will help.

Spread out the roll of paper and ask the child to lie flat on it. Then cut the paper so it is long enough to outline the child. Ask the child to continue lying flat on the piece of paper. Using the marker, ask the parent to outline the child on the cut piece of paper. Once the child's outline is drawn, the child can get up from his/her position.

Instruct the parent to let the child color and decorate the outline. Let the child pick the colors and crafts that he/she would like to use. The child can add features using decorative craft items such as eyes, hair, ears, etc.

Prompt the parent to provide positive, nurturing messages to the child during the activity (e.g., "You have a beautiful smile that brightens my day").

Encourage the parent to interact with the child during the drawing activity. For example, the parent can encourage the child by giving the child opportunities to make choices (e.g., select the crafts and the colors) and by giving positive feedback/praise to the child (e.g., "You are really concentrated on this" or "It was a good idea to cut that piece" or "You really want to do a good job with this"). In addition, encourage the parent to identify and acknowledge the child's emotions throughout the activity (e.g., "You look excited").

After the image is completed, the parent can help the child write his/her name on the paper. The parent and the child can then write down some of the positive characteristics of the child next to the completed image, such as "fun," "loving," "smart." Children can then present the image that they have drawn and talk about themselves through the drawing and how they feel about their drawing or the characteristics they have described.

Next, the same activity is repeated with a parent lying flat on the paper. Ask the child to outline the parent with markers (the therapist can do it if the child is too young). Once the parent's outline is drawn, ask the parent and the child to color and decorate the parent's outline together. Again, the parent and the child can write down positive characteristics of the parent on the completed image. The parent and the child then can talk about the parent and how they feel about the drawing.

Discussion

According to Erickson (1963), when children internalize their bodily self, their physical mastery and its cultural meaning, they develop a realistic self-esteem that helps them learn effective ways of preparing for the future. This internalization occurs during the constant, collaborative communication between parents and children where parents function as a consistent source of feedback (Siegel, 1999). Self-esteem has been described as involving a cognitive judgment of one's abilities or appearance and the affective reaction to these cognitive judgments (Nida & Pierce, 2000). This activity may enhance both the cognitive and affective components of self-esteem. The activity will help children become aware of their physical and emotional selves and achieve a sense of identity while opening up space for parents to support, accept, be patient, and provide encouragement for their children. By engaging in such a positive and bonding play activity, parents will get the chance to enhance their connection with their children. At the same time, observing the interactions will allow the therapist to assess family dynamics.

References
Arkin, C. (1997). Nurturing your child's self-esteem. Accessed April 6, 2010 from http://ohioline.osu.edu/bb-fact/pdf/bb_k_2.pdf.

Erickson, E.H. (1963). *Childhood and society*. New York: W.W. Norton.

Nida, R.E., & Pierce, S. (2000). Children's social and emotional development: Applications for family therapy. In E. Bailey (Ed.), *Children in therapy*. New York: W.W. Norton.

Siegel, D. (1999). *The developing mind: Towards a neurobiology of interpersonal experience*. New York: Guilford.

About The Authors

Rajeswari Natrajan-Tyagi, PhD, LMFT, is an Assistant Professor in the Marriage and Family Therapy Program at Alliant International University in Irvine, California. She has her master's degree in Social Work from Madras School of Social Work in Chennai, India, and a master's and doctoral degree in Marriage and Family Therapy from Purdue University, Indiana. Her clinical interests are working with culturally diverse populations and with children. Her research interests are in the areas of immigration, cross-cultural training, systemic training, self-of-therapist issues, cultural competency, and qualitative process research methodologies. She has authored several publications and has presented at local, national, and international conferences.

Nilufer Kafescioglu, PhD, is an Assistant Professor of Psychology at Dogus University in Istanbul, Turkey. She received her bachelor degree in Psychology at Ege University in Turkey, her master's degree in Clinical Psychology at the University of Indianapolis, and her doctoral degree in Marriage and Family Therapy at Purdue University, Indiana. She has been providing psychotherapy to children, families, and couples in diverse settings. She has authored publications on topics such as violence prevention programs with child caregivers, cross-cultural research on attachment theory, multicultural supervision, and couples coping with chronic illness. She has presented at numerous local, national, and international conferences.

Sibling Rivalry
Source: Pauline Youlin

Goals
- Increase open communication among family members
- Reduce conflict between siblings
- Increase the rate of positive verbal comments and pleasurable exchanges between siblings

Materials
- Sibling Rivalry worksheet (included)
- Pens
- Prizes

Advance Preparation
Copy the Sibling Rivalry worksheet (make one copy for each participating sibling).

Description
Note: This activity requires two sessions.

In session, the therapist explains the nature of the "game" by requesting that the children spend the next week or two (the time between one session and the next) by "spying" on their sibling and attempting to get as much information as possible about his/her likes/dislikes, activities, and daily schedule. Clients are not told what the categories on the Sibling Rivalry List are ahead of time so that they do not focus only on the questions to be asked but instead experience the adventure of getting an overall sense of their sibling. The purpose of the game is to create a new awareness of being connected with a sibling. Not informing players of the categories means that their learning will take place within several different contexts instead of keeping their focus on winning the game.

At the following session, each sibling completes the Sibling Rivalry Worksheet, then the therapist facilitates the sharing of responses. Whoever has the most correct matching answers will win a small prize (candy bar, small toy, etc.).

The therapist not only points out the correct answers as encouragement that they know each other so well but also gently uses the incorrect answers to continue engaging them in conversation about their different interests. The discussion can focus on the following questions:

1. Name something you learned about your sibling that you did not know about him/her before doing this activity.
2. What was the most interesting or surprising thing you learned about your sibling?

3. What is something you and your sibling have in common?

Discussion

Children enjoy competition, especially when pitted against a worthy adversary such as a sibling. Children also have a natural propensity toward engaging in the excitement of "spying" which, in this context, speaks to a genuine interest in learning about a close family member. Even with siblings who have severe communication problems and conflictual relationships, this game promotes humor, a sense of connection, and positive communication through shared interests and hobbies. Siblings often continue learning new things about each other even after the game is over, which promotes continued bonding beyond the therapeutic session. Interspersing some of the "spying" questions with questions that otherwise require some real knowledge of the sibling (i.e., best memory of a sibling, a quality admired about a sibling) initiates an awareness of just how much the siblings actually *are* connected and, when they share qualities that they like about each other, they experience a sense of positive self-esteem.

About The Author

Pauline Youlin, MS, MFTI, is a Marriage and Family Therapist Intern in Corona, California, who currently works in a clinical setting with children, adults, and families. She has worked in the school setting with adolescents struggling with substance abuse problems.

© Pauline Youlin

Sibling Rivalry List

	Sibling	You
Favorite toy or belonging		
Favorite afterschool activity		
Favorite food		
Least favorite food		
Favorite fruit		
Favorite day of the week		
Least favorite chore		
Favorite sport to watch/ play		
Favorite item of clothing		
Best subject in school		
Favorite season of year		
Closest friend		
Something good that happened this week		
Something upsetting that happened this week		
Career/Job would love to do in the future		
Best memory of your sibling		
Quality you most admire about your sibling		
If I could take vacation anywhere		
Something that makes me happy		

Silence Ball
Source: Shlomo Ariel

Goals
- Increase sensitivity to body language and nonverbal cues among family members
- Increase family members' ability to decipher and produce nonverbal messages
- Develop appropriate physical boundaries within the family
- Learn and practice self control

Materials
- Spongy rubber ball the size of a small basketball
- Objects that can mark goal posts and demarcate goal areas such as chairs or pillows
- Masking tape
- Large sheet of paper and marker or blackboard with chalk or a whiteboard with appropriate markers
- Toy video camera*
- Relatively large doll representing a man or a woman*
- Toy microphone*
- Visor hat and a brimmed hat*

*These items can be purchased or an appropriate substitute will do, for example, a pen as a toy microphone, a cellular phone as a video camera, a big pillow as a man or a woman, and other kinds of hats.

Advance Preparation
This game can be played by a family of at least four members. If there are more than four, an even number of members will be divided into two teams and the odd man out will be the referee. Otherwise the therapist can serve as the referee.

The game can be played in a space that is five square yards in size (45 square feet) or in a large room.

Create two goal posts at the two opposite ends of the room, using objects such as chairs, pillows, etc. Create a center line across the middle of the floor using masking tape.

Description
Divide the family into two teams, for example, father and daughter vs. mother and son or mother, daughter and older son vs. father and two younger sons. If there are three or more members in each team, one member can serve as the goal keeper. The teams may be reshuffled after several rounds.

Each team will be placed in its own half of the "field." The referee will stand by the center line, holding the ball.

Draw a chart with team membership and the names of the players on the sheet of paper, blackboard or whiteboard.

Explain to the family that they are going to play a special version of team handball, which will help them communicate and understand one another without words and treat one another with sensitivity and respect. The rules are explained as follows:

"The duration of the game is 10 minutes. Each team attempts to score as many goals as possible. Each goal scored earns two points for the team that scored the goal. One can cross the center line and approach but not enter the goal area of the other team. The ball can be handed over or thrown over to a member of one's own team. One can walk or run with the ball in his/her hands. The ball will be transmitted from one player's hands to another player's hands only. No kicking the ball and no throwing the ball on purpose at another player's body. The ball can be caught by the rival team while in the air but it cannot be forced out of a player's hands. If the ball falls on the floor, it can be picked up by the player who reaches it first. Touching any part of the body of a member of your own team or of the other team is considered an offence. Uttering a word or producing any other sound (laughing, shouting, sighing, groaning) during play time is also considered an offence. An offence will cost the offender's team a loss of two points. Only the referee has the right to determine whether an offence has been committed or not. The referee is allowed to speak during the play, but can only say words that are relevant to his/her function as a referee. The referee has the right to stop the game for a while by declaring: "Stop playing!" Any player is allowed to ask for a short time out in order to ask a question or make a comment by showing an agreed-upon hand gesture. A record of goals scored and points deducted due to offences will be kept by the therapist, written on the sheet of paper (or blackboard or whiteboard)."

Place the doll on a chair or a table and make it hold the toy video camera, directed toward the players. Say: "Let's pretend this cameraman is going to videotape the game to show it on TV."

Put on the visor hat and speak into the toy microphone, pretending to be a TV handball announcer and say something like this: "Watch Soundless against Noiseless, Silence Ball live!" Then, during the game, describe, as an announcer, the various players' moves in real time.

Your verbal description will also include some expressions reflecting the players' difficulties, feelings, and achievements. For example, "John seems to be upset because he has lost the ball to Jane, but he is keeping quiet." "Mary almost bumped into Dad but managed to avoid touching him."

Write the points scored or deducted on the paper (or blackboard or whiteboard).

If there are only four family members, the therapist should switch between the roles of referee, announcer, and score recorder, changing hats and tone of voice to mark the role shifts. This is slightly difficult, but not impossible.

After the game is done, take off the visor hat and put on the brimmed hat. Ask the players for permission to "be interviewed for TV about the game." Speaking into the microphone, ask each of them questions about their experience during play, letting them answer into the microphone. The questions will focus on the players' feelings, difficulties, and achievements. For example, "I saw Jane waving her arms toward you, desperately trying to attract your attention. Did you notice?" "How did it feel for you not to utter a word or a sound for ten minutes?"

If a family member, usually a younger child, has expressed frustration for having been responsible for too many offences, suggest another round of the game with same teams to give him/her a chance to perform better.

Discussion

One of the sources of malfunctioning discussed in the human interpersonal communication and the family therapy literature is insufficient sensitivity to non-verbal cues and in general under-developed nonverbal communication competence. The research literature points to a strong correlation between non-verbal communication skills on the one hand, and to awareness of and respect for body boundaries and personal space on the other hand (Knapp & Hall, 2009; Manusov & Patterson, 2006; Norris, 2004).Unskillful use of nonverbal communication can cause interpersonal difficulties in families and peer groups. Lack of attention to nonverbal cues is characteristic of what Minuchin (1974) termed *disengaged families*. On the other hand, lack of respect for body boundaries and personal space due to chaotic, impulsive communication is typical of what he termed *enmeshed families*. The technique of Silence Ball aims to improve the functioning of both disengaged and enmeshed families. Its therapeutic power is derived mainly from the fact that it enables family members to actually experience a communication mode in which attention to nonverbal cues, respect for body boundaries and personal space and self-control are rewarded whereas the opposite is penalized. Success in maintaining such an activity for the duration of 10 minutes is self-reinforcing. It provides the family with tangible proof that they really can reach a higher level of interpersonal communication.

The use of a referee, camera operator, game announcer, and an interviewer are designed to add an element of self-reflection and conscious awareness.

References
Ariel, S. (2002).*Children's imaginative play: A visit to Wonderland*. Westport,

CT: Greenwood/Praeger.

Ariel, S. (2005).Family play therapy. In C.E. Schaefer, J. McCormick, & A. Ohnogi (Eds.),*The international handbook of play therapy.* New York: Jason Aronson.

Ariel, S., & Peled, O. (2000).Group work with children and adolescents in an integrative therapeutic framework. [Hebrew Text. Unpublished English Translation is available]. *Mikbatz: The Journal of the Israeli Association of Group Therapy,*5,42–60.

Knapp, M.L., & Hall, J.A. (2009). *Non-verbal communication in human interaction.* Florence, KY: Hadworth Publishing.

Minuchin, S. (1974). *Families and family therapy.* New York: Routledge.

Manusov, V., & Patterson, M.L. (2006).*The SAGE handbook of non-verbal communication.* Newbury Park, CA: Sage.

Norris, S. (2004). *Analyzing multi-modal interaction: A methodological framework.* New York: Routledge.

About The Author

Shlomo Ariel, PhD, is a Supervisor of Clinical Psychology and Family Therapy in Israel. He is the director of the Integrative Psychotherapy Center and the Israeli Play Therapy Institute in Ramat Gan, the founder and current president of the Israeli Play Therapy Association, and a member of the training committee of the International Family Therapy Association. He is widely published in the fields of psychotherapy integration, culturally competent psychotherapy, play therapy theory and research, and play therapy. He provides training and consultation in his areas of expertise in Israel, Europe, and the Unites States.

Sneaking
Source: Steve Harvey

Goals
- Increase communication about difficult behaviours
- Increase the frequency of positive interactions between parents and the child
- Develop a joint focus
- Increase physical attunement

Materials
- A video recorder to tape the session can add a helpful dimension to this activity, but it is not essential

Description
This activity is designed for children in their early to mid-primary years who have relational problems with their parents.

The roles for this game are verbally presented to the family and cast before it begins. The roles are as follows:

1. Sneak
2. Catcher
3. Judge/Game Master

The game is played by one parent and the child together. The activity is presented in a competitive format in which the parent and child are trying to win. The therapist initially takes on the role of Game Master and presents, announces, and judges the game as it proceeds.

The game starts with the child in the role of the Sneak and the parent in the role of the Catcher. The therapist can join the game in one of these roles if the parent and child need to have their parts modelled.

The action of the game starts with the child on one side of the room and the parent on the other. The parent, as the Catcher begins with his/her back to the Sneak and looks toward the wall. The child then tries to sneak up close enough to touch the parent on the back without being seen in the action of moving. The parent can turn at any time while the child is attempting to move closer. If the Catcher turns in time to see the Sneak moving, the Sneak then must return to the original starting place on the far side of the room. The game action then starts again.

The only way for the Sneak to get close enough to the Catcher to win is to watch the adult very carefully and to stop or freeze his/her body when the Catcher turns so that no movement is seen. The Sneak, literally, must sneak. Conversely, the Catcher must listen for movement and anticipate when to turn around in order to see the Sneak moving. The Sneak must demonstrate control over his/her body in order to move quietly and stop when the Catcher turns around. The Sneak must also be observant to the Catcher's body so that he/she can move without the Catcher turning in time to see the action.

As the game proceeds, the roles are reversed so that the child also plays the Catcher and the parent plays the Sneak. The therapist as Game Master is often in the position to judge if the Catcher actually was able to see movement or if the Sneak was truly able to freeze his/her body. Adjustments can be made for younger children or for children with impulse control difficulties.

If the therapist has a camera and ability to use play back within the session, reviewing the video can be helpful in settling disagreements over whether the Sneak was actually seen moving or if the freeze was completed. These recordings can also be used to develop a verbal narrative or imaginary story about the recorded action with both the parent and child adding ideas to the plot and character development.

Discussion

Parents and children who have relationship difficulties often do not have the ability to share their attention with each other. This can become very apparent in their nonverbal communication. Even when parents try to talk with their children, the clash in nonverbal communication distracts from even their best verbal efforts.

This game helps parents and children begin to orient themselves to each other in a physical and playful manner. The competitive aspect inherent in the activity can help provide motivation for parents and children to share a nonverbal focus together in a more positive way. Both the parent and the child must control his/her body and be physically aware of the other to play the game successfully. The result of the game is that the parent and child can develop an enjoyable way to share each other's company in a coordinated and physical way.

In families where loud arguing dominates interaction, for example, parents and children can become accustomed to not looking at each other's physical presentations. Sneaking provides an opportunity for interactions that are essentially nonverbal, yet require significant attention on the part of the other family member. Often children are able to move very close to their parents without being noticed.

The theoretical background involving physical play among families and how such activities can be developed is presented more fully elsewhere (Harvey, 2003, 2006).

References

Harvey, S.A. (2003). Dynamic play therapy with an adoptive family struggling with issues of grief, loss, and adjustment. In D. Wiener & L. Oxford (Eds.), *Action therapy with families and groups*. Washington, DC: American Psychological Association Books.

Harvey, S.A. (2006). Dynamic play therapy. In C.E. Schaefer & H. Kaduson (Eds.), *Contemporary play therapy*. New York: Guilford.

About The Author

Steve Harvey, PhD, RPT-S, BC-DMT, is a Licensed Psychologist in the United States and is registered as a Psychologist with clinical and educational scopes of practice in New Zealand. He is a Registered Play Therapist Supervisor and a Board Certified Dance Movement Therapist. He is currently the Consultant Psychologist for the Child and Adolescent Mental Health Service for the Taranaki District Health Board in New Plymouth, New Zealand. He helped pioneer the use of Play Therapy approaches with families and has written several professional chapters and articles in the field published in *The International Journal of Play Therapy, Contemporary Play Therapy, Play Diagnosis and Assessment*, and *Blending Play Therapy with Cognitive Behavioral Therapy: Evidence-Based and other Effective Treatment Techniques*. He has presented and consulted extensively internationally on topics related to the use of family play in the evaluation and treatment of attachment and psychological trauma in children.

Stories Within
Source: Brian Douglas

Goals
- Increase open communication within the family
- Externalize the problem
- Begin to see, visually, the problem and the hoped-for change

Materials
- Photographs or pictures clipped from magazines
- Sample directives (included)

Advance Preparation
Ask the client to bring to the next session a large collection of photographs. Alternatively, provide a collection of photographs or magazine clippings that depict a wide variety of subject matter. The family members should have many options to choose from.

Prior to the session, decide on the treatment issues to be explored with the family and prepare the directives accordingly. Choose from the sample directives included below or create ones that are appropriate to the family's situation.

Description
Lay the collection of images on the table or floor. Ask each family member to pick an image or a collection of images depending on the issue being explored. For example, the therapist could ask, "I would like you to each pick two images from the collection before you. I would like the first image to be the one that most reminds you of anxiety. For the second image, choose one that best shows your life without the interference of anxiety." The therapist should point out that this does not need to be a long process; the members should pick an image that quickly stands-out to them.

The conversation begins once the pictures have been selected. Process questions should facilitate open communication and externalization. For example:

1. Explain why you chose these pictures.
2. What memories or stories do you think about when you look at these pictures?
3. What feelings (both negative and positive) do you experience as you look at these pictures?
4. What else would you like to tell us about these pictures?
5. What similarities and differences in your family did you notice about the pictures that each of you chose?

Discussion

Judy Weiser, a therapist who integrates PhotoTherapy techniques in her clinical work with clients, states that "PhotoTherapy techniques use ordinary personal snapshots and family photos (and the feelings, memories, thoughts and information these evoke) as catalysts for therapeutic communication and personal healing, reaching areas inside a person that words alone cannot access" (1999). This PhotoTherapy technique (called "Photo-Projectives") can be particularly helpful with families who struggle to find the words to express their thoughts and feelings.

With a visual and tangible item such as a photograph, clients can show the therapist the problem or solution and talk about why that particular image represents their struggles, barriers, hopes and dreams. This technique is a helpful way to enhance conversation and has limitless possibilities.

Externalization is a narrative technique that can help clients speak more freely about the problem. Separating the person from the problem often allows people to shift their previously held views about themselves (White, 2007).

A possible note of caution: If working with clients who have been abused and part of that abuse involved photographs, make sure that working with photographs will not act as a trigger.

References

Weiser, J. (1999). *PhotoTherapy techniques: Exploring the secrets of personal snapshots and family albums* (3rd ed.). Vancouver, BC: PhotoTherapy Centre Press.

White, M. (2007). *Maps of narrative practice*. New York: W.W. Norton.

About The Author

Brian Douglas, MSW, RSW, is a Clinical Social Worker who currently works for the Waterloo Region District School Board as a Social Worker and Attendance Counselor and also maintains a private practice in Kitchener, Ontario. He has a Master of Social Work degree from the University of Toronto and is registered with the Ontario College of Social Workers and Social Service Workers. He completed a Certificate in Couple and Family Therapy through the University of Guelph.

Stories Within
Sample Directives

"I would like you to each pick two images from the collection before you. I would like the first image to be the one that most reminds you of anxiety. For the second image, choose one that best shows your life without the interference of anxiety."

"I would like you to each pick two images from the collection before you. I would like the first image to be the one that brings about sad feelings. For the second image, choose one that best shows happy feelings."

"I would like you to each pick two images from the collection before you. I would like the first image to be the one that evokes a memory that you would like to forget. For the second image, choose one that evokes a memory that you treasure."

"I would like you to each pick two images from the collection before you. I would like the first image to be the one that most reminds you of a problem in your family. For the second image, choose one that best shows your family life without that problem."

"I would like you each to pick one image from the collection before you. I would like that image to be the one that reminds you most of your family."

"I would like you each to pick two images from the collection before you. I would like those images to show how you each see the struggle(s) your family is experiencing."

"I would like you to each pick one image from the collection before you. I would like that image to be the one that makes you feel most calm."

243

Storytelling Card Game
Source: Norma Leben

Goals
- Establish a safe and open therapeutic environment
- Identify key issues to address in therapy
- Increase open communication
- Encourage creative storytelling

Materials
- Standard 52-card deck

Advance Preparation
Arrange a flat space for the card game. Place the cards face down near the flat surface so all participants can easily access them.

Description
The therapist explains that each family member will take turns picking up the top two cards from the stack of playing cards. Members create a story by incorporating their two cards into the story. For example, a Queen and a "9" card might prompt a storyline such as, "There once was a lovely queen who lived in a castle surrounded by nine dragons." The therapist starts first and moves the story forward positively. The therapist shows how to lay down the cards to make a spiral storyline (see illustration).

The next player draws the two top cards from the deck and continues the imaginative story, building on his/her predecessor's storyline. This continues until all the cards have been incorporated into the story, or until each player has had a predetermined number of turns.

Discussion
This activity incorporates game play and storytelling that engage family members in the therapeutic process. Themes relevant to issues the client presents typically emerge during the story.

The therapist can participate in the story creation to infuse healing messages. For example, a child (with a history of abuse) draws a Queen and a "2" and says, "There was a queen bee who buzzed around and stung these two boys real bad." The therapist might continue the storyline with "6" and "8" cards by saying reassuringly, "The boys ran to their neighbor in apartment six who helped the boys by putting eight bandages on their bee stings."

The therapist shows the members how to arrange the cards in a spiraling circle as the cards are played. This pattern helps to promote the flow and continuity of the storytelling.

Reference
Leben, N. (1993). *Directive group play therapy: 60 structured games for the treatment of ADHD, low self-esteem, and traumatized children.* Pflugerville, TX: Morning Glory Treatment Center for Children.

About The Author
Norma Leben, MSW, LCSW, ACSW, RPT-S, CPT-P, is a licensed clinical social worker and play therapy supervisor in Texas. She has worked as a CPS supervisor, school drop-out team leader, residential treatment supervisor, agency executive director, and international trainer and public speaker. She has written and produced over 45 books, publications, and audio/video recordings on parenting and play therapy techniques in English and Chinese.

Tiger, Mouse, and Monkey Work Together: An Animal Parts Party for Families
Source: Mary Jo Jones, Barbara Spanjers, Cynthia Mota

Goals
- Identify conflicting emotions regarding problematic situations or circumstances
- Verbalize conflicting emotions through a metaphorical voice
- Identify the positive resolution to the conflict

Materials
- Paper bags
- Glue
- Scissors
- Decorative materials such as markers, glitter, felt, googly eyes, stickers, etc.
- Variety of animal templates (obtainable from craft books or websites), stuffed animals, or puppets
- Wise owl toy or puppet

Advance Preparation
Identify the conflicting emotions in the problematic situation or circumstance within the family prior to the activity.

Description
Note: Because of the potential complexity of the intervention, this activity may take longer than one session to complete.

Through this intervention, the family journeys through the process of accepting and integrating their conflicting and problematic emotions. Satir and Baldwin (1983) describe four basic sequences of a parts party: (1) meeting the parts; (2) witnessing the conflict between the parts; (3) transforming the parts; and (4) integrating the parts. These four sections are integral, and the therapist (e.g., as Wise Owl) guides the family through them. Although the therapist/guide directs the overall intervention, the action within each sequence should be more family-centered and not overly directive.

Introduce the parts party concept to the family, and invite family members to choose or create animal representations of their conflicting emotions. For example, a tiger may represent anger; a mouse may represent fear or vulnerability; and a monkey may represent mischievousness, acting out, or guilt.

The therapist should initially set ground rules by explaining the function of the Wise Owl as the guide. The Wise Owl will act as a "guide" by controlling the action, ensuring that each family member is heard, and maintaining the safety of the session.

Next, follow these four steps:

1. Meeting the Parts – This portion focuses on the animals becoming aware of each other, and how they might act when meeting for the first time. It may be necessary for the therapist to play some of these roles for the family to fully comprehend the role of each part.

2. Witnessing the Conflict Between the Parts – Satir and Baldwin (1983) state that "the Guide freezes the action and asks each part to tell what his plans are and what each needs to make his plan work." Adapting this for family therapy, it becomes clear that each animal has a plan based on its nature, and not everyone can get what they want. For example, there is chaos as the angry tiger (new parent who is frustrated that their child will not behave) chases after the fearful mouse (child who is anxious because he/she has been replaced by the new sibling), the mouse tries to escape, and the mischievous monkey (child who is acting out to gain attention) throws coconuts to gain attention.

3. Transforming the Parts – The animals' goals appear mutually exclusive and success for one means loss for another. For example, the tiger cannot eat if the mouse runs too fast (parent will push child away with continued anger), and the mouse cannot survive if the tiger catches her (child is in need of positive reassurance). The animals recognize that they need to cooperate with one another so all their needs can be met. The therapist/Wise Owl directs the parts to figure out how to help each other "so that they can maximize their value to their owner" (Satir and Baldwin, 1983). For example, if the tiger can ask the monkey to play with the mouse so the mouse is not afraid, then the mouse will survive and the monkey will have something constructive to do.

4. Integrating the Parts – As the conflicting parts gain awareness of what they need so they can cooperate with each other, transformation occurs. In the final stage, the family is brought to an understanding of how all of their parts can be integrated in order to coexist and function in harmony. Once all the parts have had their say and can cooperate well with one another, each part introduces itself in its transformed state. For example, the mouse states, "I am your ability to express your fears." After all have spoken, Wise Owl asks if each family member is ready to accept all parts of him/herself.

Discussion

According to symbolic experiential family therapy theory, family problems are rooted in the "denial of impulses and suppression of feeling" (Nichols & Schwartz, 2006). Children who grow up in families where the expression of emotion is stunted often become adults who are unable to connect with their core emotions and instead experience undefined anxiety, which is accompanied by maladaptive relational responses. Therapists can supplement the emotional nurturing of the family through therapeutic activities that promote the family's acceptance of their own difficult or conflicting emotions.

The Animal Parts Party intervention is useful in helping families work through their conflicting emotions regarding circumstances such as divorce or the birth of a new sibling. Through creating symbolic animal representations of their emotions and experiencing the conflicts between "animal parts," the family can achieve an understanding and integration of those conflicting emotions that are causing confusion and distress in response to a new or ongoing situation.

To solidify gains made through this intervention, the therapist should refer back to the parts party in future sessions, especially when conflicting emotions emerge. Revisiting a successful integration will help boost the family's confidence in managing emotions. The parts party may be repeated with the same or different animals, as the need arises.

Parts parties lend themselves well to multiple variations. The therapist is free to provide different types of stuffed animals, or even other media, such as puppets, art supplies, or storytelling. Parts can be represented by the family members invited to the session; or all the parts can be acted out by one family member. The parts invited to the party may be anything that creates conflict for the family. These may be feelings, perceived parts of other people (e.g., a parent), or any other constructs that are at odds and can be reconciled or processed by the family.

Due to the somewhat abstract nature of this activity, the therapist should use his/her clinical judgment to determine if the family members are good candidates for the parts party. This activity would be contraindicated for use with very young children or family members with severe cognitive impairment.

The mind-set of the therapist in approaching this intervention is also crucial. The therapist must be comfortable within the medium of play and puppetry and must have the capacity to spontaneously react to the content as it progresses. The therapist will need to get into the act of making Wise Owl come to life, while maintaining the structure and course of the play content so therapeutic progress can be made.

References

Nichols, M.P., & Schwartz, R.C. (2006). *Family therapy: Context and methods* (7th ed.).New York: Pearson Education.

Satir, V., & Baldwin, M. (1983). *Satir step by step: A guide to creating change in families*. Palo Alto, CA: Science and Behavior Books.

About The Authors

Mary Jo Jones, MS, MFT-I, is a State Intern in Nevada. She is the Clinical Coordinator for a large agency that services the mental health needs of foster youth and specializes in trauma-based services. She has authored several publications, including *Crucial Conversations: A Book Review*.

Barbara Spanjers, MA, and Cynthia Mota, BA, are currently pursuing their Master Degrees in Marriage and Family Therapy at the University of Nevada, Las Vegas.

Toss the Ball
Source: Trudy Post Sprunk

Goals
- Increase playful interactions
- Increase open communication among family members
- Assess family relationships and dynamics
- Identify areas for change within the family

Materials
- Soft ball that can be easily and safely tossed
- Watch or timer

Advance Preparation
Arrange seating to ensure ease and safety during ball tossing.

Description
Explain that for five minutes family members will take turns gently tossing the ball to other family members. As they toss the ball to someone they are to say something **nice** to that family member. The pattern is repeated for five minutes and/or until every person has heard at least two nice things about themselves.

Ask each person to describe their experience of what other family members said that was nice to them. For example, ask:

1. What was it like to say nice things to everyone?
2. How did you feel when another member in your family said something nice to you?
3. Did you receive any unexpected comments?

After processing, start the game again, however, this time ask them to say something they would **enjoy doing** (but are not currently doing) with the person to whom they throw the ball. Allow this to continue for five minutes, followed by processing the experience.

The third component of the game involves what is said when one catches the ball. The person who catches the ball is instructed to say something they would **like to change** about themselves and what prevents their ability to make that change. Allow time for the family to process and develop strategies for change. Possible discussion questions include:

1. List two things that would serve as aids to making the change that you would like to make.
2. On a scale of 1 to 10, how important is this change to you? To others in your family?

3. In what ways would your family life be improved after these changes were made?

Lastly, when one tosses the ball to another, the recipient shares an idea about what they could do to **improve family life**. After five minutes, encourage the family to consider all the suggestions and decide how and if these suggestions can be incorporated into their family life.

Discussion

This activity begins with playful positive interactions that foster family cohesiveness. In addition, expressing nice things directly to each other offers the potential of establishing an increased level of emotional intimacy and a change in communication style. The game asks that participants share activities they would enjoy doing with each other, which could provide even more opportunities for positive family interactions.

The second half of the game focuses on change for improving family life. The therapist must carefully guide the family in a discussion about how changes could be made and the advantages of making these changes. During the discussion of changes the family works together as a problem-solving team with common goals. As in all psychotherapy, the therapist uses wise clinical judgment when exploring in-depth issues of this nature.

This game highlights the curative powers of play, such as overcoming resistance, communication, creative thinking, relationship enhancement, understanding and empathy, mastery, and enjoyment (Schaefer, 1993). The game is engaging and exciting and as such, it is a helpful intervention in child-focused family therapy.

Reference
Schaefer, C.E. (1993). *The therapeutic powers of play*. New York: Jason Aronson.

About The Author
Trudy Post Sprunk, LMFT-S, LPC-S, RPT-S, CPT-S, is a Licensed Marriage and Family Therapist and Supervisor who has been practicing psychotherapy since 1971. She has presented at international, national, and local conferences and has been interviewed on radio and television. She is certified as an EMDR Specialist and is a Registered Play Therapist Supervisor. She is past-president of the Association for Play Therapy and president and co-founder of the Georgia Association for Play Therapy.

W 4:
Wish, Worry, Why, & Will
Source: Brijin Gardner

Goals
* Provide a safe environment for family members to express feelings, needs, perceptions, beliefs, and problems
* Assess family relationships and dynamics
* Increase open communication among family members

Materials
* Four index cards (preferably laminated) or foam squares
* Permanent marker
* Cotton balls
* Large glass of water
* Masking tape

Advance Preparation
Prepare the cards by writing the following words on separate index cards: **WISH, WORRY, WHY,** and **WILL**. Tape the four cards onto a wall or door in random order. Place the cotton balls and water nearby. Depending on the size of the room and needs of the family, a masking-tape "throw" line is put down to add structure.

Description
The cards with the "W" words written on them are taped to the wall and the words are read aloud. Guide a conversation about each word and how they apply to the game as follows:

Wish = Say anything you may be wishing for or something you want. Maybe an object, an event, or something you want to do or change. Wishes can have a magical value.

Worry = Tell about something in your life that you are concerned or nervous about; share something that is taking up space in your brain.

Why = A question – something you want an answer to. If a player selects this "W," then he/she gets to direct a question to another player. The person must answer the question in one or two sentences, without lectures or additional questions. (The therapist must help reinforce and create safety by stepping in if a member struggles to accept this rule.)

Will = This word means determination, motivation, and force. What are you going to do about something in your life? What are you motivated to change? What are some actions you might be willing to take?

Explain the game as follows:

"Players alternate turns selecting a 'W' word to throw a wet cotton ball at. There is not a set number of turns; the game is played until the family either runs out of cotton balls and water or until players run out of 'Ws' to talk about. When it is your turn, you announce which 'W' word you are aiming for (before you dip the cotton ball in the water to throw). Even if your cotton ball misses, you must talk about the word you verbally selected. If WHY is picked, that player can ask a question of anyone in the room – the selected person must answer the question and not respond with another question. They must wait their turn to ask a question back (by aiming at WHY). All other 'Ws' require the player to answer on his/her own."

At the end of the game, or possibly in a separate parent session, ask some of the following process questions:

1. What was it like to hear your child, sibling, or parent ask or say…?
2. What was it like to hear your child, sibling, or parent answer your question(s)?
3. How did it feel to listen to what they had to say?
4. What, if any, part of this game would you change?
5. What else would you like to share with your child, sibling, or parent?

Discussion

This game provides an engaging forum for the sharing of information and facilitates open expression among family members. This structured activity compels players to listen, which can be very powerful for a child who does not feel heard or valued. The game also allows for kinesthetic and sensory input, as there is movement, playing with water, and throwing!

The therapist can participate in the game to help model or guide the family in a specific direction. The therapist must be attentive to the process as well as the verbalizations and responsiveness of the family members. If a member of the family is stuck, passive-aggressive, visibly upset, or not participating, the therapist can step in and ask if he/she can toss a cotton ball. The therapist will ask a specific person in the group WHY? For example, why is it hard – are they feeling alright about how the game is going or about the answer they received?"

It is often helpful to meet with parents in a separate session prior to playing this game to prepare them for therapeutic expectations and possible issues the children or teens may bring up. It is paramount to help parents understand the weight and value of this game to ensure children are able to express their thoughts and feelings in a safe atmosphere.

About The Author

Brijin Gardner, LSCSW, LCSW, RPT-S, is a Clinical Social Worker practicing in the Kansas City area. She has worked extensively in the school setting with students diagnosed with behavior disorders and emotional disturbances. She maintains a private practice specializing with children, adolescents and families. She also provides training in play therapy and supervision, and has presented several times at the Association for Play Therapy Annual Conference and at the International Theraplay® Conference. She has written articles and book chapters relating to her work with groups and adolescents and her Theraplay® applications.

Waberjocky Island
Source: Ken Gardner and Lorri Yasenik

Goals
- Increase parent attunement to children
- Identify aspects of parent sensitivity and responsiveness to children's emotional needs/states
- Identify current levels of family adaptability and cohesiveness
- Provide a playful context for family members to interact and work toward a common goal

Materials
- Blanket large enough for all family members to comfortably sit on
- Scarves – one per family member
- Dress-up hats – one per family member
- Construction paper –six sheets (8 ½" x 11")
- Story sequence cards (included)
- Card stock or ten index cards
- Candy/treat –one piece per family member
- Small treasure or gift box (optional)
- Stapler

Advance Preparation
Place the blanket on the floor and position it so that all members can sit on it comfortably at the same time.

On five pieces of construction paper, draw a "stepping stone" shape; on the remaining sheet of paper draw a large "X" to mark the spot for the treasure. Place the stepping stones and the paper with the "X" in a straight line beginning at one end of the blanket and leading away from the blanket.

Place the candy/treats in the treasure or gift box. Place the box on the paper marked with the "X".

Place the hats on the floor beside the blanket and set one hat aside for the parent, noting that this is the captain's hat.

Photocopy the story sequence cards onto card stock and cut out each one, or copy onto index cards. Staple the story sequence cards together in order from one to ten. Place the ten story sequence cards inside the Captain's hat.

Description
Prepare the parent to lead this activity by reviewing the family instructions (see

below) as well as the ten story cards. Ask the parent to consider how he/she might "animate" and/or elaborate the story sequence to ensure that family members feel included. Emphasize that the parent may choose to extend or shorten segments of the story, based on responses of family members. It is also important at the end of the activity that the parent, as captain, feeds a special treat to each person and helps the family or "crew" work together and come up with one wish for their family.

The therapist reads the following instructions to the family:

"You are going to get to go on a special boat trip to a wonderful island called Waberjocky Island. The boat is designed to fit everyone and the way to row it and make it go is by sitting in a circle and linking yourselves together by holding on to the ends of the scarves, as if you are making a big chain or rope. The faster you move or sway in a circle, the faster the boat will go. But if you need to slow down, you just sway in a slow and gentle way. Now, to get ready, find a place on the boat and link yourselves together with your scarves (the therapist should point to the blanket area). One final thing that you should take on this trip is a hat, which may come in handy. However, these are special hats and will only help if the captain picks it out for you. So, Captain, please choose a hat for each member of your crew. There is one more special hat – the Captain's hat – because inside, it has all the directions and clues you need to get to Waberjocky Island where you will find the Waberjocky treasure."

Have the Captain (the parent) lead the next part of this activity by reading aloud the Story Sequence Cards and coordinating the tasks.

After the trip, facilitate discussion by asking the following questions:

1. What was the most fun part of this journey?
2. What was your Waberjocky wish?
3. How could you tell if some part of this wish came true?
4. If you could go on a smaller journey together, tomorrow, where would you like to go? What would you want to take along?
5. How were you able to get through all of those obstacles like the tunnel, waterfall and big waves?
6. Captain, how did you know those hats would work for each member of your crew?
7. How in your daily life as a family might you signal or tell someone in your family that you would like his/her support or that you want to work together?

Discussion
This activity provides various opportunities to examine attachment behaviors such as seeking closeness or proximity, responding in a sensitive and timely manner to a

child's expressed feelings or needs, and providing nurturing responses. From a structural/systems perspective, the parent is purposefully assigned the role of a leader or captain who is to coordinate the tasks or activities (particularly interactional and family-based tasks) of making one wish, finding a hat that seems "right" for each member, and feeding each member of the crew.

The process questions at the end of the game facilitate discussion among family members; they also provide another means for the parent to communicate about the special or unique things they noticed about family members and their ability to work together as a "crew."

The therapist, in observing and tracking the process, should also be prepared to offer comments on how family members supported each other during their journey. The therapist also needs to be prepared to amplify or expand upon feelings and interactions to help highlight for the parent ways in which family interactions communicate needs for comfort, safety, support, or reassurance.

About The Authors

Lorri Yasenik, MSW, RFM, CPT-S, RPT-S, and Ken Gardner, M.Sc., R.Psych, CPT-S, are the Co-Directors of the Rocky Mountain Play Therapy Institute. The Institute is an internationally recognized professional training program dedicated to offering relevant and experiential learning opportunities in child and play therapy. Lorri is a Certified/Registered Play Therapy Supervisor, a Clinical Social Worker, and a Registered Family Mediator who has been working with children and families in the areas of treatment of trauma, high conflict separation and divorce, and a range of situational and developmental issues during the course of her therapy career. Ken is a Clinical Psychologist and Certified Play Therapy Supervisor who specializes in the areas of learning/adjustment, children with development challenges, and achievement motivation. Lorri and Ken have extensive experience as consultants and trainers and regularly teach for college and university programs in the areas of play therapy, mediation, assessment, and counseling. They are the authors of the book, *Play Therapy Dimensions Model: A Decision Making Guide for Therapists.*

Waberjocky Island
Story Sequence Cards

Card #1: "We are going on a special boat trip to Waberjocky Island. Once we arrive at the island we will have the chance to find the Waberjocky treasure."

Card #2: "We are in the boat and the waves are very gentle and rolling. Let's all hold on to our scarves, so they go around the boat in a circle, and gently sway or move with the waves."

Card #3: "A few clouds roll in and there is a nice warm, gentle tropical rain. To help keep dry, we can make a roof or canopy by joining our scarves."

Card #4: "Look out! There are some big waves and rapids ahead. Everyone hold on to your scarves and row fast to get through them."

Card #5: "Now our boat is coming close to an island – but not Waberjocky Island. Look, there is a nice waterfall for us to go under. Let's tighten up together and make the scarf roof tight so we can stay dry."

Card #6: "Wow, this is a long trip and we need to drink some water. Does anyone have a hat so we can scoop up some water to drink?"

Card #7: "We got through the waterfall and need to go through one last tunnel to get to Waberjocky Island. It has a small opening – we better get close together and crouch down to get through."

Card #8: "Looks like we are here at the entrance to Waberjocky Island. Now we are supposed to get off the boat and follow the stepping stone path to find the treasure on the spot marked by an X." (Everyone helps one another out of the boat.)

Card #9: "The card (found on the X marking-the-spot stepping stone) says: The captain should feed everyone one of the special Waberjocky treats."

Card #10: "Lastly, let's join arms and make one wish together for our family."

Walk a Mile in My Shoes
Source: Alison Smith

Goals
- Encourage family member's to share feelings and perspectives with one another
- Increase ability to empathize with family members
- Increase open communication among family members
- Increase family cohesion

Description
Ask the family if they have ever heard the saying "Walk a Mile in My Shoes." Ask members to share what they think the saying means. To encourage participation, offer possible meanings of the saying. For example, is it suggesting that we get more exercise by walking?

Explain that the saying is about "understanding and entering into another's experiences and feelings." Explain that sometimes people have circumstances in their lives that we may be unaware of that can affect our relationship with them.

Next, ask all family members to stand up and remove their shoes. Ask them to place their shoes in front of them. Then "swap" shoes among the family members. Give family members shoes that may not fit or that will have an awkward fit. Be mindful to give young family members flat shoes as to avoid injury.

Ask the members to put the shoes on and take a lap around the room or down a hallway. Remind everyone to go slowly and be careful. The members may have difficulty walking in someone else's shoes.

Encourage family members to "be" the person whose shoes they are wearing. They may talk, act, and respond to others just as the shoe's owner would. It may be beneficial for members to replay a recent family argument or disagreement, while staying in character of the person whose shoes they are wearing. After everyone has had a try, ask them to return to their original spots and put their own shoes back on.

Help the family to process their feelings and thoughts about their experience. The following process questions can guide the discussion:

1. What was it like to walk in someone else's shoes?
2. What was the most difficult part?
3. What was fun about walking in someone else's shoes?
4. What do you think it feels like to be ___ (the person whose shoes you were walking in)? What do you think makes this person feel happy? What do you

think makes this person feel upset?
5. Now, what do you think the saying "Walk A Mile in My Shoes" means?
6. What have you learned today about others in your family?

Discussion

This activity builds empathy by helping family members understand and enter into another's experience. By literally walking in a family member's shoes, it allows participants to think about struggles that the other person may encounter. This activity increases family members' sensitivity and understanding of one another's positions. This in turn facilitates more authentic family relationships.

Family conflicts are often a result of not considering another's perspective. This activity helps family members to think about why a family member may have reacted to a particular situation. Through this activity, old perceptions and set patterns of thinking are discussed, and challenged, and family members are encouraged to consider new perspectives. Empathy is built as family members engage in this experiential activity.

About The Author

Alison Smith, M.S., is a Child and Adolescent Therapist in Indianapolis, Indiana. She is a Licensed School Counselor providing individual, group, and family therapy. She received her Bachelor Degree from the University of Indianapolis and her Masters in School Counseling from Indiana University.

What Would They Say?
Source: Greg Lubimiv

Goals
- Assess family relationships and dynamics
- Identify the family interactional patterns that are contributing to the problematic behavior
- Increase open communication among family members
- Share feelings that underlie conflict within the family
- Increase family cohesion

Materials
- Sentence Completions (included)
- Index cards
- Marker
- Game such as Jenga™, Crocodile Dentist™, Pop Up Pirate™
- Paper
- Pens
- Prizes (optional)

Advance Preparation
Create 20 to 30 sentence completions that only require one-word answers. Make sure the questions suit the family members and that there is a reasonable answer. Sample questions are included below.

Write the questions onto index cards. Place the cards on the table, face down, so that each family member can easily access them.

Description
The family plays a game that incorporates turn taking, such as Jenga™, Crocodile Dentist™, or Pop Up Pirate™. The game should be one that moves fairly quickly so that family members do not have to wait a long time for a turn. Ensure the game is appropriate for the youngest child as well as for the oldest.

Decide which family member will go first. If this is difficult for the family to decide, roll a die, choose a number, play rock paper scissors, or use some other chance method to decide who will go first. The turns then go clockwise.

When a turn is over because the tower has fallen or the pirate has popped, that player picks the top card from the sentence completion card pile and reads the sentence aloud. If the family member cannot read, then the therapist can read the question aloud. The person who selected the card secretly writes down his/her answer and the other family members guess what that person's answer is and they write down their guesses. This is why the name of the game is "What Would They Say?" If the child cannot write, he/she can whisper the answer to the therapist who then writes the child's response on a piece of paper. Ensure the other family members cannot see the child's answer. The responses are then read aloud. Each correct answer scores one point. It is important to emphasize that an important rule of the game is to accept whatever answer a family member may give.

The game continues until each family member has had a predetermined number of turns.

Once the family is appropriately engaged, responses can be explored in more depth. For example, in response to "When I get mad you can tell because I... shout", ask "Who else shouts in the family?"

If a family member becomes upset with an answer, remind him/her of the rules and offer support, or ask another family member to provide some support.

At the end of the game the person with the most points wins. To make the game noncompetitive, challenge the family to reach a certain score. If there are 20 questions and 4 family members the highest score is 60 (because one person does not guess each round as they completed the sentence). Choose a score that the family has a chance in achieving. In this case, a combined score of 30 means the family wins. In later games, raise the target score to provide a greater challenge.

After the game, process by asking the following questions:

1. What was the most interesting or surprising response?
2. What did this game reveal about who you know best/least in your family?
3. What did you like best about this game?

Discussion

This game engages family members and helps them to communicate more openly. Games are an effective tool to use with families. As Schaefer and Reid (2001) highlight, games "invite the relaxation of defenses that would normally inhibit expression of feelings, thoughts, and attitudes in normal social discourse. Thus, one often sees a high level of affective involvement in game play."

The order and pacing of questions in this game is important. Begin with neutral questions and then move to questions that require greater emotional risk. End the game on a positive note with questions that elicit happy feelings.

The use of prizes is an optional part of the activity, as the prospect of winning something motivates the family members and adds an element of engagement.

Reference
Schaefer, C.E., & Reid, S.E. (2001). *Game play: Therapeutic use of childhood games.* New York: John Wiley & Sons.

About the Author
Greg Lubimiv, MSW, CPT-S, is the Executive Director of the Phoenix Centre for Children and Families, a children's mental health centre in southeastern Ontario, Canada. As well, he is involved with Invest In Kids, assisting in the development of an innovative parenting program that starts in pregnancy and continues to the child's first birthday. He has worked in the field of children's mental health since 1981 and has been involved as a clinician, trainer, and administrator. He has specialized training in the field of play therapy and family therapy and has authored a number of books and articles on this and other topics, including *Wings for Our Children: The Essentials of Becoming a Play Therapist* and *My Sister Is An Angeline,* a book helping children cope with sibling death. He has a Masters of Social Work and is a Certified Play Therapist Supervisor with the Canadian Association for Child and Play Therapy. He has been presented with the Monica Hebert Award for contributions to the field of Play Therapy.

What Would They Say?
Sample Sentence Completions

My favorite color is…

My favorite food is…

My favorite fruit is…

My favorite vegetable is…

My favorite ice cream flavor is…

My favorite animal is a…

My favorite television show is…

My favorite thing to do is…

If choosing between ice cream and apple pie I would choose…

Between going for a walk and watching a good movie I would choose…

My favorite room in our house is…

Between a bath and a shower I prefer…

If I could choose to have any hair color I would choose…

If someone calls me a name I feel…

When I have a bad dream the first person I would tell about it would be…

The person in my family who helps others the most is…

The person in my family who gets angry the easiest is…

The person in my family who cries the most is…

The person in my family who laughs the most is…

© Greg Lubimiv

What's the Weather?

Source: Laura Lazarus

Goals
- Identify and express a range of emotions
- Increase open communication among family members
- Increase understanding among family members
- Gradually discuss volatile topics with reduced tension and conflict

Materials
- Paper
- Coloring materials such as markers, colored pencils, crayons, etc.

Advance Preparation
Arrange a flat drawing space for each family member. It is important that the sheets of drawing paper are not in direct eyesight of each other. Arrange the paper and coloring materials so that each family member has easy access to them.

Description
Instruct the family as follows:

"I would like you to draw a picture that shows what type of weather describes how you feel most of the time. Just as there are many different types of weather (sunny, cloudy, foggy, snowy, rainy, and so on), there are also lots of different types of feelings. You can draw a picture that shows two or three different types of weather, because you may experience different feelings at the same time. You can use any of the drawing materials here to make your weather picture."

Explain that this is a creative endeavor, and there is no right or wrong way to go about the process.

For younger children, give an example of how a type of weather is similar to a feeling (e.g., a thunderstorm may be a symbol for anger).

Talking during the drawing phase is discouraged, as well as looking at one another's work. Giving members as much time as necessary is important so that when they are finished their drawings are as complete as possible.

After the drawings are complete, family members can share their drawings with one another and discuss the various emotions that were illustrated in the weather drawings.

The following questions can be helpful when processing the activity:

1. Identify some of the types of feelings in your picture.
2. What are some of the similarities among the pictures?
3. What did you learn about other family members through this activity?
4. Tell about a time when you experienced the feelings illustrated in your picture.

Discussion

This drawing activity encourages family members to express emotions in a creative, non-threatening manner. Using various types of weather as a concrete symbol for emotions can help clients to identify and express their feelings. The drawings can be used as a springboard for further discussion about their feelings, and can be referred to in future sessions in terms that will be familiar (i.e., "What's your weather today?").

Using art is particularly useful with families who are not masterful with words. Kwiatkowska (1967) suggests that the informality and indirectness of art techniques lessens defenses and controls in communication and the symbolic representation in a family's drawing can clarify areas of conflict.

Family cohesion is enhanced as members share their artwork and notice similarities among the drawings.

Reference

Kwiatkowska, H.Y. (1967). Family art therapy. *Family Process*, *6*, 37–55.

About The Author

Laura Lazarus, MA, is a Therapeutic Day Treatment Counselor in an elementary school in Manassas, Virginia, where she works with children who suffer from a variety of emotional and behavioral disorders. She has also worked with at-risk children and their families as a home-based counselor. She received her Master of Arts in Clinical Psychology at Argosy University's American School for Professional Psychology in Washington, D.C. She is currently pursuing LPC credentials.

When I...
Source: Trudy Post Sprunk

Goals
- Increase open communication among family members
- Improve listening skills
- Assess family relationships and dynamics

Materials
- When I... Worksheet (included)
- Scissors
- Pencils

Advance Preparation
Arrange seating so that each family member can write privately on a flat surface. Make multiple copies of the When I... Worksheet.

Description
Provide each family member with three worksheets for each family member present except themselves. For example, if it is a family of four, everyone will need nine worksheets.

Explain the activity by giving the following example: A son might request that Mom tell two feelings she has when he says, "I love you." The mother then shares two feelings and discusses her experiences when he says "I love you."

Next, the son would ask Mom to name two feelings she experiences when he hits his sister. Again, the mom shares two feelings and discusses her experience of his behavior. This procedure continues with a combination of sharing and processing feelings until each person has participated.

Ask process questions such as:

1. What was it like when your_____(mom, dad, sister, brother) responded by telling you two feelings he/she has had when you _____(take out trash etc.)?
2. What two feelings did you think he/she might share?
3. What surprised you the most about the responses?

Discussion
The "when I" approach to family therapy facilitates meaningful interactions and communications with all family members. Since all members are encouraged to openly and honestly express their feelings to each other, everyone is an active

participant. Each is encouraged to recognize and accept the feelings of others as well as to express feelings clearly. Listening, sharing, accepting, and processing are all key components to this activity, which increases emotional intimacy and enhances communication within the family.

By engaging in these key aspects of successful relating while in the therapy office, it is hoped that they will become generalized and become a part of the family's pattern of daily interactions.

About The Author
Trudy Post Sprunk, LMFT-S, LPC-S, RPT-S, CPT-S, is a Licensed Marriage and Family Therapist and Supervisor who has been practicing psychotherapy since 1971. She has presented at international, national, and local conferences and has been interviewed on radio and television. She is certified as an EMDR Specialist and is a Registered Play Therapist Supervisor. She is past-president of the Association for Play Therapy and president and co-founder of the Georgia Association for Play Therapy.

When I...
Worksheet

Examples

Mom, tell me two feelings you have when I...

    1. Say I love you
    2. Hit my sister
    3. Forget to feed the dog

_____, tell two feelings you have when I...
(Family member's name)

1_____

2_____

3_____

                                             _____
                                                 Your name

When I Was Your Age:
PhotoTherapy Techniques for Families
Source: Judy Weiser

Goals
- Improve communication among family members
- Increase parents' understanding of their children's worldview by remembering what it was like for them at that age
- Encourage parents to discuss details of their own childhood to increase the children's knowledge of their parents' younger hopes and fears, feelings and dreams
- Increase trust between children and parents once they realize they have had similar childhood feelings, worries, hopes, and experiences
- Increase the frequency of positive interactions between the parents and the children

Materials
- Good-quality photocopies of photographs of each parent taken when the parents were the same age as each of their children is now. If photos of the parents at those particular ages cannot be found, the parents can "remember" or "imagine" a moment in their childhood and draw simple stick-figure sketches to use as the photographs. NOTE: Using original photographs puts them at risk of accidental damage. It is better to use photocopies of the originals.
- Interview questions (included)
- Pens
- Paper
- Video or audiotape (optional)

Advance Preparation
If it will be difficult for all family members to continuously view the photos being discussed throughout the interview, it might help to digitally pre-scan each of the photos so they can be displayed on a screen or digital frame (or wall), or use a photocopier to enlarge them and tape them to a wall.

Carefully consider which parent to begin with. The reason for this is that for the first parent these questions will be fresh (not heard before when the other parent did it), and when the second parent does the same exercise, he/she will have heard the questions already and had time to prepare (or rehearse) the answers.
Also, decide which child should start (i.e., chronologically or randomly by drawing straws).

Similarly, decide how to proceed after the first child interviews the first parent. For example, have the same child interview the other parent via a photo of that parent at the same age, or have another child interview the parent who went first.

The therapist needs to decide in advance what to do if there is not enough time for all of the children to interview both parents during the one session: should all the children interview only one parent in that session, or should the child who starts, interview both parents, before another child starts again with the first parent at the different age? The therapist must decide what will work best for the family's situation and tell the family what the procedural rules will be before starting.

Review the interview questions and modify them as needed to fit the particular family's situation. Photocopy one sheet of interview questions for each family member to use when they are observing (and making notes) during each of the child–parent interviews.

Description

This activity can take different amounts of time, depending upon the number of children in the family and the amount of discussion afterwards, so there needs to be flexibility in planning the activity to fit into the set appointment time.

Provide each child with a sheet of interview questions. Make sure that those "recording" the session have working pens or pencils and know that their job is to document what they think is important to remember and discuss later.

Explain to the family that, while they look at a photo of the parents as children of the same age, each child in the family will get to interview each parent about what his/her life was like at the same age they are now. Each child will first ask the questions on the list, and then he/she can add any of his/her own questions after the list is finished.

They should be told that if the person who is being interviewed does not know the answer, he/she can just say so and try to make a hunch at one that would likely be very close to the real answer. The person answering can voice his/her answers as if being the child at that time, or he/she can use his/her adult voice to talk about the photo from "back then."

No one is permitted to interrupt the child–parent interview by talking, disrupting, or leaving the room (unless it is a bathroom emergency, in which case the person must leave quietly). If the therapist feels that some guidance or elaboration is needed, then he/she may interrupt.

Have the child begin by asking the parent the following general question: "What was your life like at the age you are in that picture?" Once the parent has finished his/her spontaneous summary, the child should begin asking the questions on the interview list in order to get additional information. The therapist should not interrupt unless it is truly necessary; "trusting the flow" of the dialogue itself is important. However, if necessary, the therapist should gently remind the parent and child that the questions are about feelings as well as thoughts, and so it would be helpful for the parent to share his/her thoughts about the "why" of each answer given and some of the feelings attached to it.

Both the child and the parent are permitted to take notes if desired (but this is not necessary). However, all others in the room should be taking notes as they follow along.

After the child has asked all the questions on the list, then any other questions that come to mind can be asked.

After the interview has ended, the two-part discussion can begin: first the "de-briefing" of the two participants, then asking the others to share their observations, thoughts, feelings, and insights.

The therapist should ask the child:
1. How was your parent's childhood similar or different from yours at your age?
2. What things did you learn about your parent's life at that age that you didn't know before?
3. Did anything you learned about your parent today surprise you? If so, what?
4. Did anything you learned about your parent today upset or disturb you? If so, what?
5. What feelings did your parent describe?
6. Were there any connections between what your parent was like at that young age and the problems the family is trying to get help with today?
7. Is there anything you would like to ask or tell your parent as a result of what you learned about them today?

The therapist should ask the parent:
1. What seems different about your child's childhood and yours at the same age?
2. What things did you learn about your life at that age that you hadn't really realized before? What things surprised or upset you?
3. What feelings did you find yourself talking about – and why did you have those feelings at that age?
4. Do you ever have any of those childhood feelings in your life today?
5. Did you see any connections between what your life was like at that young age and the problems your family is trying to get help with today?
6. Is there anything you would like to ask or tell your child, as a result of what you shared with him/her today?

The observers can then have an opportunity to speak and ask questions. They should not be interrupted while they are speaking. When they are finished, the therapist can facilitate a general discussion among all the family members.

The above process can be repeated according to which method the therapist determined would work best. That is, having the same parent interviewed by a different child or having the other parent interviewed by the first child, before moving on to next child.

Discussion

This activity is designed to permit individual family members to encounter each other in more fullness as unique individuals, in addition to their more stereotypical roles when relating to each other as parent and child.

What makes PhotoTherapy techniques valuable in therapy is that, when you look at a photo (or, just as importantly, simply remember one), the moment inside its borders instantly comes "alive." You see it as if it is happening right now – being viewed in three dimensions as if it is real, and you are there in the scene, not realizing that your eye is not the lens of a camera – even if it was taken decades ago.

This quality of the viewer instantly "being there" inside the photo that is being encountered in its "all at once-ness" unconsciously connects him/her with any feelings and memories associated with that moment – whether the photo is one from his/her own life or one never seen before that just reminds him/her of related situations and unconsciously triggers feelings embedded in those memories.

This is the reason for asking participants to view real photographs and be interviewed as if they were that age, instead of just asking them to relate old memories. It is important for the parent to actually *be* his/her young self for a few minutes and view the world (and reply to the questions) from inside that perspective. Asking people to tell stories to help explain photos of their lives will always yield a different (and deeper) quality of information than just asking them to talk about their past.

When the parents take the time to think about *being* a specific young age (what it was like, how it felt, how they understood complicated things from their limited perspectives, how they encountered feelings without much idea how to handle them, how their own issues at that age are often very similar to their child's right now, and so forth), it can help them better understand their child at the same point in development and hopefully see things better through the eyes (and age) of that child.

Similarly, knowing that their parents were once young and occasionally silly and that they did things their own parents did not approve of, helps the children realize their parents are people whose identities are made up of many more things than just being their parents. These combined learnings help the participants move beyond the limitations of being simply parent and child and encourages them to get to know each other more fully as unique individuals whom they might want to get to know better in the future.

While chatting about the old photos of the parents when they were young, the parents and children share pleasurable experiences in common, bringing them closer together. This in itself creates a more trusting bond, especially since it is being witnessed by other family members whose very presence validates the shifted reality.

Although the therapist can often detect these patterns and interactional dynamics more quickly or more deeply than family members themselves, it will be more therapeutically beneficial to let the family members first share their own observations and conclusions before hearing the therapist's version. Since such discussion at the end of this activity can easily go longer than one might expect, the therapist is cautioned to structure the timing of each part of the activity to ensure that sufficient time for debriefing and good closure is provided.

It is ideal to videotape the session for the sake of future viewing (both for later therapy sessions and for family history in general), but using taping or playback equipment is not a requirement. Even if it is done, the "recorders" should still be writing down their own observations and thoughts.

References

Weiser, J. (2004). PhotoTherapy techniques in counseling and therapy: Using ordinary snapshots and photo-interactions to help clients heal their lives. *The Canadian Art Therapy Association Journal, 17(2)*, 23–53.

Weiser, J. (2002). PhotoTherapy techniques: Exploring the secrets of personal snapshots and family albums. *Child & Family. Journal of the Notre Dame Child and Family Institute, 5(3)*, 16–25.

Weiser, J. (1999). *PhotoTherapy techniques: Exploring the secrets of personal snapshots and family albums* (3rd ed.). Vancouver, BC: PhotoTherapy Centre Press.

Weiser, J. (1988). PhotoTherapy: Using snapshots and photo-interactions in therapy with youth. In C.E. Schaefer (Ed.), *Innovative interventions in child and adolescent therapy*. New York: John Wiley & Sons.

About The Author

Judy Weiser, R.Psych., A.T.R., Founder and Director of the PhotoTherapy Centre, is a psychologist, art therapist, consultant, trainer, and early pioneer of PhotoTherapy techniques (using people's personal and family snapshots to access feelings and memories during the therapy process).She is the author of the classic text *PhotoTherapy Techniques: Exploring the Secrets of Personal Snapshots and Family Albums* (now in its third printing), as well as numerous professional articles, book chapters, and a video/DVD on the subject. She also created and maintains the primary informational resource and networking website for the field (*PhotoTherapy Techniques in Counseling and Therapy*) as well as a Discussion Board and Facebook Group. Long considered the world authority on PhotoTherapy, she has given over 300 workshops, lectures, and training intensives about these techniques (and related applications of Therapeutic Photography) in over 50 cities worldwide during the past 30 years.

© Judy Weiser

When I Was Your Age:
PhotoTherapy Techniques for Families
Interview Questions

Please ask the child in that picture to answer the following questions about his/her life at that time and to explain a bit more about the reason why he/she thinks this was the answer.

Each question should begin with the phrase, "When you were the age that I am now, [insert the question to follow]?"

1. What memories or stories come to mind when seeing this picture again now?
2. What feelings does this picture evoke now that you see it again?
3. What was your favorite thing to do when you played?
4. What was your favorite food? What food did you hate the most?
5. Who was your "best friend," and what was it like being with that person?
6. How did you get along with your sisters and brothers?
7. What did you want to grow up to be?
8. Did you like school? What was the best and worst part of school?
9. What did you do after school or on weekends?
10. Did you prefer to be alone, or with other people? Why?
11. Where did you like to go when your parents were not with you (or when they didn't know where you were going)?
12. What kinds of problems did you have at that age? How did you solve them?
13. Did your family have problems at that time? If so, how did they solve these?
14. What chores were you expected to do? Did you always do them? What happened if you didn't?
15. What family rules did you have to obey? Which rules did you hate the most?
16. What kinds of things did you do that got you into trouble with your parents?
17. What would they do if they were angry or upset with you?
18. What worried you the most? What frightened you the most? What were you most afraid of? And, how did you cope with these things?
19. What made you happy? sad? bored?
20. What made you angriest and how did you express that?
21. Did you ever hit anyone? Did anyone ever hit you? What were the circumstances?

22. What things would make you cry?

23. When you were upset or crying, who would you seek out to comfort you and make things better?

24. Do you think your parents gave more attention to (or preferred) you – or one of your brothers or sisters? Why?

25. Would you have preferred to spend more time with your mom or your dad? Why?

26. Is this picture a true depiction of you at that age? If not, then what would need to be changed to make it more real?

27. Is there anything missing from this photo that should have been there to make it more complete a picture of you at that age? If yes, what would that be?

28. What else would you like to tell me about this photo?

Wilderness Trail
Source: Madhu Kasiram

Goals
- Establish a therapeutic relationship at multiple levels: between therapist and clients, among family members, and across different families
- Witness common wonders
- Negotiate common obstacles

Materials
- Accessible wilderness trail
- Appropriate hiking gear, such as shoes, jacket, hat, etc.

Advance Preparation
Identify several walking trails that are at an appropriate level for the family members and where nature's "wares" are on display.

Description
Explain to the family or families that they are taking this trail together to experience nature and to talk about that experience while they are hiking. Let them know that they will be required to take responsibility for voicing any specific needs they may have while on the trail, for example, needing to take a rest.

The therapist will be hiking with the participants and will use different nature points to stimulate discussion and encourage attentive listening among the participants. During the hike, the therapist can facilitate this discussion by using the following questions and comments:

1. Comment on this structure/rock formation/sunset, etc.
2. Encourage participants to compare and comment on each other's perceptions.
3. How can you relate the above aspect of nature to your life situation?
4. What lessons can you derive from nature in helping you with your difficulties?

The therapist's questions and comments may encourage the natural telling of a story, or may involve using the story themes as metaphors for overcoming hardship (Thulani, 2004) or celebrating victories.

The therapist will not assign specific places or roles on the trail, as the natural order followed by the participants will yield rich information on leadership and participation styles. However, to ensure everyone participates in meaningful ways and that their stories and/or roles are appropriately affirmed, the therapist may use deliberate theoretical constructs from narrative, structural, or Milan family therapy.

Discussion

The twin injustices of HIV/AIDS and poverty in sub-Saharan Africa and indeed in South Africa (Kasiram, 2009) make it challenging to meaningfully engage with emerging family structures such as the child-headed family (Mturi & Nzimande, 2006). These families in particular have a need to "do hope" (Weingarten, 2000) since they live with hopelessness that often stems from the multiplicity of adult responsibilities. This has prompted practitioners to look "outside the box" for creative ways to connect meaningfully with such children and families.

The weather, landscape, and abundant natural resources in South Africa offer a wide variety of ways to engage in a discrimination-free, easily accessible environment. Practitioners of family therapy, groupwork, and community work have recorded optimal gains through their use of the natural environment in their localities (Brink, 2000; MacDowell, 2004; Thulani, 2004). Natural environments with warm, sunny skies and open, uncluttered views appear to warm the spirits of participants, particularly children who often do not question "motives" for using different contexts for practice.

Walking together as a family amidst nature builds and strengthens relationships, especially since it is difficult to be silent when there is a joint witnessing of the wonder of nature. Taking hikes along wilderness trails encourages the development of meaningful relationships as both task and process goals (Miller 2010, http://www.talkingcure.com), and it is clear that these relationships can help the family find ways to work together as they face hardships and challenges.

References

Brink, J. (2000). Take a walk on the wild side. Workshop presented at the 8th International Conference, South African Association of Marriage and Family Therapy, Cape Town.

Kasiram, M. (2009). Trauma, HIV/AIDS and healing: What can a systems overview and family therapy offer? Plenary paper presented at the International Family Therapy Association Conference, Portoroz, Slovenia.

MacDowell, M. (2004). The spirit of wilderness: The benefits of a wilderness trail for child-headed families. Paper presented at the 9th International Conference, South African Association of Marriage and Family Therapy, Durban.

Miller, S.http://www.talkingcure.com accessed 25/05/2010.

Mturi, A.J., & Nzimande, N. (2006). Exploring the link between changing family patterns and HIV/AIDS in South Africa. In M. Kasiram, Partab, and B. Dano (Eds.), *HIV/AIDS in Africa: The not so silent presence.* Durban: Printconnection.

Thulani, Z. (2004). Wilderness diversions. Paper presented at the 9th International Conference, South African Association of Marriage and Family Therapy, Durban.

Weingarten, K. (2000). Witnessing, wondering, and hope. *Family process,39*, 389–402.

About The Author

Madhu Kasiram, PhD, is a Professor of Social Work at the University of KwaZulu Ntal. Her area of interest is in adjusting traditional family therapy theory and techniques to better fit the South African context where micro-systemic strategies are often regarded as an unaffordable luxury because of the favoring of community-based or other developmental interventions. Her work includes how to creatively embrace multiple systems within the paradigmatic framework in which family therapy is rooted.

World Creation
Source: Christopher Belous

Goals
- Increase understanding among family members
- Increase communication among family members
- Identify comparable and compatible components among family members

Materials
- Markers
- Large sheets of paper (one per family member)

Advance Preparation
Arrange a flat drawing space for each family member. It is important that the sheets of paper are not in direct eyesight of each other. Arrange the markers so that each family member has easy access to them.

Description
Explain to the family that they will be exploring their own perceptions and communication styles through the following intervention. Also be sure to tell them that this is a creative endeavor, and that there is no right or wrong way to go about the process.

Provide each family member with a sheet of paper and markers. Explain the activity as follows:

"On your sheet of paper, I want you to draw your world. Try and draw the best representation of who you are and what your world is like in as much detail as possible. You can use any amount of color and choose any style and technique you wish. You can have as many continents, oceans, and other features as you would like. You can have people and important events as part of your world. I would appreciate it if you would label each part of your world, so that we can talk about these later. Be sure to include some kind of communication system in your world, such as how everyone talks to each other, and if there is communication with anything else – some people have drawn telephone lines, others satellites, some have even drawn phone booths. It is up to you."

Talking during the drawing phase is discouraged, as well as looking at one another's work. The point is for family members to create as whole and unique a representation of their worlds as possible, without undue influence from others. Giving the members as much time as necessary is important so that when they are finished their worlds are as complete as possible.

After the drawings are complete, family members can observe one another's drawings. Ask each member to lead a "journey" through his/her world and be the tour guide of his/her planet.

The following tips and probes can be helpful when processing the activity:

1. What is the name of the world, city, and continents?
2. What does the world have that is unique?
3. How does the world communicate? What about with other worlds?
4. Are there any natural resources (i.e., water, land, mountains, weather, animal life, plant life)?
5. Who are the significant inhabitants (i.e., family, strangers, friends, themselves, significant others)?
6. What do the colors, shapes and sizes of the objects mean?
7. Does the location of the objects have any meaning?
8. Are there borders? Are they clearly defined? Fuzzy? Non-existent?
9. Who is in control of each section of the world? Is it them? Someone else?
10. Where are the clients in the world?
11. Who lives where?
12. Is there danger present? If so, who/what is in danger? Who/what serves as protectors?
13. Are their laws in this world? Who makes the laws? Who obeys them? Who makes sure they are obeyed?

Feel free to ask additional questions and explore emotions and thoughts behind the decisions of the clients.

Discussion

One of the most common presenting issues for family therapy is communication. This activity promotes communication and active listening among family members. It allows family members to become familiar with one another's world views and helps them to gain a higher level of understanding of one another.

The activity gives the family the ability to describe in as much detail as they would like their perceptions of the world in which they live. The activity also helps clients communicate important life events.

As well, the activity can be used as an assessment tool for the therapist, to consider issues of significant past traumas, current boundaries, relational dimensions (connection and loneliness), and ability to communicate. This will allow the therapist to discover important events and determine interventions for future treatment sessions.

About The Author

Christopher Belous, MA, LLMFT, CFLE, CCT, is a doctoral student in the Couple and Family Therapy program at Michigan State University. He is a Certified Family Life Educator, and has obtained Certification in College Teaching from the Graduate School at Michigan State University. He is actively engaged in research and clinical work with individuals, couples, and families.

Yuehong Sandplay Encouragement Method
Source: Yuehong Chen Foley

Goals
- Assess family relationships and dynamics
- Increase positive communication and interaction among family members, such as talking calmly, giving clear messages, making eye contact, listening, taking turns, and following rules
- Increase family cohesion by practicing encouragement skills, such as giving meaningful appreciations and thoughtful compliments

Materials
- Sandtray half-filled with sand
- Small bin
- Variety of miniature objects or figurines representing different categories such as people, animals, plants, buildings, vehicles, etc.
- Table and chairs
- Large sheet of paper
- Tape
- Marker
- Paper
- Pen
- Polaroid or digital camera
- Printer

Advance Preparation
Place the miniature objects and figurines in a small bin that can be easily passed among family members. Tape the large sheet of paper to the wall. This will be used to document the story that the family creates.

Description
Introduce the activity by stating, "We are going to create one sandworld together, create one story together, and then share appreciations of each other. The rules are: The sand stays inside the sandtray only. When making the sandworld, you only touch the miniature figurines or sand when it is your turn. When creating the story, you only speak when it is your turn. Then we will share appreciations of each other and take a photo of our sandworld."

Step One: Building a Sandworld Together
Have family members sit so they can all reach the sandtray. Explain the first step of the activity as follows: "We are going to create a sandworld together. Each person will take turns choosing and putting one object from the bin into the sandtray within five seconds, then he/she will pass the bin to the next family member.

Please watch quietly and wait for your turn." The therapist can put an object in the sand first, or ask a volunteer to put an object in first. After each person has five or six turns, the therapist states, "Let's stop the building phase here. Now, let's look at the sandworld quietly and think about what is happening in it."

Step Two: Making a Story Together

Explain the next phase of the activity by stating: "We will make one story about this sandworld now. Each person will say one sentence of 10 words or less. Try to use one word from the person before you and connect your ideas. Speak loudly and clearly so the whole family can repeat your sentence." After each person has six turns, say "The End of the Story." The therapist can write down each sentence on the large sheet, or ask a family member to volunteer to write them down.

Step Three: Appreciations

Tell the family: "Now we are going to take turns appreciating each other. You can say one appreciation to each person at your first turn. If you would like to say more appreciations from your everyday life at home please wait for your next turn. Be sure to keep eye contact with the person you are appreciating. Try to say your appreciations in 10 words or less. You can say specifically what you liked about the person during sandplay, for example: you waited for your turn quietly; you listened and followed rules carefully; you passed the bin to others kindly and quickly; I like your ideas. Have a family member volunteer to write down the appreciations as they are being said.

Step Four: Taking a Picture of the Sandworld

Say to the family: "Now, let's take a picture of our sandworld. Then we will print it and keep it in a special folder, along with the story and the appreciations."

Step Five: Postplay Discussion

Discuss with the family the process that evolved during the activity. Ask process questions such as:

1. What was it like to work together to create the sandworld and story?
2. What do you think about the sandworld and story that you created?
3. How did it feel to give and receive appreciations?
4. What surprised you the most about this activity?

Discussion

Many families have problematic relationships because they interact in a disrespectful manner and they have poor communication skills. This activity provides the family with an opportunity to practice interpersonal skills such as listening, maintaining eye contact, repeating, taking turns, giving clear messages, following rules, and giving meaningful compliments. The therapist can highlight the positive interactions that emerge during the activity to strengthen family functioning.

Encouragement in the form of sincere appreciations and compliments from family members recognizes the efforts and achievements of the person, focuses on the strengths and assets of the person, and integrates the family members' awareness. Encouragement improves the participants' self-acceptance, trust in others, and courage to change in the process of building self-esteem and quality relationships (Adler, 1927).

This activity is also a good assessment tool. It provides opportunities to observe the ways that family members interact with one another. The choice of specific sandtray items, the themes expressed in the story, the postplay discussion, and the link of the story to the family's real-life situation provide valuable insights about the family.

Sandtray play is therapeutic because it involves kinesthetic multi-dimensionality in time and space, invites imagination and experience of thoughts and feelings, and opens the person's energy to connect the intellectual, the soul, the heart, and the body (De Domenico, 1988). The process of building, sharing, and comprehending the sandplay in the presence of receptive family members offers multiple opportunities to realize harmony between the inner and outer worlds. The structured behavior procedures provide a safe and orderly environment for the family to start their therapeutic journey.

Collaborative storytelling is an added therapeutic dimension to this activity. Collaborative storytelling develops interpersonal skills and builds family cohesion.

References

Adler, A. (1927). *Understanding human nature*. Trans. W.B. Wolfe. New York: The World Publishing Company.

De Domenico, G. (1988). *Sandtray worldplay: Comprehensive guide to the use of the sandtray in psychotherapy and transformational settings*. Oakland: Vision Quest Into Symbolic Reality.

About The Author

Yuehong Chen Foley, PhD, LPC, is the founder and President of Responsible Child, LLC. She provides play therapy to children and filial therapy services to their families. She has published numerous research articles in the field of play therapy, and has worked as a school counselor and behavior interventionist in public schools for seven years.

Special thanks to Dr. Gisela De Domenico for her teachings and editorial review.

Section Three:
Termination Techniques

Chapter Overview: Termination Techniques

Termination from therapy is the culmination of the process and products of all that has gone on in prior sessions. A positive termination requires clinical sensitivity to the family's needs. Ideally, the end of therapy should come in a planned way, be a joint decision between the therapist and the family, bring psychological closure to good therapy, and be a positive experience for each family member.

The family is ready to end therapy when the treatment goals have been achieved. It will be easier to recognize when to terminate treatment if these goals have been clearly defined in the initial phase of therapy. The basic elements of good terminations include the following: "Give the family notice; set an ending date; explore the feelings about ending; expect testing, crises, and everything seeming to fall apart; better yet, predict the crises for them so they realize that it is all part of the ending process; review all the skills learned and progress made" (Taibbi, 2007). It is also important to celebrate the family's achievements in therapy (Odell & Campbell, 1998) and to obtain feedback from the family about what therapy has been like for them. As Roberts (1993) puts it, "We are making too many assumptions in the field of family therapy about how families view treatment and we need to hear more clients' voices."

When the inevitable crises occur during the termination phase of treatment, it is helpful to reassure the family that they have learned the skills necessary to handle the problem. The family may need to be coached to use their problem-solving skills, but the therapist should intervene in as minimal a way as possible.

An important goal of termination is to empower the family by helping them to recognize their capacity to handle their issues on their own in the future. Enabling the family to see the changes they have made allows the therapist to disengage from the system.

Family members may worry that the presenting problem will recur when therapy ends or that the progress made may not continue. The therapist should acknowledge the family's fear and help the family explore early warning signs of relapse. In addition to exploring the fear, the family can be asked "to actually try, in a limited way, to recreate the problems they were having when they initiated therapy" (McCollum, 1993). Reenacting a relapse can be done using play, art, or psychodrama.

The therapist must be cognizant of feelings of loss often associated with ending therapy, and to process these feelings in a sensitive manner. Termination is also a time to review and celebrate therapeutic gains. Creative termination activities and closing rituals should be integrated into final sessions. The techniques in this section help to create positive endings for families.

Farewell Fortune Cookies
Source: Sueann Kenney-Noziska

Goals
- Provide a positive termination experience
- Increase open communication regarding termination
- Emphasize and review therapeutic gains

Materials
- Fortune cookies
- Tape
- Tweezers
- Questions (included)

Advance Preparation
Purchase fortune cookies (available at most grocery stores in the oriental food section). If possible, individually wrapped cookies should be purchased.

Therapeutic questions are written on strips of paper, which are folded and taped onto the outside of each individual cookie. If cookies are not individually wrapped, the therapeutic questions can be rolled up and inserted inside the fortune cookie using a pair of tweezers. In the latter case, clients will have two fortunes inside each cookie – one traditional fortune and one "therapeutic" fortune.

Description
Family members take turns selecting one "farewell fortune cookie" and responding to the corresponding therapeutic question. The therapist facilitates the activity and expands on responses as needed.

At the end of the activity, the family members can each eat their fortune cookie.

Discussion
Termination is an important aspect of therapy and warrants clinical attention. As therapy comes to a close, techniques should emphasize processing emotions relating to termination as well as reviewing therapeutic gains and focusing on the future (Jones, Robinson, & Casado, 2003). This technique utilizes the symbolism and metaphor of fortune cookies to focus on the client's future, instill hope, explore and review the therapeutic process, and support closure of the therapeutic relationship.

The therapeutic questions for this intervention focus on different aspects of the termination process. Questions were formulated based on clinical literature that delineates tasks appropriate for the termination stage of treatment, including such things as therapeutic closure, exploring the future, reviewing therapeutic gains, and preparing the client for termination of therapy (Jones, Robinson, & Casado, 2003). The questions provided for this technique are intended to serve as a clinical guide and should be modified for the unique needs of the family.

References

Jones, K.D., Casado, M., & Robinson, E.H. (2003). Structured play therapy: A model for choosing topics & activities. *International Journal of Play Therapy*, 12(1), 31–47.

Kenney-Noziska, S. (2008). *Techniques-techniques-techniques: Play-based activities for children, adolescents, and families*. West Conshohocken, PA: Infinity Publishing.

About The Author

Sueann Kenney-Noziska, MSW, LISW, RPT-S, is a Licensed Independent Social Worker and Registered Play Therapist Supervisor specializing in using play therapy in clinical practice with children, adolescents, and families. She is an accomplished author, instructor of play therapy, guest lecturer, and internationally recognized speaker who has trained thousands of professionals. She is founder and President of Play Therapy Corner, Inc., is actively involved in the play therapy community, and is author of the book Techniques-Techniques-Techniques: Play-Based Activities for Children, Adolescents, and Families.

Farewell Fortune Cookies
Questions

What is one thing you have learned in therapy?

What is one problem or obstacle you have overcome?

What is one mistake from your past you have learned from?

Name one person you can turn to for support/help.

How do you feel about ending therapy?

What is your family able to do better now?

What qualities do you have that will help you succeed in the future?

How can you use what you've learned in therapy in your future?

© Sueann Kenney-Noziska

Healing Animals
Source: Liana Lowenstein

Goals
- Identify progress made in therapy
- Discuss individual and family strengths
- Increase hope for the future

Materials
- Two sheets of paper for each family member
- Drawing materials such as markers, crayons, or pastels
- Tape

Advance Preparation
Arrange a flat drawing space for each family member. It is important that the sheets of paper are not in direct eyesight of each other. Arrange the drawing materials so that each family member has easy access to them.

Description
Provide each family member with a sheet of paper and a variety of drawing materials. Ask them to get into a relaxed position and to close their eyes. Then say, "Imagine a family of animals…this animal family has been through great hardship…take some time to imagine what it is like to be this animal family…when you are ready you can open your eyes and draw this *wounded* animal family."

Allow 10 minutes for completion of the drawings. Ask the family to draw in silence without any talking during the drawing segment. It is helpful to say, "Don't worry about your drawing. You will be able to explain it after you have finished."

Once the drawings are complete, ask the family members to close their eyes again. Say, "Imagine this same family of animals…this animal family has survived something very difficult…they are strong…take some time to imagine what it is like to be this animal family…when you are ready you can open your eyes and draw this *healing* animal family."

After the members have finished drawing their two animal families, display all the pictures, ideally by taping them to a wall. Invite the family to discuss their images. For example, ask:

1. What similarities/differences exist among the drawings?
2. What three words best describe the wounded animal families?
3. What three words best describe the healing animal families?
4. What helped the animal families overcome their hardships?
5. What important life lessons have the animal families learned?
6. How will the animals use their strength to overcome hardships in the future?
7. What do your drawings reveal about your family life?

Discussion

This drawing activity is incorporated into the ending phase of therapy. The aim is to help the family explore the changes they have made over the course of treatment and to create a new awareness of how they have overcome adversity.

Family members can communicate through the artwork things that they cannot articulate through spoken words. This is one of the many advantages of using art in family therapy. The art process "can often bypass well-entrenched defenses that manifest themselves as obstacles to the family members' interpersonal understanding of each other. Additionally, the art process may allow the possibility for family members to articulate emotions and thoughts through a visual means, which unlike the verbal dialogue allows individual self-expression to be made permanent through the art product" (Kerr, Hoshino, et al., 2008). Working with families using art allows them to see, express, and understand things differently.

The animal family creates a metaphor that facilitates symbolic exploration of underlying feelings. When family members complete their drawings separately and then share them with their family, unique perceptions are explored and similarities and differences among family members are discussed (Revell, 1997).

The process questions focus on growth, strength, and survival, as these are important themes to highlight in the termination stage of therapy. Through this intervention, the family is provided with the message that they have survived hardship and they can utilize this strength to get through difficult times in the future. This gives the family a sense of validation and hope.

References

Kerr, C., Hoshino, J., Sutherland J., and Parashak, S. (2008). *Family art therapy: Foundations of theory and practice*. New York: Routledge.

Revell, B. (1997). Using play and art therapy to work with families. In B. Bedard-Bidwell (Ed.), *Hand in hand: A practical application of art and play therapy*. London, ON: Thames River Publishing.

About The Author

Liana Lowenstein, MSW, RSW, CPT-S, is a Social Worker and Certified Play Therapy Supervisor in Toronto. She maintains a private practice, provides clinical supervision and consultation to mental health professionals, and lectures internationally on child and play therapy. She has authored numerous publications, including the books *Paper Dolls and Paper Airplanes: Therapeutic Exercises for Sexually Traumatized Children, Creative Interventions for Troubled Children and Youth, Creative Interventions for Bereaved Children*, and *Creative Interventions for Children of Divorce*.

Helping Hands
Source: Trudy Post Sprunk

Goals
- Increase awareness of each family member's helpfulness
- Verbally appreciate each family member's positive contributions to family life

Materials
- Large sheet of white paper or poster board
- Washable markers
- Wet cloth or paper towels

Advance Preparation
Place the paper or poster board on a flat surface that can be easily reached by everyone.

Description
Request that each family member choose a marker that is a different color than other family members' markers. Then ask members to place one of their hands on the poster board and trace multiple copies of that hand. Slight overlapping of the hand drawings is permissible.

Next, ask members to write inside the outlines of their hands the things that they do or say that are helpful and/or beneficial to their family. Their writing is to be done silently. The therapist may need to write for young children. Upon completion of the writing, family members share what they have written. The therapist encourages a discussion of the thoughts and feelings each member has about what they and others provide for the family unit.

To process the activity, the therapist could ask:

1. How did each person feel about what they provide to the family unit?
2. Name two or three more activities/behaviors each of you would like to provide for your family.
3. Tell how you would be able to add these activities/behaviors to your daily/ weekly routine.
4. Name one thing you like that another family member provides.

Discussion
This technique, used near termination, can increase family awareness of how each member contributes to the well-being of their now more functional family. Reviewing and appreciating how each contribution strengthens relationships assures the family that they can continue to work together without the need for additional therapy at this time.

General goals a therapist reviews regarding termination include the following:

1. Healthy family communication, including effective communication about feelings.
2. The ability to problem solve as a cohesive unit.
3. Healthy inter- and intrapersonal relationships.
4. Differentiation of self.
5. Resolution of their referring problem.

This activity provides the therapist with an opportunity to determine how well the family has achieved each of the above goals.

About The Author

Trudy Post Sprunk, LMFT-S, LPC-S, RPT-S, CPT-S, is a Licensed Marriage and Family Therapist and Supervisor who has been practicing psychotherapy since 1971. She has presented at international, national, and local conferences and has been interviewed on radio and television. She is certified as an EMDR Specialist and is a Registered Play Therapist Supervisor. She is past-president of the Association for Play Therapy and president and co-founder of the Georgia Association for Play Therapy.

Last Session Family Card Game
Source: Liana Lowenstein

Goals
- Review and validate therapeutic gains
- Verbally identify and discuss feelings about ending therapy
- Provide a positive termination experience

Materials
- Question cards (included)
- Card stock or index cards
- Scissors
- Standard 52-card deck
- Cookies

Advance Preparation
Photocopy the questions provided onto cardstock and cut them into cards, or copy the questions onto index cards.

Description
If the family played the First Session Family Card Game at the beginning of their therapy (see Section One), then introduce the activity by stating, "We are going to play the same card game that we played in our first session, but this time the questions will help you talk about your experiences in therapy, your accomplishments in therapy, and your feelings about ending therapy." If the family did not play the First Session Family Card Game, then say, "We are going to play a game that will help you talk about your experiences in therapy, your accomplishments in therapy, and your feelings about ending therapy." The rules are explained as follows:

"Take turns picking the top card from the deck of cards. If you get a card with an **even number**, pick a card from the question card pile and **answer the question**. If you get a card with an **odd number**, pick a card from the question card pile and **ask someone in your family to answer the question**. If you do not feel you can answer the question, you can ask your family for help. If you pick an ace, ask someone in your family for a hug. If you pick a jack, do 10 jumping jacks. If you pick a Queen or King, you get a cookie. At the end of the game, everyone who played gets a cookie."

The therapist can observe the game play, highlighting individual and family changes he/she has seen during the course of treatment and reinforcing strengths.

After the game, facilitate discussion by asking the following questions:

1. What do you think was the purpose of this game?
2. Whose answers were most like how you feel?
3. What positive changes did you notice in how your family interacted during this game, compared to how you interacted at the beginning of therapy?

Discussion

When working with troubled families, the therapist must handle the termination phase of treatment with particular sensitivity. Terminating therapy can be seen as a mourning process and as a re-enactment of earlier experiences of loss. During this phase of the intervention process, family members may experience feelings of sadness, anxiety, rejection, and abandonment. Conversely, they may be happy about ending therapy, feel relieved, or feel proud of their therapeutic gains. The therapist must help each family member express his/her feelings about ending therapy and normalize and validate these feelings. Termination is also a time to punctuate and celebrate therapeutic achievements. The question cards in this game were created with these goals in mind.

This activity is intended to be used when a family is ready to terminate therapy. If the family participated in The First Session Family Card Game, then they can be asked to reflect on what has changed and how it felt to play the game now from when they first played this game.

Termination, if handled correctly, may have a surprising degree of therapeutic potential (Treacher, 2003). The ending phase of therapy can be an empowering process and can help family members focus on therapeutic progress. It is recommended that a graduation ceremony be held with the family as a way of recognizing and celebrating their progress. For further details on planning a graduation ceremony, see Lowenstein (1999).

References

Lowenstein, L. (1999). *Creative interventions for troubled children and youth.* Toronto, ON: Champion Press.

Lowenstein, L. (2006). *Creative interventions for bereaved children.* Toronto, ON: Champion Press.

Treacher, A. (2003). Termination in family therapy: Developing a structural approach. *Journal of Family Therapy,11(2)*, 135-147.

About The Author
Liana Lowenstein, MSW, RSW, CPT-S, is a Social Worker and Certified Play Therapy Supervisor in Toronto. She maintains a private practice, provides clinical supervision and consultation to mental health professionals, and lectures internationally on child and play therapy. She has authored numerous publications, including the books *Paper Dolls and Paper Airplanes: Therapeutic Exercises for Sexually Traumatized Children*, *Creative Interventions for Troubled Children and Youth*, *Creative Interventions for Bereaved Children*, and *Creative Interventions for Children of Divorce*.

Last Session Family Card Game
Questions

What is a positive change you have made during your time in therapy?	What is a positive change someone in your family has made during your time in therapy?	Change seats with the person who you think worked the hardest in therapy.
Tell about a skill you learned in therapy that you can use to deal with problems that arise in the future.	Tell about something you have learned about someone in your family during your time in therapy.	What helped you the most during your time in therapy?
Name someone who can help you when you have a problem or a worry.	Fill in the blank: Something our family needs to continue to work on is...	What is your family able to do better now?
What was your favorite activity that you did in therapy?	Fill in the blank: My proudest moment in therapy was when I...	How do you feel about ending therapy?
What advice would you give to another family who are experiencing a similar problem that brought you to therapy?	What advice would you give your therapist about working with families?	Families often teach therapists valuable lessons. Ask your therapist to tell something your family has taught him/her.

© Liana Lowenstein

Thank-You Cards
Source: Amber L. Brewer

Goals
- Create an enjoyable ritual for family therapy termination
- Identify progress made during therapy
- Strengthen family relationships

Materials
- Colored paper or construction paper
- Markers
- Party favors such as party hats, balloons, and loot bags
- Celebration treats such as pizza and cake
- Assortment of age-appropriate games and toys

Advance Preparation
This activity is to be used after the family and therapist agree that therapy goals have been achieved and the family is ready to discontinue therapy.

Meet with the parents prior to the second-to-last therapy session to discuss and plan a Graduation Celebration for the last session. Explain that the purpose of the Graduation Celebration is to honor and celebrate progress made in therapy. Discuss appropriate elements of the Graduation Celebration, such as decorations, party favors, loot bags, treats, party games, etc. Arrange the details of the Graduation Celebration with the parents and decide who will be responsible for bringing the various items.

Create a thank-you card to present to the family in the final session. Express in this thank-you card your appreciation for the lessons learned from the family as well as for the progress the family has made.

Description
Note: This activity occurs over the last two sessions of treatment.

The Second-To-Last Session
To prepare the family for the activity, inform them during the second-to-last therapy session that you would like to have a "Graduation Celebration" for the last session of therapy. Ask the children whether they have ever attended a graduation ceremony.

Explain that graduation is a way to celebrate when someone finishes something important, and that the upcoming Graduation Celebration will be a party, held to honor their completion of therapy.

Tell the family that, because it is a party, there will be games and food. However, explain that prior to the party, you would like each of them to write thank-you cards to all the other members of their family. Inform the family that they will be reading their cards to each other during the Graduation Celebration. In these cards, family members are to (1) express appreciation for things other family members have done for them, and (2) identify positive changes they and other family members have made throughout the course of therapy. Family members then create their thank-you cards. The therapist or the parents may help young children compose their letters as needed. The content of each letter may be as simple or elaborate as the author would like.

Inform the family that after the cards are read, they can play their favorite game(s) for the remainder of the session. Offer to bring some toys and games; however, the family can bring toys and games from home as well. Encourage the family to select toys or games that include all family members and that are not overly competitive in nature. Emphasize that the reason for playing the game is not about winning but rather about bringing the family closer together and enjoying one another.

The Last Session
On the day of the Graduation Celebration, review with the family what the agenda will be for that session. Remind the family that the Graduation Celebration does not mean they have graduated from their problems; rather, it means that they appear prepared to handle problems on their own at this time. Explain that, just like students sometimes return to school after graduating (e.g., going to college after they complete high school), the family may at some future period return to therapy. Tell the family that this would not mean the family has failed but that they need to come back to "therapy school" for just a little more learning.

Next, invite family members to read their thank-you cards to each other. Applaud the growth that each member has made. When the family has finished reading their cards, read to them the card you prepared beforehand. Express your thoughts on the strengths and growth you have seen in individual members and in the family as a unit since they first came to see you. Talk about what makes that family special.

Discuss with the family what they will do to keep building on the progress they have achieved in therapy. Have them name some specific plans for staying strong and handling possible future problems. Express your hopes for the family's future.

For the rest of the session, invite the family to eat their treats, enjoy the party favors, and play together with the games or toys of their choosing.

Discussion

This activity offers several benefits to families who are preparing to transition out of therapy. First, it frames termination as a reason to celebrate and draws upon a fun and familiar ritual (i.e., a party) that can ease the family through the therapy completion process. Second, the activity creates a forum in which families consolidate helpful changes they have made and commit to future growth after therapy ends. Furthermore, when family members express praise and appreciation to each other, they continue to strengthen their relationships. Members who have a history of chronic fighting are often surprised and pleased to hear compliments from other members. Sometimes, family members write letters of appreciation to the therapist, which can help them to express their thanks and to say good-bye. Young children, who require help from others to write their words, may choose to draw a picture depicting their feelings about the therapist or other family members.

Narrative Therapy founders White and Epston (1990) emphasize the value of using therapeutic letters in counseling contexts. Family thank-you Cards can be considered a type of therapeutic letter that family members write to each other. Because family members are the authors of the letters, they (vs. the therapist) become the primary therapeutic agents during the last session. Thank-you cards capture positive sentiments that can be stored and re-read later, during difficult periods of life, when family members are in need of comfort and encouragement.

Reference

White, M., & Epston, D. (1990). *Narrative means to therapeutic ends*. New York: W.W. Norton.

About The Author

Amber L. Brewer, PhD-ABD, LMFT, provides therapy at a counseling agency in Utah. She specializes in integrating play therapy techniques into family therapy to treat child-focused problems and has presented on the subject at multiple national conferences. Her authorship includes published articles and a book review on such topics as attachment and therapy alliance, bereavement, and divorce.

References and Suggested Reading

Ackerman, F., Colapinto, J.A., Scharf, C.N., Weinshel, M., and Winawer, H. (1991). The involuntary client: Avoiding "pretend therapy." *Family Systems Medicine, 9(3)*, 261–266.

Anderson, C.M., & Stewart, S. (1983). *Mastering resistance: A practical guide to family therapy.* New York: Guilford.

Ariel, S., Carel, C., & Tyrano, S. (1985). Uses of children's make-believe play in family therapy: Theory and clinical examples. *Journal of Marital and Family Therapy, 11(1)*, 47–60.

Ariel, S. (1986). Family play therapy. In R. van der Kooji & J. Hellendoorn (Eds.), *Play, play therapy, play research.* Netherlands: Swets and Zeitlinger.

Ariel, S. (2005). Family play therapy. In C.E. Schaefer, J. McCormick, & A. Ohnogi (Eds.), *International handbook of play therapy: Advances in assessment, theory, research, and practice.* New York: Jason Aronson.

Bailey, C.E., & Sori, C.E.F. (2000). Involving parents in children's therapy. In C.E. Bailey (Ed.), *Children in therapy: Using the family as a resource.* New York: W.W. Norton.

Bailey, C.E. (2005). *Children in therapy: Using the family as a resource.* New York: W.W. Norton.

Baim, C., Burmeister, J., & Maciel, M. (Eds.) (2007). *Psychodrama: Advances in theory and practice.* London: Routledge.

Bedard-Bidwell, B. (Ed.). *Hand in hand: A practical application of art and play therapy.* London, ON: Thames River Publishing.

Berg, I.K., & Steiner, T. (2003). *Children's solution work.* New York: W.W. Norton.

Bitter, J.R. (2009). *Theory and practice of family therapy and counseling.* Belmont, CA: Brooks/Cole.

Blatner, A. (1992). Theoretical principles underlying creative arts therapies. *Journal of the Arts in Psychotherapy, 18*(4), 405–409.

Blatner, A. (1996). *Acting-In: Practical applications of psychodramatic methods* (3rd ed.). New York: Springer.

Blatner, A. (2000). *Foundations of psychodrama: History, theory, and practice* (4th ed.). New York: Springer.

Bowen, M. (1978). *Family therapy in clinical practice*. New York: Jason Aronson.

Boyd-Webb, N. (Ed.) (2007). *Play therapy with children in crisis (3rd ed.)*. New York: Guilford.

Colapinto, J. (1991). Structural family therapy. In A.S. Gurman & D.P. Kniskern (Eds.), *Handbook of family therapy: Vol. 2*. New York: Brunner/Mazel.

Carey, L. (1999). *Sandplay therapy with children and families*. New York: Jason Aronson.

Carey, L. (2006). *Expressive and creative arts methods for trauma survivors*. London: Jessica Kingsley Publishers.

Carter, B., & McGoldrick, M. (Eds.). (1999). *The expanded family life cycle: Individual, family, and social perspectives (3rd ed.)*. Boston: Allyn & Bacon.

Carter, E., & Orfanidis, M.M. (1978). Family therapy with the therapist's family of origin. In M. Bowen (Ed.), *Family therapy in clinical practice*. New York: Jason Aronson.

Combrinck, L.G. (2006). *Children in family contexts: Perspectives on treatment (2nd ed.)*. New York: Guilford.

Corsini, R. J., & Wedding, D. (Eds.). (2004). *Current Psychotherapies (7th ed.)*. New York: Wadsworth Press.

Corsini, R.J. (Ed.). (2001). *Handbook of innovative therapies*. New York: John Wiley & Sons.

Crenshaw, D. (2007). *Evocative strategies in child and adolescent psychotherapy*. New Jersey: Jason Aronson.

Dattilio, F.M., & Jongsma, A.E. (2010). *The family therapy treatment planner*. New York: John Wiley & Sons.

Dayton, T. (1990). *Drama games*. New York: Innerlook.

De Domenico, G.S. (1995). *Sandtray-worldplay: A comprehensive guide to the use of sandtray in psychotherapeutic and transformational settings*. Oakland, CA: Vision Quest Images.

Freeman, J., Epston, D., & Lobovits, D. (1997). *Playful approaches to serious problems*. New York: W.W. Norton.

Friedlander, M., Escudero, V., & Heatherington, L. (2006).*Therapeutic alliances in couple and family therapy*. Washington, DC: American Psychological Association.

Gershoni, J. (Ed.). (2003). *Psychodrama in the 21st Century: Clinical and educational applications.* New York: Springer Publishing Company, Inc.

Gil, E. (1994). *Play in family therapy.* New York: Guilford.

Gil, E. (2003). Family play therapy: "The bear with short nails." In C.E. Schaefer (Ed.), *Foundations of play therapy.* New York: John Wiley & Sons.

Gil, E., & Sobol, B. (2000). Engaging families in therapeutic play. In C.E. Bailey (Ed.), *Children in therapy: Using the family as a resource.* New York: W.W. Norton.

Goldenberg, H., & Goldenberg, I. (2007). *Family therapy: An overview.* Pacific Cove, CA: Brooks Cole.

Goodyear-Brown, P. (2009). *Play therapy with traumatized children: A prescriptive approach.* New Jersey: Wiley.

Harvey, S.A. (1994). Dynamic play therapy: Expressive play intervention with families. In K. O'Connor & C. Schaefer (Eds.), *Handbook of play therapy: Vol. 2. Advances and innovations.* New York: John Wiley & Sons.

Harvey, S.A. (2009). Family problem-solving: Using expressive activities. In A. Drewes (Ed.), *Blending play therapy with cognitive behavioral therapy.* New York: Wiley & Sons.

Henggeler, S.W., Schoenwald, S.K., Borduin, C.M., Rowland, M.D.S., & Cunningham, P.B. (1998). *Multisystemic treatment of antisocial behavior in children and adolescents.* New York: Guilford.

Hertlein, K.M., & Viers, D. (2005). *The couple and family therapist's notebook: Homework, handouts, and activities for use in marital and family therapy.* New York: Routledge.

Homeyer, L.E., & Sweeney, D. (2010). Sandtray therapy: A practical manual. New York: Routledge.

Hoshino, J. (2003). Multicultural issues in family art therapy. In C. Malchiodi (Ed.), *The clinical handbook of art therapy.* New York: Guilford.

Hubble, M., Duncan, B., & Miller, S. (2000). *The heart and soul of change: What works in therapy.* Washington, DC: American Psychological Association.

Kenney-Noziska, S. (2008). *Techniques-techniques-techniques: Play-based activities for children, adolescents, and families.* West Conshohocken, PA: Infinity Publishing.

Kerr, C., Hoshino, J., Sutherland, J, and Parashak, S. (2008). *Family art therapy: Foundations of theory and practice.* New York: Routledge.

Klorer, P.G. (2006). Art therapy with traumatized families. In L. Carey (Ed.), *Expressive and creative arts methods for trauma survivors*. London: Jessica Kingsley Publishers.

Klorer, P.G. (2000). *Expressive therapy with troubled children*. New York: Jason Aronson.

Kwiatkowska, H.Y. (1967). Family art therapy. *Family Process, 6*, 37–55.

Landgarten, H.B. (1987). *Family art therapy: A clinical guide and casebook*. New York: Routledge.

Leben, N. (1993). *Directive group play therapy: 60 structured games for the treatment of ADHD, low self-esteem, and traumatized children*. Pflugerville, TX: Morning Glory Treatment Center for Children.

Linesch, D. (1993). *Art therapy with families in crisis*. Philadelphia: Brunner/Mazel.

Lowenstein, L. (1999). *Creative interventions for troubled children and youth*. Toronto, ON: Champion Press.

Lowenstein, L. (2002). *More creative interventions for troubled children and youth*. Toronto, ON: Champion Press.

Lowenstein, L. (2006). *Creative interventions for bereaved children*. Toronto, ON: Champion Press.

Lowenstein, L. (2006). *Creative interventions for children of divorce*. Toronto, ON: Champion Press.

Lowenstein, L. (2008). *Assessment and treatment activities for children, adolescents, and families: Practitioners share their most effective techniques*. Toronto, ON: Champion Press.

Lowenstein, L. (2010). *Assessment and treatment activities for children, adolescents, and families VOLUME TWO: Practitioners share their most effective techniques*. Toronto, ON: Champion Press.

Lubimv, G. (1994). *Wings for our children: Essentials of becoming a play therapist*. Burnstown, ON: Burnstown Publisher.

Lubimiv, G. (2009). *All in the family: Using play with families*. Unpublished manuscript.

Malchiodi, C.A. (2003). *Handbook of art therapy*. New York: Guilford Press.

Malchiodi, C.A. (2005). *Expressive therapies*. New York: Guilford.

Malone, P.T., & Malone, T. (1987). *The art of intimacy*. New York: Prentice Hall.

McCollum, E. (1993). Termination rituals. In T.S. Nelson and T.S. Trepper (Eds.), *101 Interventions in family therapy*. New York: Haworth press.

McGoldrick, M., Gerson, R., and Petry, S. (2008). *Genograms: Assessment and intervention (3rd ed.)*. New York: W.W. Norton.

Moffatt, G. (2002). *A violent heart*. Connecticut: Praeger.

Moffatt, G. (2004). *The parenting journey*. Connecticut: Praeger.

Moreno, J. L. (1977). *Psychodrama* (Vol.1). Beacon, NY: Beacon House, Inc.

Napier, A.Y., & Whitaker, C.A. (1978). *The family crucible*. New York: Harper & Row.

Nelson, T.S., and Trepper, T.S. (Eds.) (1993). *101 Interventions in family therapy*. New York: Haworth press.

Nichols, M.P., & Schwartz, R.C. (2007). *Family therapy: Concepts and methods*. New York: Allyn & Bacon.

Odell, M., & Campbell, C.E. (1998). *The practical practice of marriage and family therapy: Things my training supervisor never told me*. New York: Routledge.

Oster, G., & Crone, P. (2004). *Using drawings in assessment and therapy: A guide for mental health professionals*. New York: Routledge.

Pardeck, J.T. (1988). Family therapy as a treatment approach to child abuse. *Child Psychiatry Quarterly* 21(4), 191–198.

Patterson, J., Williams, L., Edwards, T.M., Chamow, L., & Grauf-Grounds, C. (2009). *Essential skills in family therapy: From the first interview to termination* (2nd ed.). New York: Guilford.

Perrow, S. (2008). *Healing stories for challenging behaviour*. London: Hawthorn.

Revell, B. (1997). Using play and art therapy to work with families. In B. Bedard-Bidwell (Ed.), *Hand in hand: A practical application of art and play therapy*. London, ON: Thames River Publishing.

Riley, S., & Malchiodi, C. (2004). *Integrative approaches to family art therapy*. Chicago: Magnolia Street Publishers.

Rivett, M., & Street, E. (2009). *Family therapy: 100 key points and techniques*. New York: Routledge.

Roberts, J. (1993). Termination rituals. In T.S. Nelson and T.S. Trepper (Eds.), *101 Interventions in family therapy*. New York: Haworth press.

Rubin, J.A. (1999). *Art therapy: An introduction*. Philadelphia: Brunner/Mazel.

Rubin, J.A. (2005). *Child art therapy*. New York: John Wiley & Sons.

Schaefer, C.E. (Ed). (2003). *Foundations of play therapy*. New York: John Wiley & Sons.

Schaefer, C.E., & Carey, L.J. (1994). *Family play therapy*. New York: Jason Aronson.

Schaefer, C.E., & Kaduson, H. (Eds). (2006). *Contemporary play therapy*. New York: Guilford.

Schaefer, C.E., McCormick, J., Ohnogi, A. (Eds.) (2005). *International handbook of play therapy*. New York: Jason Aronson.

Schaefer, C.E, & Reid, S. (Eds). (2001). *Game play: Therapeutic use of childhood games* (2nd ed.). New York: John Wiley & Sons.

Sherman, R., & Fredman, N. (1986). *Handbook of structured techniques in marriage and family therapy*. New York: Routledge.

Shirk, S.R., & Karver, M. (2003). Prediction of treatment outcome from relationship variables in child and adolescent therapy. *Journal of Consulting and Clinical Psychology, 71(3)*, 452–464.

Singer, J.L. (1996). Cognitive and effective implications of imaginative play in childhood. In M. Lewis (Ed.), *Child and adolescent psychiatry: A comprehensive textbook*. Baltimore, MD: Williams and Wilkins.

Sori, C.F. (2006). *Engaging children in family therapy: Creative approaches to integrating theory and research in clinical practice*. New York: Routledge.

Sori, C.F., & Sprenkle, D.H. (2004). Training family therapists to work with children and families: A modified Delphi study. *Journal of Marital and Family Therapy,30(4)*, 479–495.

Stormshak, E., & Dishion, T. (2002). An ecological approach to child and family clinical and counseling psychology. *Clinical Child and Family Psychology Review, 5*, 197–215.

Taffel, R. (1991). How to talk with kids. *Networker, 15(4)*, 39–45; 68–70.

Taibbi, R. (2007). *Doing family therapy: Craft and creativity in clinical practice* (2nd ed.). New York: Guilford.

Treacher, A. (2003). Termination in family therapy: Developing a structural approach. *Journal of Family Therapy,11(2)*, 135-147.

Trepper, T.S. (2002). Show me one more time. In D.A. Baptiste (Ed.). *Clinical epiphanies in marital and family therapy: A practitioner's casebook of therapeutic insights, perceptions, and breakthroughs.* Binghamton, NY: The Haworth Press.

Wachtel, E.F. (1994). *Treating troubled children and their families.* New York: Guilford.

Wark, L. (2003). Explaining to parents the use of play in family therapy. In C.F. Sori & L.L. Hecker & Associates, *The therapist's notebook for children and adolescents: Homework, handouts, and activities for use in psychotherapy.* Binghamton, NY: Haworth.

Weiser, J. (1999). *PhotoTherapy techniques: Exploring the secrets of personal snapshots and family albums* (3rd ed.). Vancouver, BC: PhotoTherapy Centre Press.

Yasenik, L., & Gardner, K. (2004). *Play therapy dimensions model.* Calgary: Rocky Mountain Play Therapy Institute.

Zwerling, I. (1979). The creative arts therapies as "real therapies." *Hospital and Community Psychiatry, 30(12)*, 841–844.

Professional Organizations

Family Therapy

American Association for Marriage and Family Therapy: www.aamft.org

American Family Therapy Academy: www.afta.org

Association for Family Therapy in the UK: www.aft.org.uk

Division of Family Psychology, American Psychological Association: www.apa.org

European Family Therapy Association: www.europeanfamilytherapy.eu

International Association of Marriage and Family Counselors: www.iamfc.org

International Family Therapy Association: www.ifta-familytherapy.org

Israeli Association for Marital and Family Therapy: www.mishpaha.org

Victorian Association of Family Therapists: www.vaft.asn.au

Queensland Association for Family Therapy: www.qaft.com.au

Art Therapy

American Art Therapy Association: www.arttherapy.org

Australian National Art Therapy Association: www.anata.org.au

British Association of Art Therapists: www.baat.org

Canadian Art Therapy Association: www.catainfo.ca

International Art Therapy Organization: www.internationalarttherapy.org

Creative and Expressive Therapy

Arts in Therapy Network: www.artsintherapy.com

Australian Creative Arts Therapy Association: www.acatainc@hotmail.com

Canadian Creative Arts in Health, Training, and Education: www.cmclean.com

Expressive Therapies Institute: www.expressivetherapies.com.au

International Expressive Arts Therapy Association: www.ieata.org

Israeli Association of Creative and Expressive Therapies: www.yahat.org

European Consortium for Arts Therapies Education: www.uni-meunster.de/ecarte

National Coalition of Creative Arts Therapies Associations: www.nccata.org

PhotoTherapy Centre: www.phototherapy-centre.com

Drama Therapy and Psychodrama

American Society of Group Psychotherapy and Psychodrama: www.asgpp.org

British Association for Drama Therapy: www.badth.ision.co.uk

British Psychodrama Association: www.zambula.demon.co.uk

National Association for Drama Therapy: www.nadt.org

Play Therapy

Association For Play Therapy: www.a4pt.org

Canadian Association For Child And Play Therapy: www.cacpt.com

British Association of Play Therapists: www.bapt.info

International Society for Child and Play Therapy: www.playtherapy.org

Play Therapy Australia: www.playtherapyaustralia.com

Play Therapy Australasia: www.playtherapy.org.au

Sandplay Therapy

British and Irish Sandplay Society: www.sandplay.org.uk

Canadian Association for Sandplay Therapy: www.sandplay.ca

International Society for Sandplay Therapy: www.sandplayusa.org

Sandplay Therapists of America: www.sandplayusa.org

Also by Liana Lowenstein

Creative Interventions for Troubled Children and Youth

More Creative Interventions for Troubled Children & Youth

Creative Interventions for Bereaved Children

Creative Interventions for Children of Divorce

Assessment and Treatment Techniques for Children, Adolescents, and Families:
Practitioners Share Their Most Effective Techniques
(Volumes One through Three)

Cory Helps Kids Cope with Divorce: Playful Therapeutic Activities for Young
Children

***For further information about the above books and upcoming
publications, go to www.lianalowenstein.com